ESTABLISH THE WORK OF OUR HANDS

A MEMOIR: STORIES FROM THE GREY AND
THE GREEN TO THE BLUE AND THE BROWN

RON POLINDER

LifeRich
PUBLISHING

LifeRich Publishing is a registered trademark of The Reader's Digest Association, Inc.

LifeRich Publishing books may be ordered through booksellers or by contacting:

LifeRich Publishing
1663 Liberty Drive
Bloomington, IN 47403
www.liferichpublishing.com
844-686-9607

Scripture quotations marked (NIV) are taken from the Holy Bible, New International Version®, NIV®. Copyright © 1973, 1978, 1984 by Biblica, Inc.™ Used by permission of Zondervan. All rights reserved worldwide.

Cover pictures by: Jeff Littlejohn (top picture) and Mike DeYoung (bottom picture)

Sketch of Rev. Rolf Veenstra by Elmer Charlie Yazzie
Sketch of Grandpa Polinder by Bill Swinburnsen

ISBN: 978-1-4897-4024-3 (sc)
ISBN: 978-1-4897-4025-0 (e)

Library of Congress Control Number: 2022901804

Print information available on the last page.

LifeRich Publishing rev. date: 04/07/2022

CONCERNING THE TITLE

The choice of a book title rarely comes easily. I have pondered this for some years. But I trust it was the Holy Spirit who one day presented the final words of Psalm 90:17b: "…establish the work of our hands for us—yes, establish the work of our hands."

I have long-loved Psalm 90, and particularly prayed that seventeenth verse, as it related to the task of family, school, church, politics and more. Thus, *Establish the Work of Our Hands*. Note not the work of *my* hands, because virtually all my professional and personal life was done in community.

This thought is wonderfully supported by Ephesians 2:10—"For we are God's handiwork, created in Christ Jesus to do good works, which God prepared in advance for us to do." Thus, this book includes descriptions, writing, and stories of a life lived out serving God and his Kingdom.

The subtitle is somewhat more obscure: *Stories from the Grey and the Green to the Blue and the Brown*. Having grown up in Western Washington, one learns early on what it is to have grey skies and green landscape—it is a way of life, an orientation to how you view the Creation. In moving to New Mexico, we discovered big, blue skies like never before, and brown--so much brown, or reddish brown with its stunning Red Rocks. While we learned to love the blue and the brown, our default disposition was still the grey and the green.

Until we met Theresa, a junior in high school who had just returned from a trip to Grand Rapids with her mother, a former Wingate student. I ask Theresa, "What did you think of Michigan? Her response, "Too green, I missed the brown." Never in all my decades had I heard such a statement. But therein is a lesson—symbolizing two different worlds.

We had the privilege of moving among and between those two worlds, not just geographically, but culturally. Thus, a memoir of the adventures and stories of our journey in the colors of God's good Creation.

DEDICATION

To Colleen

- loving and respectful daughter of Al and Harriet,
- beautiful, amazing Mother to Shawn Mitchell, Stacia, Shawna and Rustin and Grandmother to eleven,
- loyal sister to Gloria and Vic, and enough relatives to fill the page,
- the best friend of enough to fill another page, including Judy,
- my best friend for most of our school years and then 44 years of marriage, until June of 2012. And she still speaks into my life, all the time.
- As her mom would say, "showers of blessings."

CONTENTS

FOREWORD BY JIM DE KORNE

In 2005 I was working with Christian Schools International (CSI) and planning the annual summer convention for principals and school leaders in the US and Canada. One afternoon Ron Polinder contacted me and offered, "Why not Rehoboth for the next location?"

And that's exactly what happened. In the summer of 2006 – with Ron's expert guidance and creative energy – nearly 500 principals and other school leaders from literally around the world gathered at the humble Rehoboth campus 103 years after its official beginning, celebrating accomplishments, crossing cultural divides, and gaining new perspectives.

Betty Yazzie and other school mothers flipped fry bread over an open fire. Navajo, Zuni, and people of other tribes mingled with the guests from the Wooden Shoe Clan. Together, everyone offered thanks to God for his blessings.

Most of the visiting participants were already aware of the existence of Rehoboth. It was not "foreign" to them in that sense. Yet – as they experienced just a small and brief glimpse of cross-cultural life in and among their native brothers and sisters – their exiting remarks mirrored the sentiments of the Queen of Sheba visiting Solomon … the half had not been told.

That short story is instructive in two ways that are relevant to these notes on Ron Polinder and his attached memoirs that I hope you will read, ponder, and appreciate. First, it clearly demonstrates Ron's heart. And second, it embodies Ron's deep commitment to learning that must be integrated with practice. Faith without works is dead.

If you have ever lived or worked in the Rehoboth area you will smile at the actions, and maybe even slightly grimace at the all-too-real foibles of well-intentioned but not always culturally-savvy participants. If you have ever lived or worked in the Lynden WA area you will appreciate the deep roots of the community as well as the long learning curve of young and old residents alike.

Isn't that true for all of us, everywhere? And isn't it also so easy to forget that fact?

In our current cultural moment we are prone to an arrogant outlook that assumes that we must be the first humans to ever encounter – and solve! – our present panoply of problems.

Not so.

And Ron's wonderfully told stories illustrate that beautifully.

One of the many things I appreciate about where I currently live (Colorado USA) is the way in which traveling a short distance provides a totally new view. Most people know the familiar outline of our local mountain, Pikes Peak. Yet drive around the backside and it looks completely different.

I was privileged to personally walk alongside (and learn from) Ron for several years and a few of the events described in his book. And it is refreshing and thought-provoking to read his personal account of the situations we both experienced.

Ron is a listener and a learner. That's what makes his perspective valuable.

Recently a good photographer friend John Van't Land was at a 4H animal presentation and let his grandson use a spare camera. After the event he was amazed at his grandson's photos — not necessarily for their technical excellence but for their subject matter. Closeups of a steer's face, a shot of a horse's tail, an empty water bottle with a clover. John was fascinated that standing next to each other at the very same occasion, he and his grandson had produced such very different views of the exact same event. As you will discover in the pages that follow, Ron — more than John — can relate to that grandson.

The adage that comes to mind is "We don't see things as they are. Instead, we see things as we are"—Anais Nin (1903-1977).

I trust that, with me, you will see in these pages the warm authentic heart of Ron Polinder describing the warm authentic people he has had the privilege to work alongside. Indeed, he really does want to bring us all together.

That is the beauty of Ron's memoir. In our age of instant categorization and resulting polarization, Ron provides a gallery of authentic vignettes that are sincerely humorous, sometimes critical, yet always hopeful. He gives each of us the gift of seeing the normal course of life, with a dollop of New Mexico green chili added, as something to be noticed, tasted, and celebrated.

As Ron would say, "That would be terrific!"

Read the book. Be inspired. See life with new eyes.

FOREWORD BY DON KOK

This is about a couple of kids from the same era, one growing up on a dairy farm in Northwest Washington, the other a farm in Wisconsin. Both were enfolded by animals, rich soil, and changing seasons while immersed in the rhythm of work and play amongst family and friends. We were molded by the faithful witness of Christian parents, the gift of a Christian education from grades 1 – 12 (no kindergarten for either of us back on those days), and the privilege of attending Calvin College where we were taught to think about life from a Biblical perspective.

Somewhere during those years, we were both drawn to help shape other minds, hearts, and lives through the profession of teaching, specifically becoming educators within Christian schools. Over time, we were encouraged to give school administration a try, learning to hire and walk alongside teachers, monitor student achievement and behavior, coordinate schedules, review curriculum, help plan school events, solve problems, and "other duties as assigned." In 1993, I became the K – 8 principal at Lynden Christian School where I met someone by the name of Ron Polinder, high school principal. He was the elder statesman, I the relative rookie. As time passed, we attended the same church, our families were in a household of faith together, and we had occasion to counsel each other related to that endeavor called parenting. We were colleagues for seven years, calling or meeting when either of us thought we had a bright idea, when there was a knotty situation, when we needed a word of encouragement or wished to share a humorous incident. We laughed together a lot. We disagreed occasionally, but we never quarreled.

There were any number of times when I would call Ron and tell him that I was hoping to introduce or implement a particular program in the school. He would invariably ask me how that program fit into the vision and mission of the school. Had I thought about that? Yes. Well, no. Certainly not like him. Ron always had the ability to reflect upon and clarify a topic from a Biblical worldview, and then to wisely put those perspectives into spoken or written word. He made so many of us think. Head, heart and hands working together beautifully to bless others.

In 2000, Ron and his wife Colleen were called back to Rehoboth Christian School where he was to be the interim superintendent for just one year. Yeah, right—just one year? He served there for nine years. We no longer were going to work again as fellow administrators in the same school. His departure left a deep vacuum in my professional and personal life. But during those years we stayed in touch, and since Ron's return to Lynden, we have been able to deepen our friendship even further. It is my understanding that some types of trees withstand significant forces over the years because their roots are intertwined. Yes, indeed.

In this book *Establish the Work of Our Hands*, Ron shares a host of experiences that involve family, friends, farm, schooling, work, disappointments, joys and sadness, deep sadness; vignettes to which so many can relate. But because Ron has been such a prolific thinker and writer over the years, he has also incorporated in the book glimpses of mission and philosophical statements, newspaper articles, letters to the editor, reflections, and critiques.

This is also a memoir filled with the "gift of the stranger" and the heart of hospitality – characteristics of Ron that have endeared him to numerous people. Because of those sweet relationships, he has included some eulogies and memorials flowing from the deep recesses of his heart reflecting both sorrow and serenity.

Be encouraged to read this book. Reflect on the work of his hands, your hands, and our hands, together.

THANKS FROM THE AUTHOR

I must start with Elaine Vos, a Lynden mom who did some editing for my Pastor, Ken Koeman, and my friend and Elaine's Dordt College professor, James Schaap. If she was endorsed by them, surely she would be a good fit for my book. And she has been terrific—pleasant, insightful, skilled. In addition to the editing task, she helped me navigate the process with the publishing guidelines and the technology. Never have we shared a cross word. Elaine has been a gift from God.

Good friends have read all or portions of the book: Kevin Pawlowski, Allen Likkel, Don Kok and Jim DeKorne, the latter two also writing the forwards. What good brothers these are, gentle, kind and helpful, better than I deserve.

There have been others who responded with affirmation about certain stories or events. And the dozens of characters who are the story, friends, colleagues, neighbors, relatives, my siblings and children, about whom I have written with or without their permission.

Dad and Mom, Henry and Mina Polinder, who gave me roots and wings, and a lot of love for a kid who could become big-mouthed and over-bearing. Yet, never did I have to question their care and compassion.

Finally, there is Judy, my wife and partner now for eight years, with whom every struggle became her as well, with a listening ear and sensible advice. And virtually every story received her tender blessing, with smiles and affirmation. Thank you Judy!

PREFACE

Something About Papa

This memoir is intended for my grandchildren, and maybe for their children. Other friends and relatives may choose to take a peek, for which I would be honored. But I do hope my grandkids will at some point in their lives read this so as to learn about Papa and Nana, the times in which they lived, and how they thought—about life, and faith, and a whole lot more.

I will appear as the primary author, though most everything written here was also reviewed by Nana (I will at time use "Nana" and other times "Colleen"). Of course, later it will be Grandma Judy. Virtually everything had their blessing.

A worthy question to ask is, "What makes Papa think he is a writer, and his material is worthy of your reading?" This is my journey and justification.

My first sense of writing something worthwhile came in the 7th grade. Mr. Lee VanderArk, our English teacher, was teaching us how to write compositions. He insisted we buy a thesaurus and gave us permission to use the biggest words we could find that seemed to fit.

I choose to write an essay about my horse, Rusty, a great horse, and I set out to try to describe him. When we got our papers back, I received an A-. Altogether, there were three A-'s in the class, and Mr. VanderArk made that known publicly.

As a Freshman at Calvin College all of us faced the dreaded Freshman English. The rumor was that most students got a D or F on their first composition. It was part of Calvin's tradition of putting the "fear of God" into this roundup of rookies. But I got a B- from the honorable Professor Steve VanderWeele. His Freshman English was the only English or Writing course I ever had.

Somewhere in my years teaching at Ft. Wingate, I wrote a proposal regarding how to better teach our low achieving student. I also wrote a letter of concern to Christian Reformed Home Missions about some issues of concern at Rehoboth. I got compliments for such writing and began to feel more confident.

When I was a young elementary principal, we started a monthly "Parent News" just for our Grade 1-6 parents. The response was quite remarkable, this being the first attempt to communicate to the parents. The next year, we sent home a weekly "Parent News," and it has gone on for all the decades since.

In moving home to Lynden in 1982, I took a part-time job with Concerned Christian Citizens (CCC). Our "Communique" publication went to a couple thousand people, and a much more diverse crowd. It was because of that writing that Dick Beardsley from the *Bellingham Herald* called me to be one of 12 community columnists, writing an article a month. Again, larger audience—now it is getting scary. I labored over those columns.

That led to a call from Bob Keller, asking me to write a chapter in a new book to be entitled *Whatcom Places*. The fuller story of that experience comes later in the book.

Upon our return to New Mexico in 2000, I was invited to write columns on the religion page of the Gallup Independent, which I did periodically over six or seven years. And there was the occasional request for an article in *Christian Home and School*, the *Christian Educator's Journal*, *The Banner* and a several other obscure places.

To be sure, I have never thought of myself as a first-rate writer. But somehow, without any particular training, I became a decent writer, at least I was invited and/or given numerous writing assignments. And I write much as if I am talking—first your Auntie Karen and later others echoed that I write with "voice."

To talk about my writing skills is subservient to whether one's writing is directed toward "a long obedience in the same direction" (Eugene Peterson). Does Papa's writing make sense, does it honor the Scriptures, is it more than a worldview, but a way of life?

Thus, as noted above, the title, and the verse from Psalm 90:17b "Establish the work of our hands, yes, establish the work of our hands." Please Lord, unto the 3rd and 4th generation!

Family and the Farm, Stories and the Stool

This is a memoir, a partial chronology, a collection of stories about both our personal and professional lives. It includes family narratives and accounts of farm-life, which occupied generations of Polinder living.

And it includes some opinion, even critique, of the big issues we faced through the years. I hope you find them worth your time to read, and maybe even have a chuckle or two along the way.

There is also this strange reference to a stool—what might that be? In our tradition of Dutch Calvinism, there was a steady emphasis on Christian schooling. There was often reference to this triad of home, church, and school. And the image used to describe it was a three-legged stool. I would often say to prospective parents: "Christian education begins at home, it is furthered in the church, and then the school can do it best work."

In significant ways, this explains our lives, both Nana and me, but also our children, and grandchildren. I am thankful for this pattern, now at work unto the 5th generation, going back to my grandparents, though I don't know the particulars of their Christian education.

Many cultures around the world look to their elders to provide wisdom. Of course, I dare to hope that my grandchildren will find a morsel or two of wisdom in this book. I have experienced numerous remarkable moments when I marveled at the way younger people "honored their father and mother" or others in their extended families. Our culture worships youthfulness, too easily disposing of their elders to a care center. Our Navajo and Latino friends resented such a pattern—they respected the "elderlies," as Navajos so often called them, and looked to them for guidance.

As I reflect on my life's journey even in these pages, I often think of that line from the *Fiddler on the Roof* in the song "Sunrise, Sunset," written by Jerry Bock and Sheldon Harnick: "One season following another, laden with happiness, and tears." In short, I have had plenty of both—deep, intense suffering, but also overwhelming joy, and, like railroad tracks, they run alongside each other.

Most importantly, I pray that God will be honored by what is written here. He has blessed Nana and me so abundantly. And sacrificed Himself for us, and you. So in sheer gratitude, I offer up this endeavor. "May these words of my mouth and this meditation of my heart be pleasing in your sight, Lord, my Rock and my Redeemer" Psalm 19:14.

What/Who to Include?

Already this memoir is too long. How dare I write still more? But how can I skip "Bob and Carol, Ted and Alice?" With trepidation, that some will be hurt by my sin of omission. And not only certain people, but significant stories that changed my life or those around me? So, I can only apologize from the outset, and ask your forgiveness.

How to read the book?

I can't imagine that anyone would read the whole thing. I hope that you read "in" it. Check out some of the characters and stories, and that may lead you to explore others. I will be honored by your exploration.

CHAPTER 1

Ron, Eleanor, Sherm

With our pet cow, named "Pet"

Sneaking "scratch" to the chickens

The Early Years (1946 – 1950's)

What was it like to be a kid if you were born in 1946 in Lynden, WA? One does not remember all that much—we lived in an old house on the family farm. Life was simple: school, church, farming, some social life, mostly with extended family.

I did not go to kindergarten—most of us didn't. School started for me in 1952; born in September, I was five. Suddenly I was amid all these new kids! I don't recall knowing a single person. But that quickly changed, and friendships developed. I was a decent student, but not the brightest and the best. As the years passed, history and geography were favorites, but math by grade five became a problem.

We sang, starting every day with 15 or 20 minutes of hymns and choruses with piano accompaniment, often two classes joined. Of course, recess and noon hour were the favorites, playing football and softball, but not basketball in those days. We had a splendid woods of tall cedar trees (where the current middle school is built) and we played there, building forts and climbing trees.

We went to church twice every Sunday. My earliest memory was in the basement of Third Christian Reformed Church, before there was an upstairs. The second service was in the afternoon at 2:15, though it shifted to evening service in our middle school days. We learned to behave, but much of it was over our head. We dressed up, even with white shirts and suits at an early age. I am thankful for the habit—the message was 'Church was important.'

After church, we went to Grandma's house; one week "Freddy's grandma" and the next week "Dort's grandma"—that is what we call them. As kids, we mostly listened in on the adults, hearing the news of the community, all shaping our values along the way. The grandmas served a generous lunch, and then we would head for home around 5:00 to do the milking and chores.

Social life beyond the extended family was limited. We did not have neighbor kids to play with, except Billy Stuurmans in my case. But Billy loved to pretend we were hunting, which his dad did. Since my dad was not a hunter, I thought it was dumb. We loved it when our folks would invite over or visit one of the family friends—the DeJongs, the Stuurmans, the Bovenkamps.

And of course life was so much about the farm. Dad was milking by 6:00, and we were supposed to be out by 7:00, though sometimes we didn't listen to mom's efforts to get us out of the sack. We slept upstairs in the old house, with no heat, except a hot water bottle on cold nights. We hustled to do chores because we had to have breakfast and then off to 8:45 school. After school we would have a snack, and then out to the barn. We would usually be back in the house by 7:30 for supper and homework—or special TV programs like *The $64,000 Question* or *Maverick*.

I was able to join 4-H at age nine, which did provide us some social life with kids from Lynden public, a good experience. But equally important were the lessons learned about agriculture in our 4-H meetings and at the Fair. In the summer, it was filling silo and making hay. By age six, I was expected to drive tractor for the hay wagons, always fearing that there would not be enough room between bales, and thus incurring the wrath of Uncle Fred.

For years we shared farm work and equipment with Uncle Fred and close neighbors Clarence and Cornelia Ludden. Eventually Uncle Fred broke off, but we worked back and forth with the Luddens for many years. The Luddens did not have children and were not church-going people, so when we had lunch at their house, there was no opening prayer, all of which are learning experiences. But we loved Cornelia's warm homemade bread and were family friends and farm "partners." I remember Dad telling me to go mow Clarence's hay, and I was quite sure Clarence did not know it—but we looked out for each other. Such was family farming and neighborliness. The Ludden estate was given for scholarships to graduates of both Lynden and Lynden Christian Schools.

Great Uncle John Spaan owned the John Deere dealership (where current museum is housed) and sponsored a men's team for many years. Clarence Ludden was the coach, and my dad after he quite playing, was the assistant for several years. Uncle Fred was the first baseman, until brother Sherm took over. Given Sherm's promotion, I replaced him as batboy, and inherited his uniform. (We were the only team in the county to have a batboy with a uniform. I was far too proud of it.) I learned a lot from those talented young players, not all of which was wholesome. Clarence would pay me a quarter after each game, which often went into my piggy bank. These teams were highly skilled, but were relentless in razzing the opposition. Sportsmanship was seldom practiced, and the next day(s) in the hay field those games were reviewed almost play by play. All of which was high entertainment. Along with the Fair, softball was our only summer leisure.

One additional pleasure of the early years was a horse named "Rusty." Dad and Mom, along with their good friends Don and Minner DeJong, decided to buy a horse in partnership for their son Gerb (a year older) and me. Their strategy was to trade the horse back and forth each month, so as to create a desire for the horse to return to be able to ride again. Too often, kids grow weary of a horse as it loses its novelty, but for Gerb and me, it was always a treat to again be able to ride Rusty for that month.

Rusty was a terrific horse, well-mannered, classy. We got him when Gerb and I were in 7th and 6th grades respectively, and we rode him until we were out of high school. Rarely did we put a saddle on him—always bareback. I think we only shoed him once. Sister Marge and Doris DeJong also followed the same pattern, though Doris was more inclined. Regardless, it was one of the great gifts of growing up, to learn to love and ride a horse—thanks to our parents!

School Daze (1952-1968)

I remember nearly every teacher I ever had, starting in 1st grade through graduate school. I will not bore you with all of them, but I believe I learned important things or had memorable experiences with most.

You will note that there was no kindergarten. I have jested about how smart I would be if only I had kindergarten.

Elementary:

1st grade—Mrs. Bush: A kindly, elderly lady, I don't remember ever being chided by her. My parents went to parent/teacher conferences and she shared but one sentence (I learned some years later). She said, "He's a boy!" That was it. Dad and Mom thought there might be more to the story.

2nd grade—Mrs. Heutink: She was less kindly. I remember on four occasions being sent out in the hall, which was the punishment of choice in those days. It was the year that I had stitches placed in my nose given a foolish accident. Upon returning to school a couple of days later, I was hit in the eye by a bat thrown by Teddy Lautenbach, yielding a swollen, black eye. Years later, Mom shared her disgust that the teacher did not call. But note the "years later"—never would my parents criticize or undermine a teacher.

3rd grade—Miss Bouwman: She was 19, after either one or two years of training at Calvin College. It was the year that Nana moved to Lynden and started at Lynden Christian. We actually were both in the slow-reading group, indicating that my oral reading was substandard. Miss Bouwman was altogether sweet as a teacher—we loved her, and Nana decided that year to become a third grade teacher.

4th grade—Mrs. Nymeyer: She was a newlywed. I recall liking my year—in particular we started to study history and geography, which soon became my favorites. Always did riddles during lunch. Nana was not in the same room. J

5th grade—Mr. Nymeyer: Husband to Mrs. above. Not a good year for me. I struggled in math, and every year since. But I still loved history and geography—I remember going through all the U.S. presidents, and all the regions of the United States. The Nymeyers were having their first baby, and my practical mother made me bring a plastic/rubber pants as a gift. Also, twice I took daffodils, growing wildly in the field on the way to the bus—at mom's urging.

6th grade—Miss Harthorn: Single woman, quite attractive, but we were not nice to her. I'm embarrassed. She cried at times. Nana and I were in the same room, and we became sweet on each other. In fact, we traded rings, meaning "going steady." What a joke—snuck to town to buy an 80-cent ring. We rarely talked, just looked across the room and smiled. Miss Harthorn moved to GR, and during our college years, Nana and I went to visit her. I think I apologized for my mischief.

7/8th grades—this is when we started changing classrooms:

Mr. VanderArk—Elsewhere I wrote about his giving me a good grade on a composition that I wrote. Also, he directed the middle school choir, and taught us how to sing parts—that was a big deal. We learned by using "My God How Wonderful Thou Art." He was also the basketball coach, but I had broken arms both years, so was unable to go out for the team.

Mr. Hendricks—He was also the principal, and a very good teacher. In the 7th grade, he was hired part-time to write the civics textbook, "Under God," coming to school each day with a few new pages to add to our notebook. We thought that was pretty cool, and I believe it helped me develop my love for the study of government.

Mrs. Gelensye—Our math teacher, and she was tough, especially if you did not get your assignments in on time. She would have names on the blackboard with how many assignments were missing. It was humiliating for a certain group of students. If you misbehaved, she had a way of pressing her thumb into your collarbone area. Numerous students discovered they had this painful location, which I miraculously managed to avoid.

High School—a few highlights:

Mr. Korthuis—our history teacher, and my favorite. I was a pretty good student of history and he seemed to appreciate that and took an interest in me. We have remained friends to this day, though he moved to Montana shortly after my years at Lynden Christian. He was a serious Christian; devout, I would claim. He wrote at least a couple of books related to his life and profession. He lost his wife Elaine after many years of paralysis following a car accident. Very sad, but he is now happily remarried.

Mr. Friesen—our choir director, and a good one, though we did not always behave well. He looked to me for leadership of our tenor section, and for the choir hour in general. I know I disappointed him at times. Nana had him for band. She was a good trombonist. We asked him to sing at our wedding and visited him a few times in subsequent years.

Mrs. Wymore—she was not five feet tall, but nobody got the best of her. She was divorced and had a son—very unusual for the early 60's. In addition to being a fine teacher, she was also a beautiful singer. I remember when she took her ukulele to class and sang us ballads. She also directed the choir at Third Church, with great skill.

She got my attention one grading period when she gave me an F in senior English. It was the semester I was milking Uncle Sherm's cows, getting up early, and too often going to bed late, given my dating patterns with Nana. I would sleep through her class at times, and she grew weary of us ne'er-do-well senior boys—flunked a bunch of us. I did much better the next grading period.

I think she grew weary of the lack of sophistication of our school, and Lynden in general. After three years, she departed for Eastern Christian in New Jersey, a big loss to our community. She was a Calvin grad, and I remember her talking about certain professors with such awe—I believe it influenced Nana and me.

One of the most eventful moments in high school was getting cut from the basketball team during my Junior year. I wrote about this in an article for the Bellingham Herald, which drew a nice response (see "Basketball Lessons"). I realized that I was more talented in music than basketball—it was a good lesson and I am thankful for it.

In summary, I am thankful for my Christian education. I had many good teachers, but not all. I think Lynden Christian was a good school, but not a great one. In going to Calvin, I came to see how behind I was compared to students from other schools around the country. To be sure, my aptitude for math and science was weak. Yet, the culture of the school, reflective of the broader community allowed for too much mediocrity and inappropriate behavior. We should have been held to higher standards, though the community did not demand it—in fact they often resisted it.

But I could have been a much better student had I worked harder. I was a slow reader, and always a procrastinator. It plagued me into college as well. Yet, I was able to graduate from Calvin, though not with a great GPA. But I listened quite well and caught on to what Calvin was trying to teach—about our Reformed tradition, about the Kingdom of God and our call to serve that Kingdom. All said, I'm grateful!

Farm Life:

Aerial picture of the farm, taken in the 60's

Ronelee cows on sale

Sister Marge perplexed her name isn't included

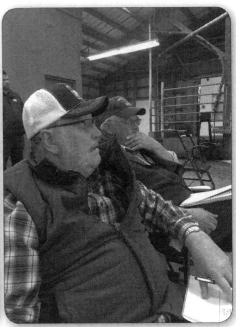

The brothers watching

My Ronelee Home

It was once Bylsma Road, Route 2, which became 8075 Polinder Road, sometime in the early 60's, and later 670 Polinder. We called it Ronelee Farm, named after the three eldest siblings, then born. But deeper than the name and numbers, was what we called "home." Home is a rich, beautiful word, almost biblical—some have said: "home is where the heart is." For nearly six decades that farm was still home; even when leaving for college in 1964, I left home practically but not emotionally.

When we decided in 2009 to again move home to Lynden, our Native friends protested, "Why are you leaving us?" My response was, "We are moving back to our Rez." That answer Native folks can understand because they are not home in some city, large or small—they are at home on their Rez. The case was settled.

Strangely, even though we lived in New Mexico for 23 years, we always felt like sojourners. It was never home for me, though we loved it and it was a second home. But my affection for that farm on the road bearing our name in the community and state we loved could not be undone.

What was it that attached me to what I claim as home? There is not one explanation:

Dad and Mom—isn't that the major among minors? Driving those miles from New Mexico all those years was highlighted by seeing Dad and Mom again. Thus, in January of 1982 when Mom was taken from us, I could barely manage the trip home; it would not be home—home was slashed in half.

Our Farm—I still call it "our" farm—how dare I? As of this writing, I own a mere 15 acres down the road. I have part ownership in a few cows, but the farm has sold. Under my name was no birthright, no investment, no equipment. Truth be told, I was too often slothful with my chores, I did not have the eye for cattle that Sherm or Eleanor had, and by the time I was 18, I decided that farming was not my calling. Yet I would cling to the audacious notion that I had some ownership in Ronelee Farm.

Ronelee Holsteins—I loved it that we "showed" cows. I was always proud of our cows, but usually scared of our competition. Did we measure up? Sometimes yes, and sometimes we stood down the line, often thinking we should have "stood" higher in the final placing. I had the good fortune of having really good 4-H animals, and often placed first. And I worked hard to prepare for "fitting and showing" which I intended to win, and usually did. As a family, we took the fair seriously, the best week of the summer. For 60+ years, Ronelee Holsteins were highly regarded in the show ring.

When our kids came along, Uncle Sherm was always generous with finding good 4-H calves for them to take to the Fair. So too, our grandkids! Thus, our passion was sustained—hard work, but we loved it. And we found deep satisfaction, even pride, when they won.

Family Affair—None of us were excused from farm duties, also known as chores. Dad of course set the pace, but Mom was no stranger to barn work. Neither were any of us five kids, though the oldest three likely were the most involved. Dad was a leader in the Dairy industry, and often gone for meetings and trips. With confidence, he turned responsibility over to Mom, who did her best to crack the whip on us kids. Sherm and I still marvel at the responsibility we were given, and the diligence with which we followed through.

I remember keeping track of all the birthing and the breeding, and then preparing all the registration papers. We drove tractor, mowed, crushed, raked, baled. We filled silo, bucked bales, loaded wagons. Marge and I take pride in how much the two of us could accomplish come haying season. Karen, the tail-ender, was not exempt—she spent her hours in the milking parlor.

All to say, it was truly a family farm, likely now lost on the American landscape, but we had the privilege of participating in these unique decades of history. I believe we are all thankful.

Of course, the times they were a-changing—and Sherm and Phyllis and their family took over the operation for a 40-year-run. Still, we all watched from a distance, always yet claiming a portion. Sherm was open to our interest and inquiries. I probably paid the most attention, but we knew full well it was not our operation.

And now this enormous development—the farm is selling as Sherm and Phyllis recognize the realities of age and health. We are both thankful and sad, all of us. But the emotions of us younger siblings are smallish compared to the elder Sherm and Phyllis. For them, this is mammoth, massive, enormous—we surely recognize this reality.

But they, and all of us, now return to our roots, our spiritual roots, which must be deeper than all of the above sentiment. This farm never really did belong to us, nor Sherm, nor our parents. We are mere stewards of the land and animals that God placed in our care. We grew up memorizing Psalm 24:1a, that the "the earth is the LORD's, and everything in it." We sang in school "See the farmer sow his seed, up the field and down…God will make the golden corn, grow where all is brown" ("A Seed Song," by Frederick A. Jackson). In church we grasped that "Our World Belong to God" (A Contemporary Testimony of the Christian Reformed Church).

Ronelee Farm was a gift to us, and now we give it back to God, passing it on the Plagerman's, praying that the farm flourished under our watch, and is found to be in better condition and cultivation because four generations of Polinder's lived out their faith in this sacred space called Ronelee Farm.

For this, my home, I bow my knee in gratitude.

Showing Cows

What a strange title, some may think! But showing cows has been a big deal for our family, now for four generations.

A further explanation about showing cows at the Lynden Fair, or places beyond. There is a lot to learn about "showing," and since our family has been at it for a long time, you eventually learn the skills and tricks of the trade.

My Dad, or likely his dad, bought a purebred calf sometime in the 30's. Her name was Eva. I am not sure if Dad ever showed her at the fair—it was the Depression, and such activity may have been considered frivolous. Eva had a least two daughters, Dort and Francis, both of whom I remember. From those two cows came offspring that are still part of Ronelee Farm, especially Francis.

In 1951, Dad announced to brother Sherm, a mere 10-year-old, that he was no longer going to help with showing horses, but was going to start showing cows. My Dad drove the six-horse hitch, even an eight-horse hitch (of which there is a great picture following). But he had taught his brother Fred how to drive, and Uncle Fred was eager to take the reins. So in '52, we started taking cows to the Fair.

It didn't take long for us kids to really get into it. Our mom less so, but she figured the cow people were a better crowd than the horse people, who could be quite rowdy. Mina wanted Hank in a better environment. We were excited to be part of a new adventure and did our share of work to prepare for the Fair. I think the first year we took a half dozen, and by year two about a dozen head. It was hard work training animals to lead from a halter and learning to wash them so they were perfectly clean.

Uncle Sherm and Auntie Eleanor joined 4-H at about 11 or 12 years of age, and I was able to join a year later when I was nine. We practiced a lot, and rather soon we were at or near the top of our classes. We had good competition from Skagit County. I believe in my second year, I won fitting and showing and the "type" class with Ronette, who I showed for several years, often winning even at Puyallup Fair. At some point I switched to the younger Luella, who was even a better animal. I won more than my share. Auntie Marge too, showed for a few years and did very well.

Marge and I both had some memorable experiences at Puyallup. One year, in fitting and showing, the judge left me way out on the edge of the ring, calling most of the others in before me. I was scared, but I kept working to make sure my animal was set up properly. He was testing me. Suddenly he motioned me in—to 2nd place, next to my friend Randy Nelson. Then he had the two of us go head to head, and pulled me in first. Sadly, a year or so later, Randy was in a car accident, had a serious brain injury, and died a few years after that.

Another year, my Dad warned me I was too active, my movements too fast, too obvious. I didn't listen. Dr. Blosser gave me first place, but in his "reasons" he said I was "a wee bit of an exhibitionist." I won, but I was embarrassed. I learned to tone down my style of showmanship.

Marge had worse experiences—one year she got a white ribbon, causing my Dad to talk to the judge, pleading the case of any kids who had a clean, well-trained animal. He did not refer to his daughter, but Marge happened to walk up to Dad while he was talking to the judge—and handed him her white ribbon. He asked, "Is this your daughter?" "Yes," said Dad. Truly an awkward moment, for a dad that was not inclined to stick up for his kids.

Even worse, one year Mom and Marge got a ride to Puyallup with some distant relatives. They drove all too slowly, and then stopped at a restaurant for breakfast, ordered big off the menu, and took their time to wolf it down. Marge is near tears, knowing she is going to be late to wash her calf. Mom in turned grabbed the bill and quickly headed for the cashier. They moseyed into Puyallup maybe a half hour before show time. The good news is that Uncle Fred was there with Fred III and had taken it upon himself to wash Marge's calf. Marge loved him ever since—and went on to win the show. But that story about those slow, tight relatives never left the memory of our family.

All in all, it was a good experience, including being a 4H-er.

When Colleen and I moved back to Lynden in 1982, Staci was old enough to join 4-H. Again Uncle Sherm was generous with my kids in choosing good calves and heifers. Staci was diligent and we practiced aplenty. Sure enough, come show day, she and her calf looked like a million bucks. Nana did Staci's hair in a bun, and dressed her in "whites," as was the protocol. She won the class! I was so proud, I wondered if my buttons would pop off into the shavings. I think I also cried, wishing that my mom could have been there to see her granddaughter.

A couple of years later, Shawna started to show, and she likewise did well, winning fitting and showing more than once. And then a couple years after that, Rusty was old enough, and he too won his share in both fitting and showing and "type". Nana and I were always so pleased at how hard the kids worked, and what they learned about practice and good preparation.

But it wasn't without painful experiences. One year, Staci's heifer misbehaved and stepped hard on her foot. Shawna one year stood near the bottom of "open class," and maybe even got a red ribbon in 4-H. Rusty too had his problems, one year his calf had ringworm and thus you could not take them to the Fair. Uncle Sherm often said that it was good to learn how to stand at both ends, to get first, and to stand dead last. One needs to learn how to win, and how to lose.

And then there were my grandkids—as of this writing, both Lathan and Lerieka have had a showing experience. Papa many times took them out to the farm to practice—it was hot and smelly, and Lathan particularly hated the animal snot rubbing on her arm. But they won, both in their first year. Papa was even prouder than when his own kids won! But Lathan too had his trials, one year his animal was in heat. That makes it impossible to show well.

As noted above, all of us had the benefit of attractive, good-looking animals. The judge is naturally attracted to them.

It is a small slice of life, but important lessons were learned: hard work, persistence, patience, winning and losing, seeking perfection, enjoying competition. The Lord will use even such obscure activity as showing cows to mold our character.

Dad showing at the Fair

Lathan and Lerieka, winners

Dad teaching his brother Fred
to drive 8-horse hitch

Dad at plowing match with
team, Doreen and Heather

Our terrific horse Rusty

Receiving my first trophy for
Fitting and Showing

Mom and Dad: Tales and Yarns

It was Mark Twain who once said, "Most of what we remember isn't true."

He also said, "No real gentleman will tell the naked truth in the presence of ladies."

Finally, he is also credited with "truth is stranger than fiction."

But then there is Stanley Wiersma, or his pen name Sietze Buining, who with a twinkle in his eye said, "Never let truth stand in the way of a good story."

So who knows if what is said here is truthful. Surely we will debate it, Polander's we. And we will walk away with our opinion, convinced we got it right.

When I am finished, I hope you will have some of your own favorite lines of family lore.

We often picture Mom as that hardworking farm woman, who preferred being outside rather than a homemaker. She did well at both. And maybe we remember her serious side, which was well-developed. But we must not forget how much fun she could be, or the tales she could tell.

- Was it true that a certain lady at Third Church during an afternoon church service left with her youngster seemingly to take the lad to the bathroom. But when they walked back into church it was the hem of her dress that was caught up in her girdle. Third Church was thus given a new sample of "revealed truth."
- Was it Mom who discovered an interesting correction in the Lynden Tribune? It was the previous week that the police report revealed that a local young man had siphoned gas out of someone's car. The bigger issue was there were two by the same name in our community. Which of them could have done it? Well, a proper correction was printed by the mother of "the [so-and-so] that didn't steal gas," who to this day in the Polinder family is known as "that one who didn't steal gas."
- Mom was an early riser, and would holler to her sleepy children, "You are missing the best part of the day!" Even after Colleen and I were married and sleeping in the Guesthouse, Mom would decide at about 7:05 that is was time to wash the windows. Her method was to spray them with a hose, as if that would do much good. But it sure did wake us. Colleen never complained, but she must have wondered about her mother-in-law, who no doubt did it with a mischievous smile on her face.
- Mom was actually proud of Dad in his various leadership roles. She always wanted him to look sharp and enjoyed buying new suits on occasion. Of course, when Dad was gone, it added to

her workload, though I proved to be her most willing helper out in the barn. J Marge the house cat was of only marginal help. But Mom imitated Dad when he got yet another call to serve on some Board. Dad would indicate he was already quite busy, but he would ask some questions about the assignment, and then conclude by asking, "Well, when is the first meeting?"

- Mom and Dad were ballplayers, both loving the game of softball for their entire lifetimes. Mom was first baseman for Farmer's Equipment, Aunt Dort was the left-handed catcher. Hilda DeHaan was pitcher, Joanne Polinder Dykstra a youthful center fielder. There were the Hamstra sisters playing 3rd and shortstop, both of whom could throw very hard. Mom would complain that her hand was swollen and blue after catching their throws to first. How did she even catch them with her "pancake" of a glove? But catch them she did, and would proudly proclaim her team played "errorless ball, many a night." It was a litany the rest of us tried to live up to.

- We always had about four rows of sweet corn, and the word got out that you could buy a sack of corn at the Polinders. I can picture Mom out in the field, snapping off ears of corn and filling those burlap sacks. Often we were out there with her, holding open the sack, or likely picking some ourselves. Mom would stuff that sack full, making sure the customer got their money's worth. How much did Mom charge for a full sack? And how many sacks did she sell? My recollection is the profits went for our school clothes.

- Mom had certain phrases that she used aplenty, all of which were material for us kids to tease her about. When she was tired, "her knees were buckling" and she was "purtineer parched." When we teased her, she would say, "I have a broad back, I can take it." When she was unhappy about something or with somebody, much to the embarrassment of us kids, she would say, "I'm just going to ask some questions."

- In general, we were not a family that quickly talked about our feelings or our joys and sorrows. Thus when Mom was pregnant with Karen, for her to reveal such was a big deal, and we all know exactly the circumstances, or even where we were standing when she told us. (It was uncharacteristic for us to discuss pregnancy.)

Now for a couple of Dad's memorable moments:

- It was 1963 or '64, and the building of a new high school was under discussion. There was a well-attended Society meeting in which the matter was debated. There seemed to be strong verbal support, so then it was time at least ask for a show of hands as to who might be willing to donate at least a $1000 for the new project. Many hands went in the air, including Dad's, until he saw the hand of a someone who owed him a chunk of money. In his wisdom, Dad's hand came down, figuring his now-private pledge would have to make up for the unlikely pledge of the guy in front of him.

- With all Dad's Darigold work, he attracted plenty of farmers to our yard with complaints about how Darigold was operating. We all got sick of it, because it meant that we did more of the chores and the milking. There was Bud Hunter, once Dad's comrade, who turned against Dad, causing Mom to call him the "Backstabber."(Later in life they reconciled and became partners, with other, in Bellingham Frozen Foods.) But the most memorable visitor was Herb Munson, all of 6'6", usually in stripped overalls and those cheap, tall, black barn boots. One winter eve he walked up the back steps looking for Dad. We said he was at church working on the parsonage. Herb headed for Third Church not knowing where, or likely what a parsonage was. There were cars by the church basement's West entry, prompting Herb to inquire therein, only to discover Ladies Aid in session, which included our Mom. There stood the long drink of water, in his striped overalls and barn boots, asking for Henry Polinder. Poor mother—the embarrassment of it all. But oh how she loved to tell the story.

- Well, there was trouble in the land and Darigold was taking the heat. Dad was Board Chair, but he only had Bill Mize on his side, and three against him, led by the Hitlerian Harold Knight. Dad was up for reelection, and he knew he was in trouble. He did not even go to the annual meeting, held in the auditorium of Bellingham High School. It was a packed house, well over a thousand people. Dad dispatched Mom and me to observe, which we did from the back row. Midway through the meeting, the election results were announced, indicating that our dad got beat. Mom and I left somewhat promptly, heading to our car. Our path converged with neighbor and fellow Third Churcher, Jim Bajema, lighting his pipe. Seeing Mom, he said, "Well Mina, the bastards beat us." As Mom and I entered the car, we burst out laughing. Such cryptic analysis could not be improved upon. It remains one of the favorite lines of my youth, and likely that of my siblings. Dad stayed away from Darigold for three or four years while the company continued to go downhill. I did manage to get a summer job there and would report on "stuff" that I saw, leaving Dad shaking his head. He was re-elected at the difficult time when "the cowmilkers" organization was created prompting a couple dozen of dairymen to leave Darigold. Our Dad had the big hand in cleaning up the mess, causing endless conversations and meetings. He remained on the Board into the 90's. He was chairman for at least 23 years and left the Board with much distinction and honor.

- But I have a lovely summer memory a few years later when I was invited to an Annual Meeting at the old 1st Street gym, again quite a full house. The previous week, the troublesome Linda Zander, long one of Dad's detractors, published a letter in the Tribune, critical of everything Darigold. Dad was hot, and he took the letter to the Annual Meeting a few days later. Linda was sitting across the gym from Sherm and me, as Dad dissected her letter point by point. To our delight, Sherm and I watched her shaking her head through the ordeal. It was not Dad's style to publicly take someone to task, but he had had his fill of this difficult woman. It was one of Dad's finest hours. I don't recall if Mom was still living, but had she been present, she would have been proud of her husband.

- Dad's great concern was that his kids may get the "big head." I think he even thought that about Uncle Fred, as he would occasionally critique his driving of the 6-horse hitch. I remember cringing when Dad would remind his brother that those horses needed to be lined up as they made their turns, not having a swing horse too far out. I find myself looking for that still as I watch the driving at the fair. Dad's effort to keep us humble for me happened after softball games, when he did not ask if I got any hits, rather, "how many errors did you make?"

- A sweeter moment and memory between Dad and me happened in my Junior year of High School, shortly after I got my license. That fall on a Friday night a group of us guys were "going bowling," which was the standard ruse for the reality that we were going to a movie. In those days, movie attendance was strongly discouraged by the CRC. I finished by chores early to be on time, and got halfway to the house, and I turned around and walked back to the barn. I found Dad in the driveway and confessed that I really was not going bowling. We would be going to a movie instead. Dad's response? "That's Ok for you to go to movies, just make sure you choose good ones."

- This final word: I never questioned Dad's love for me, or any of us. One-time years later, after he married Lois, evidently they were reading or listening to Chuck Colson. Seemingly Colson admonished parents if they had not told their kids that they loved them. Sure enough, one night the phone rings at our Abbott Road house, and Dad shared Colson's word about telling your kids you love them. Then he said, "I just wanted you to know that." Mind you, he could not say "I love you, Ron"—that was not his style. But the beauty of it was that he didn't have to say those exact words—I knew my Dad loved me. But I cherished the call to this day.

Dad's Team

Mom's Softball Team

Family with baby Marge

Little Margie, little farm girl

Family with baby Karen

Little Karen with Dad playing piano

Assorted Short Stories:

The Walk to Aunt Minnie's House

On a Monday morning, Mom sent Sherm, Eleanor, and me to Aunt Minnie Polinder, across the pasture. I don't recall the purpose of the trip, likely an errand of some sort. Aunt Minnie was a warm-hearted person and offered us some leftover jellyroll from the night before. Being the youngest, maybe three or four, I got the smallest portion, to which I brashly asked, "How come I get such a stinkin' little piece?" The more mature brother and sister were of course horrified.

On the way back through the pasture, Mom, watching through the window, saw the older siblings roughing up the little brother. What now, she wondered? She soon found out, and I am sure I got a good scolding. She called Aunt Minnie to apologize. But Aunt Minnie had a good sense of humor. She thought little Ronnie was wonderfully cute.

Unfortunately, it would not be the only time I embarrassed my mother!

Joyce

My friend Faber and I were having a hamburger at the Fairway one evening, and in walked the Terpsma family. Father Gerrit was celebrating a high 90's birthday, and the kids had gathered for the event. Jerry Terpsma was a classmate of Faber, so he naturally stopped at our table to exchange greetings. I then asked where his sister Joyce was. In fact she was part of the group, and then I recognized her. I said, "Hi Joyce—you were my girlfriend in the 4th grade." Without missing a beat, she said. "You were not—Ronnie Polinder was my boyfriend." To which I said, "That would be me."

The laughter filled the Fairway!

Romance

It started already in the 6th grade where I developed a liking for that tall Haak girl—Colleen. And she returned the favor. It didn't amount to much—I don't remember ever really talking to each other. But we sure did smile at each other across the classroom.

There was the school roller skating party. But I didn't know how to skate—I was a farm kid and we didn't get to town to learn how to skate. But I talked my folks into letting me go, which they limited to about 90 minutes. I didn't know the protocol of the skating rink, but my friends helped me through the process of getting skates.

Now I had to face getting on the floor. My concern was that soon my face would be *on* the floor. I swear I was the only beginner in the house. I was all arms and legs, flailing in different directions. By the third time around the rink, I started to get some balance, and Nana and others helped me along. I was improving.

When the Ladies Choice sign came up, we all cleared the floor. And there came your Nana to ask me to skate with her. It was a holy moment. She wasn't embarrassed of me, and off we went, holding hands. When in 6th grade, holding hands is a big deal.

I should add that at some point we exchange rings, meaning we were "going steady." Of course, one did not actually give the ring to your girlfriend—you would ask a surrogate, in my case Duane Bouma, to deliver it. It worked.

Until summer, when Nana went to the berry fields and had lots of other suitors. Out of sight, out of mind—I got dumped. But that pretty blonde girl was always in my heart.

Bus Woes

I was not always a good boy—in fact, too often I was quite naughty. It especially came out when riding the bus. Mr. TeSelle was the driver, and he had the reputation of being a stickler for the rules. Sadly, that made us all the more interested in pestering him.

The large Hoksbergen family lived up on the Wiser Lake road, and a bunch of them also rode the bus. It was a dangerous combination, the Hoksbergens and the Polinders. I had done something foolish, I don't remember the particulars, but was put off the bus for a few days. But we conspired to put me in a bunch of Hoksbergens, including a couple of high schoolers, and they would "mob" me on to the bus. Well, Terrible Ted, as we called him, saw me in the middle of the crowd, and simply would not move the bus until I got off.

But that wasn't the end of it—the next morning I got called out of my 7th grade classroom at the old Grover Street school and was given a ride home by Mr. TeSelle. Dad and Mom were in the milkhouse, washing the machines, as was the morning custom. They were not happy to see me. Mr. TeSelle explained my crimes, while I had my elbows on the stainless-steel milk tank, tears streaming down my face.

Why the tears? I was guilty, embarrassed, ashamed—my parents deserved better. And so did Mr. TeSelle.

The final decision came rather easily. Ron would walk home the mile and a half the rest of the year, about three months' time. As was their pattern, Hank and Mina supported the school and those in authority. Certainly, they were not about to support a big-mouthed kid.

In those days, good parents always took the side of the teachers. If you sided with your kid, it undermined the authority of the school. It is a good lesson to learn when you become parents. And of course remember—a big mouth can get you in a lot of trouble.

Snowballs

Mom drove me to school one snowy morning my Sophomore year. There were kids throwing snowballs out in front of school. I told my mom that they could get in trouble because snowball fights were limited to the field behind the old First Street school. Not smart—to tell Mom what the rules were.

It was 2nd hour. The wet snow had accumulated on the windowsills. A window opened easily, the snow was of such texture that it would make a fine snowball and the temptation was great. With the teacher not yet in the room, I crafted the perfect snowball to throw at my friend across the room.

Of course, I missed! It hit the post of the door coming into the classroom, just as Rev. Reinsma, our Bible teacher, walked past. The splatter was obvious, and with stern face, he came in and asked who threw the snowball. I knew I was in deep weeds, but I thought if I confessed it might help my cause. Wrong again!

He hauled me into Principal Boxum's office where sat a half dozen kids who faced the same fate— we got the boot from school for the day.

Mr. Boxum loaded classmate Carol Eshuis Holleman and me into his '55 Ford, and headed to our homes, Carol's first. She lived out a ways, which meant that I would have to ride solo with the Principal back toward my place. As I recall, he tried to get into my mind. Who knows what dumb things I said in response.

Dad was gone to a meeting, but Mom was very present. Mr. Boxum explained my foolishness. Of course, Mom noted to Mr. Boxum exactly what I said three hours earlier about snowballs. Not an ounce of sympathy.

Mina was disgusted with her foolish Sophomore. I hauled a lot of manure that afternoon!

North Dakota

Nana was a proud product of Hull, North Dakota. Her Dad and Mom ran the store and post office, though Dad also worked in sale barns around the region.

Nana went to 1st and 2nd grades in a one room country schoolhouse. Would you believe that she had her own pony and rode it to school? They had a little shed out behind the school for the kids to tie up their horses. That lasted only a few years after the family moved to Lynden, when one of the little girls got kicked in the head and died. Thus ended the horse era at the country school.

They moved to Lynden in 1954 in part for work, in part for school, and in part for distancing themselves from their German Russian Catholic neighbors. The Haak family would return every year or two to Dakota, a place they still loved.

After we got married, on our drive back to Calvin, we stopped to meet the relatives in Dakota. Grandpa Haak was still living, though deeply compromised by a stroke. Grandma Haak was still busy in her kitchen, living up to her reputation of being an outstanding cook, and of course, lots of other relatives.

Nana's Haak grandparents

Nana's Rensker grandparents

Nana's Uncles and Aunts: Grandpa & Grandma Haak 3rd from the left

CHAPTER 2

COLLEEN/MOM/NANA

Romance again

After our 6th grade romance, there was a four-year gap that ended in a most beautiful way. Lynden Christian had what was called Twirp Week, in which the girls asked the boys out for a date. Though I was asked out by someone else, I heard that she was wanting to ask me for a date. Early the next week, I made my move—and as they say, the rest is history.

We double-dated with Clay and Adria Libolt, to a Thanksgiving concert at school, and then to Shakey's Pizza in Bellingham. It was terrific—and from thence we went together for nearly five years. A big decision that needed to be made was a college choice. Colleen was leaning toward Calvin, and I was inclined toward WSU, following brother Sherm. Finally, Calvin won out, in part because of sister Eleanor's stories, and the attraction to a Christian College.

Calvin College—what an adventure! Two wide-eyed Lynden kids, 2500 miles from home. We were naïve, new to the mix of fellow students from all around the continent. We were not well prepared for the rigors of Calvin, but we made it. Our social life was more important seemingly, as friendships developed that lasted a lifetime. In those days, Calvin celebrated Homecoming that included a queen and a court. That tall, attractive, winsome Lynden girl was chosen as the representative of the Freshman class. What an experience the two of us had, I being her escort, dressed respectively in gown and tuxedo, though we had no car. Pat Velzen Nederveld was the Junior rep, and she was already going with Gary Nederveld, who had a '49 Ford, and invited us along to a couple of the events. We met up again a few years later at Rehoboth and became forever friends.

Calvin was a stretch for Colleen academically—she worked hard, all the while knowing she wanted to be a teacher. She excelled in her Education courses that pulled up her GPA. Still, we had time to date and experience the richness of college life—including the spiritual insights from the classroom, chapel, and church attendance on the weekend.

It was during our Sophomore year that I developed some doubts about whether she was "the one for me." We broke up that Fall, a painful, but necessary season. Of course, Nana was soon getting dates from all kinds of guys, including one of the Senior starters on the basketball team. One evening, I saw them studying together in the library. Alas, Ron came to his senses, realizing that he may lose this amazing young woman. In the Spring of '66, we reconnected and committed.

Marriage

Wedding Day, Aug 22, 1967

Soon we began looking for engagement rings in Grand Rapids, and it was around Thanksgiving that year I gave her the ring. We aimed for the summer of '67 to tie the knot. In the meantime, because of some changes in the Calvin Curriculum, her advisor helped her see that she could graduate in 3 ½ years if she did summer school at WWU. That in turn would enable her to get a teaching job the second semester of '68 and secure our financial standing.

Thus the plans unfolded for an August of '67 wedding. She was stunning in her gorgeous wedding dress. Bethel CRC Pastor McCloud married us, and our High School music teacher Mr. Jerry Friesen was the soloist. Three of my friends from Calvin came out for the occasion. We honeymooned at Harrison Hotsprings in BC, returning quickly to attend Clay and Adria Libolt's wedding. Within a few more days, we packed our '59 Ford and headed across country.

Our first stop was in Pullman, WA where Nana's friend, Judy Elenbaas Trull, whose husband Jim was a student at WSU. From there stops in both North and South Dakota to visit the Haak relatives in Hull, ND and then to Aberdeen, SD to Grandpa and Grandma Renskers. And to our modest apartment on 1253 Bemis in Grand Rapids. All adventures for us in our early newlywed days.

Our Senior experience at Calvin was marvelous. Student teaching was first on the agenda for Colleen, resulting in a straight A, and a job at Jenison Christian. She worked hard and was soon a favorite of her principal, who would beg her to stay for the coming year. In turn, I had a full Senior year, which also included student teaching at Sylvan Christian Middle School and a final semester of coursework. Further, I was Treasurer of the Student Council.

The Eastern Ave CRC had a reputation for having an outstanding Young Couples Club and we were quick to join in, where we met interesting people, in particular Gary and Carol DeVelder. Further the preaching of Pastor Jim Kok was inspiring, which added to the Calvin challenge to engage in Kingdom work. Collectively, we were ready to go out into the world, thankful for how the Lord had led us in our education and our marriage. New Mexico—here we come!

Music

Music was a very significant part of our lives, both Nana and me—and our kids too. Nana was an excellent pianist. She could lead a congregation from the piano with great skill. All those years on the Rez, often the first question was, "Does anyone here play piano?" She did not want to be presumptuous, so Nana always waited to be asked. Those churches loved her playing, and their singing gave evidence.

But there is so much more—she started lessons at an early age and was already accompanying classroom singing in the 4th grade. In the 6th grade, she started the Trombone, and quickly mastered it. This became a problem because I had started the Trombone in the 5th grade. By the 7th grade she beat me out of 1st chair. I didn't much appreciate it, and soon my interest waned. After my Freshman year, playing 3rd Trombone, I thought it was time to quit. I should have decided it was time to practice.

Nana continued to flourish, playing first chair all through high school, and was invited to be part of a brass quartet. And she continued with piano lessons with Mrs. Carrick, who was a tough, legendary instructor. At Calvin College, she minored in music, but she thought she was a better practitioner than theorist.

Including the trombone, my experience was checkered. I think beginning in 2nd grade, I did three years of piano, but again a lack of practice will get you nowhere. But something else happened—my Grandma Polinder always insisted that there be a Christmas program before opening presents. Our family needed to be represented, and it sure wasn't going to be Uncle Sherm or Auntie Eleanor. So Auntie Marge and I sang "Tell Me the Story of Jesus." She was in 1st grade, I was in 6th. We got a warm response.

I always enjoyed our singing in school and in church. I enjoyed singing parts during congregational singing. We had a good Freshmen chorus—a lot of good male singers in our class. And then on to the adventures of High School choir.

A new director Mr. Jerry Friesen came our 11th grade year. He was a good musician and director, though our choir period could get rather rowdy. He had me prepare solo pieces for the regional "musicale" both my Junior and Senior years, the last year singing a difficult "The Lord is My Light and My Salvation." As I recall, I got a 1- both years, which was considered a good score.

On to Calvin College, where I tried out for what was called "Radio Choir" which sang for the radio program called "The Back to God Hour." It was a decent experience, but not good enough to hold my attention. I quit after a semester, which in hindsight I regret because it ended my college music opportunities. I have always wondered if I could have made the more advanced groups. Nana did not even go out for band, which ended her Trombone career. We often wondered what might have been.

In New Mexico, we both used our gifts periodically. Nana would play routinely at church, and she always accompanied me if I was asked to sing a solo. She was a good alto, and one time we sang a duet at a Wingate HS variety show.

Then the kids started coming, and each of them showed musical talent at a young age. Staci at three sang, "My momma told me something that little girls should know" (a nursery rhyme song "Let the Sunshine In"). She stole the show! Then a year or two later it was "You're Something Special" by the Gaither Vocal Band—likewise a big hit.

A few years later our whole family sang a medley of songs from Psalm 91:4a—"He will cover me with his feathers." Rusty standing on the piano bench, both girls perfectly in tune, mom singing alto, dad singing some tenor—we did it in several churches both on the Rez and at home in Lynden.

After moving back to Lynden, we were able to participate in the 75th anniversary of Lynden Christian, which included a performance of *H.M.S. Pinafore*. That happened to be the first musicale ever done at LC, so it was decided to have some alumni do it again. Marv Vanderpol was the long-time director of such, and he took on this project as well. He approached me about trying out for the role of Captain. I had never been to a Gilbert and Sullivan production, but I got talked into it.

And I am glad I did—it was one of the best months of my life. Part of the fun was the interest of all three of our kids, all of whom learned my part before I did—and likely the parts of several others. We really had a talented cast including Scott Bajema and Leta VanRy Hastings, both of whom had sung professionally. Janet VanderGriend, Jack Veltkamp, Brent Hoekema also had lead roles—after four performances, we were even asked to do an encore performance. It was a hoot!

Just a couple of years later, Staci was in high school, and she promptly tried out for the musicals and won good parts all four years. I remember *Irene*, *Pirates of Penzance* and *The Mikado*. We were always so proud of her performances—she was very talented on stage. Shawna too participated and was the lead in *Seven Brides for Seven Brothers* her Senior year. She was chosen over another talented girl because she knew how to dance, and she played the role of a mother. She performed superbly, singing "Glad that You Were Born" (by Johnny Mercer the lyricist) to absolute perfection. It still makes me cry.

Our only regret in all those years related to Rusty. He too had parts, but his Senior year he tried out for the Captain, the same part I had in *H.M.S. Pinafore*. He was not chosen, though he would have done far better than the kid that was selected. I can still see the look on his face in chapel as he looked at me shaking his head in disappointment. It was the only time "we stuck up for our kid," though we did not say anything to the directors. Rusty and I did sing a duet at his graduation.

I praise God for the beauty of music—many times it would bring me to tears. Both Staci and Shawna were part of Calvin College choirs. It was Staci's Freshman year and I was on campus for a Board of Trustees meeting. I went to her rehearsal, warmly welcomed by Mr. Mustert. At the end, he said, "Let's sing the 'Irish Blessing' for Stacia's dad." I could not contain myself—the tears flowed! I always wish Nana could have been at my side.

There were many other wonderful musical moments. At Staci's wedding, first Shawna started, even startling her fellow bridesmaids, singing "Surely the Presence of the Lord is in this place…" Moments later, Staci sang to Tom "I Could Never Promise You" (Don Fransisco)—Breathtaking!

And at Shawna's wedding, to a stilled church, from the balcony she again sang, "Surely the Presence" (Lanny Wolf). And as we walked, her music director Sean Ivory from Calvin played "I Will," an Allison Krauss piece. Stunning! Elsa Prince declared it the most beautiful wedding she had ever been at.

As hinted elsewhere, the Swedish hymn "Children of Our Heavenly Father," having been sung at Shawn's graveside service, became a staple for every baptism and every wedding thereafter. And yes—at Nana's memorial services, both in Lynden and at Rehoboth. "Though he giveth or he taketh, God his own ne'er forsaketh'—that most precious promise carried us through good times and bad (Original Swedish lyrics by Lina Sandell; translated by Ernst Olson). May I hope that my grandkids will see fit to sing the song at their weddings, and baptisms.

Nana practicing piano

Nana practicing Trombone

Nana with her friend Judy, who become Grandma Judy

CHAPTER 3

CALVIN COLLEGE (1964-1968)

Project V

Such was the name of an obscure program for a group of Calvin College Freshmen in 1964-65. Eighty of us were randomly selected to live on a particular floor, 40 girls on second floor Beets Hall and 40 guys on second floor VanderWerp Hall. We would also have the same professors—two from Religion, two from English and two from History. In my case, I had Prof. Willis DeBoer for Religion, Prof. Steve VanderWeele for English and Prof. John DeBie for history and the 20+ students in each of those classes were also in the other classes. And us guys were all from the same floor in the dorm.

I believe the intent was to create a better sense of community amongst that group of students, including the prospect of them working together on their homework. If that was the objective, I would say it worked—the guys on our floor were exceptionally close and many rich friendships developed—which is the theme behind this story. Though there was also plenty of mischief from the outfit.

For me, I have often noted that it was my Freshman year at Calvin when I really found friends. My high school friendships were all too shallow, maybe because I had a girlfriend my Junior and Senior years, that being your Nana. But at Calvin even before Thanksgiving, a group of us became very friendly. That included George Herrema from New Jersey, Terry Baker from Florida, Don Batts and Ken Klaasen both from Detroit, Rick Evenhuis from Minnesota, Ray Slager from New York, Jim Kos from Western Michigan and me from Washington State. We were obviously a diverse group in terms of geography, but we shared a common Dutch American CRC heritage.

It is hard to explain how friendship happens—certain events and characteristics and interests draw you together. In our case, it was George's laugh, it was Kos's membership on the basketball team, it was pre-med Batt's interest in physiology. His fascination with a picture of my show cow on my bulletin board, alongside Nana's was, he claimed, the strangest thing he had ever seen. But it makes for interesting conversation—Batts loved to hear me talk about cows, what made them "good-looking," and how their bodies functioned in comparison to humans.

Kos was a starter on the basketball team, so he immediately had his own cheering section—we admired his rugged, forward play. Klaasen was so doggone smart—he had his aerospace career path chosen. Baker had a modern translation of the Bible, which he was quick to share with us.

We were basically good kids who could occasionally also be downright naughty. There were way too many water fights on our floor and too much noise during study hour. We were not inclined towards alcohol, or dances. We were not a party crowd, but could we have fun and laugh uproariously, often led by George. Soon we were laughing at George rather than the original joke.

One of our best, or worst, moments was at the expense of Terry Baker. He had a date and borrowed the car of Bob Heerema, a fella from another floor. We conspired to drive the car away, Bob having another set of keys, while Terry was walking his date back to the dorm. Obviously, when Terry came back to the parking area, there was no car. Of course, the poor fella was frantic. Finally, he had to come back to his room where some of us were "innocently" visiting with his roommate George.

"Well Baker, how was the date—do you have my keys?" asked Bob.

Baker stuttered, "Well, let me explain."

Bob, not giving him a chance to explain, again says, "Baker, did you get in a wreck—I need my keys, some of us are going out for coffee."

By now Baker is frenzied as Bob, now acting perturbed, demanded, "Bake, where are my dang keys?"

By now it is time to let Terry explain, which he did with pain in his voice. Finally, Bob took the keys out of his pocket and showed them to a profoundly relieved Baker. Of course, the rest of us having observed Bob pull this off to perfection, finally were able to let loose our guffaws. To this day, all one of us has to say is, "Bake, give me my keys" and we will dissolve into laughter.

Less obnoxious than the story above, we twice took trips together. Spring vacation of our sophomore year we drove to George's house in New Jersey, enabling us to go to New York City for a couple of days. His parents treated us like royalty.

We also went to Detroit one long weekend, some of us hitch-hiking as I recall. Ken Gardner, another Detroit fella on our floor, had a sauna, which most of us never experienced before.

Our Junior year, we piled into Klaasen's car, four of us, and drove to Pease, MN to the Evenhuis's for Thanksgiving. Sadly, with the table loaded with dinner, including Mrs. Evenhuis's creamed onions, the Rev. Evenhuis showed evidence after church of having a mild stroke. Somehow that poor mom was able to still feed a table full of buffaloes.

But beyond the foolishness, were could also be very serious. We grew spiritually given our Bible class, occasional Bible studies, faithful attendance at church and endless discussions. We were slowly catching on to what Calvin College was trying to do for us. And slowly we considered our career path—what was God calling us to do?

Now 54 years later, how God has chosen to use the gifts of these pretty ordinary guys is quite remarkable:

- Ray Slager got his Ph.D in Accounting and became a tenured professor at Calvin.
- George Heerema served as a middle school Social Studies teacher, his entire career at Zeeland Christian.
- Jim Kos was a history major and high school teacher who rose in the ranks in Hamilton, MI to become the Superintendent for a couple of decades.
- Don Batts earned his MD degree and became a distinguished researcher for Upjohn working on HIV-AIDS in Kalamazoo, MI.
- Ken Klaasen earned his advanced degree in Aeronautical Engineering and spent his whole career at Jet Propulsion Lab in Pasadena working on space exploration.
- Terry Baker, now called Merlin, lives in Australia, and works with refugees. We are unsure of his spiritual life.
- Eric Evenhuis graduated from both Calvin and Fuller Seminaries, and has been a pastoral counselor for his career
- My roommate, Ron Bode, became a Social Worker, and eventually operated Senior Living homes
- Ken Van Iddekinge became an accountant at Amway for a full career.
- I have been in the school business for my entire career, mostly in Administration, working in New Mexico and Washington.

Again, we marvel at what this gang in God's good providence has been up to professionally. But the story is quite incomplete without the fuller tale of our friend Eric.

Nine friends from 2nd Floor VanderWerp

Eric Evenhuis, my roommate,
and his wife Nancy

Just recently, Eric, at age 71, found out who his father was. Eric lost his mother when he was 12 to alcohol-related issues. Her first husband left when Eric was just four. She remarried prior to her death, meaning Eric now had a step-father, who all too quickly remarried after her death, leaving Eric with a step-father and step-mother, neither of whom had a particular loyalty to him.

When the step-mother left home unannounced, Eric, still age 12, remembered a woman who had extended her concern for him at his mother's funeral. He called her and she came quickly to pick him up. He packed his suitcase and moved in with this friendly farm family.

There were other uncles and aunts, including Rev. Robert Evenhuis and his wife Faye. It was decided that they would be the best option for Eric, thus moving in with another set of strangers, these folks living in Peace, Minnesota. At last, some stability for Eric, who respected his new step-father in particular. There was an older brother in this family, but he was already an adult.

Suddenly he was in a Christian environment, which was completely new to him. Knowledge of the Bible and a Christian culture was foreign, but he took to it and adjusted quite well to his new setting. At age 17, the only college choice set before him was Calvin, so he ended up on 2nd floor VanderWerp with the assortment of guys described above. He would call it one of the biggest blessings in his life.

But the story does not end there—he had two much older siblings and he was puzzled that he did not look like either. The sister died young, and the brother was mentally unstable--he had a relationship with neither. He suspected that he had a different father than his siblings, but who had such information?

He did have a cousin, suffering from cancer, who seemed to have some grasp of family history. Finally, he called him, now 2017, and said he had a question for him and he was going to come to see him. The question—who was my father?

Cousin Jim knew full well who the father was and upon Eric's visit, identified a well-known doctor in Michigan for whom his mother, a nurse, worked. After all these decades, he had a name, and could look up family history online. Pictures showed a clear resemblance. Jim also indicated that his birth mother was quite promiscuous and had more than one abortion (long before abortion was legalized.) Is it any wonder that today, Eric is strongly pro-life—for some reason he was spared a premature death.

How is it that Eric, given his totally difficult childhood, would have the fulfilling life he now enjoys? Many people with such a painful past would more likely be in jail. But by the sheer grace of God, Eric was saved in the fullest sense of the term.

In our Sophomore year at Calvin, Eric and I were roommates. We have been life-long friends. When we see each other after years of separation, it is like we were never apart. That is the blessing of friendship, which started by God's grace in the unclear objectives of Project V at Calvin College. But it was not unclear to our Lord, who brought this disparate group of college freshmen together for his purposes.

A Hard Privilege

My Senior year at Calvin included election to the Student Council. In fact, I was Treasurer, and thus on the Executive Committee. It was a great experience—we were much engaged in significant issues, like student evaluation of professors, bringing big name entertainment to campus, and some big-name speakers too. This was the late 60's and college campuses around the nation were abuzz with demands for "student rights."

It was in the spring of '68 that Martin Luther King was assassinated, and our Student Council was much involved in organizing the two marches that followed. But that spring, there was another issue on campus, and that required the attention of the Executive Committee referred to above.

Our student newspaper was called *The Chimes*, and like many student newspapers they were always on the edge of mischief, particularly challenging the status quo at the college, the denomination, and especially the federal government. You will remember this was the era of protesting Viet Nam, civil rights, and more.

The editor of *Chimes* was our classmate Jeannine Oppewall from Massachusetts. Assistant editor was another classmate Paul Schrader, Jeanine's boyfriend and later her husband—and later still, her divorced husband. Both individuals were extremely bright. They produced a formidable student newspaper.

But there was a serious problem—their articles and stories were almost always critical of the college, the church and even the Christian faith. In fact, some of them were hostile to Christianity. Students and their parents complained that this was over the line. To be sure, Calvin had given *Chimes* considerable latitude through the years, but the antagonism of *Chimes* toward the essential Christian belief was cause for alarm.

In response, the Publications Committee was called into service, and that included five professors and four students, those students being the Executive Committee of Student Council. Of course, that included me!

We met a couple of times during the year, enough to stand in awe of the staff members on the committee. They included the venerable college President, William Spoelhof and his cohorts, Charles Miller, Henrietta TenHarmsel, John DeBie and Steve VanderWeele. It was a privilege to sit around the table with these good people, full of faith, integrity and wisdom. To this day, they remain in my mind as pillars of the College. I think that my classmates Gerb DeJong, Loren Veldhuizen, and John Weeda would offer similar respect.

After a short introduction regarding the issues, Jeannine was called in a board room in the library. I actually do not remember so much about the event, except rather early on she lit up a cigarette. As I recall, she held her ground and was not ready to publish an apology of any kind. The professors did most of the questioning while us students shyly listened.

After the Jeannine departed, it was decision time. The discussion was wide-ranging and fair-minded—there was nobody with an axe to grind. But a decision was not coming easily, though it seemed to lean toward her dismissal. I was uncomfortable with that direction and had the audacity to speak for the first time. I said, "I think it we should all go home and pray about this—we don't want to be a stumbling block."

Silence! And then the dear Professor VanderWeele said, "I think Mr. Polinder has a point..." And that is what we did—we headed to our respective homes agreeing to gather in the morning.

The morning meeting was short and to the point—we unanimously agreed to dismiss the editor of *Chimes*, Jeannine Oppewall. That sounds cold, but it wasn't. The empathy of the professors was palpable.

The news spread quickly—the provocative Paul Schrader resigned along with the rest of the newspaper staff. A couple other students volunteered to take the lead as editors, and we limped through the rest of the year. As you can imagine, it was big news on campus, though I think most of the student body supported the decision.

I think it was the correct decision, but that does not mean I did not have doubts. It was hard!

Both Oppewall and Schrader went on to make big names for themselves—Paul as a screenwriter and director, and Jeannine as a production/art director, also in the movie industry. If you look them up in Wikipedia, you would be amazed at their productivity.

So why this story? Because it's a hard story. But it was also a privilege to be at the table with those outstanding people. They were role models, and I suspect my work as an administrator was given some root in the painful process of firing the editor of our college newspaper.

Homecoming court Freshman Year

Colleen Graduation, '68

My graduation, '68

Leaving Home, for New Mexico

My Heart, I Offer: A Devotional

In 2000, Calvin published a devotional book made up of 365 devotionals written by Calvin alumni. The book was entitled "My Heart I Offer." What follows is the January 22 entry.

Proverbs 4:23

Those of us who have been raised in the Reformed tradition or adopted it somewhere along the way are wired to be rather rational about our Christian faith. We take seriously the "Christian mind," the "life of the mind," and "loving God with our mind." We are fond of verses like "be transformed by the renewing of your mind" (Roman 12:2) and we delight in books like Mark Noll's *The Scandal of the Evangelical Mind*, especially when he cites our tradition as one which has been something of a model of Christian thinking.

Make no mistake about it, Reformed thinkers have made huge contributions to the evangelical community and to the kingdom at large. We desperately need to pass on the Reformed vision and worldview to our children and far beyond. It is a great gift that at once flows from the Scriptures and helps us read the Scriptures. We are stewards of this world view and take seriously the mandate to "make disciples." But just as urgently, we will want to attend to Proverbs 4:23 which reminds us

"Above all else, guard your heart, for everything you do flows from it." The heart is the symbolic center of our emotions, feelings, and motivations. The desires of the heart, good or evil, are powerful often beyond our rationality. Rooted in the heart is the relational side of life. We would do well to nurture our relationality, to educate our emotions.

Novelist Walker Percy describes one of his characters as "one who gets all A's in school, but flunks life." Don't we all know some of these folks—old classmates, fellow church members, maybe members of our family? What goes haywire? For some it is an addiction, for others a deep wound of the past, for still others crippling emotions or habits.

In some ways this describes all of us, wounded and broken souls that we are. It is only the transforming relationship and friendship with Jesus that offers hope, this mysterious new life "which is Christ in you, the hope of glory." (Colossians 1:27) Thereby our heads are reformed and renewed, though the process starts with Calvin's motto: "My heart I offer promptly and sincerely."

Ron Polinder
Lynden

Remarks: 45th Anniversary of Calvin Graduation (2013)

EmCee: Ron Polinder

The story of Moses, the statue that each class tried to capture, wasting volumes of time thereon, brings us back to a paradox that for me is still confusing—both the fun and foolishness of our pursuit of this famous Calvin tradition. Now, I know something about this—Did you know we had a Moses committee? And I was chairman of that committee, something that has never quite made my resume. This was a highly clandestine operation—think CIA, KGB; I was the Vladimir Putin of our class. The committee represented all groups, geographies, income levels, and IQ's—all below 100. I was the lowest common denominator. Viet Nam was raging and we engaged in this foolhardiness, while former classmates were in the jungles of Southeast Asia. It's a reminder of the duplicity or our human condition.

That is not all. There were somewhere around 60 of us in the Go-Go club, with yellow shirts, maroon ties, berets—and not green berets. We cheered on the Knights—at a game in Holland against Hope, we made more commotion than the entire Hope crowd. At the Home game against Hope, with the help of Mrs. Steen, we dressed up Jack Slater like the Hope mascot, a flying Dutchman, who normally only appeared for the home games at Hope. But for this special game against Calvin, he seemingly showed up in GR, and proceeded to fire up the Hope fans.

But then appeared the Calvin mascot, a big-headed Calvin Knight, in the person of Barry Kuiper. The Dutchman suddenly trembled in fear, feigning to flee from the Calvin Knight only to be caught and slain at center-court by the fearless Calvin Kuiper. The Dutchman was carried off the floor on a stretcher by dutiful members of the Go-Go club—to the enormous joy of Calvin fans, and the utter disdain of the helpless dopes from Hope, who are still wondering what happened. Of course, I was also part of the Go Go club—How is it that the sensible Colleen stuck with me?

Some of you will also remember that steamy May morning our Freshman year. There were 31 of us scholars, staying up well passed midnight, dutifully doing our homework, and some fool on some floor said, "Let's go to Hope"—I think it was Floyd Joostens. And the 30 scholars lost their minds and followed Floyd—piling into six vehicles. We quickly purchased some gasoline so we could burn a "C" on the lawn of the Hope soccer field. And then at about 3 a.m., we ran through one of the floors of an adjacent Hope Dorm—scaring them to death. It must have been a spiritual experience for them—the end had come!

As we hustled out of Holland, the last of the cars was stopped by the now alerted police, and those five fellas spend the night in jail, Gary Lovelace in his pajemas. The rest of us arrived back on campus at dawn, only to see our counsellors/RAs waiting for us. The morning news reports on local radio reported it. We conspired to minimize the attack, to no avail. We were in deep weeds. A few days later, it was the Discipline Committee—who appropriately dished out 13 probations, 11 suspensions and seven expulsions, based on previous infractions and the seriousness thereof.

(I was in the middle group, with a two-week suspension just before exams, booted off campus to live with cousin Gord Otter. Colleen would bring me notes from missed classes.)

Senior sister Eleanor did her best to defend me, but Hank and Mina, back on the farm, would have nothing of it. True to form, the were on the side of the college.

Amidst all this foolishness, there was deeply serious stuff going on in classrooms and coffee shops at Calvin College. Ideas were being tested, a worldview was being promulgated, and many by graduation offered their hearts, "promptly and sincerely." A certain Freshman bowed his knee, and professed to his church elders his "only comfort in life and in death," fortifying and affirming his faith with some opening words from the Heidelberg Catechism Q & A 1.

How do you explain it—on the one hand, this nonsense. On the other, confessing that the fear of the Lord is the beginning of wisdom. A mystery: the folly of youth, and the grace of God.

CHAPTER 4

NEW MEXICO – FORT WINGATE (1968 – 1972)

Viet Nam

That word, that name is loaded with meaning. For those coming of age in the late 60's, it was life-changing. For far too many, it meant death.

Of course, we are talking about the Viet Nam war, or as the Vietnamese call it, the "American War." In the 60's, communism was on the march, and this former French colony was divided between North and South, the northern half of the country was already Communist controlled. The U.S took the position that communist expansion must be stopped. Already, the Soviet Union and China were threatening forces in the world, led by Communists and supporting North Viet Nam. The U.S. was determined bring democracy to South Viet Nam.

Others saw the picture quite differently—that this was a civil war between the North and the South, and that we had no business entering the conflict. It started out with merely some advisors being sent to the South, but the escalation steadily continued through the 60's and into the 70's. Thousands of young men were drafted and sent to the war. 60,000+ did not return, except in a body bag. As the war was expanding, and the death count growing, more and more protests were taking place in the country. They often grew violent. At Calvin College too, there were deep and even angry discussions about the War.

I remember taking my usual conservative position and being pro-War. Even at conservative Calvin College, large number of students were resistors, some of whom openly took to the streets, others becoming conscientious objectors, and still others dodging the draft and fleeing to Canada. This is not the place to give a fuller history of the War, but I encourage my grandchildren to do a more careful study. My purpose in this story is to share its influence on my life, and thus Nana's too.

A few times, I would take up the argument in the Calvin Commons defending the war. I didn't know nearly as much as the people on the other side of the table and should have kept my mouth shut. Further, I wasn't prepared to go to war myself. By the end of my sophomore year, I declared an Education major, not unrelated to the fact that teachers got deferments. Having heard about teaching jobs for the Bureau of Indian Affairs, I thought my deferment could be enhanced by this kind of government service. I was hardly a "profile of courage."

Yet, some nervousness set in when I got a letter in the spring of '68 to report to Detroit for a military physical. What an experience that was! Two of my friends also got the same letter, Loren Velthuizen from Iowa and Dennis Van Andel, my longtime Lynden pal. We rode a bus to Detroit, stayed in some lousy dorm, and entered a few hours of military life. The charge against military life was that you had to "hurry up and wait." The lines were long and the poor saps that were assigned to do our physicals were bored and without personality, at least so it seemed.

There was a stir in the camp, maybe just gossip, that Mohammed Ali was also in the facility. Ali was a resistor, had purposely flunked his intelligent test, and possibly was being retested. We never confirmed his presence, but he was an international figure because of his boxing accomplishments, and his conversion to Islam.

As hoped for, we got a letter of deferment some weeks later. But the country was in turmoil with protests marches nationwide, in some cases violent. Students were killed at Kent State University. It was the same spring that President Lyndon Johnson announced he would not run for re-election and that Martin Luther King was assassinated. Civil Rights marches and anti-war rallies were tearing the country apart. Even though the dead were being shipped back to the US by the hundreds, we were told we were winning the war. It was a lie, being told by leaders like Westmoreland, Rusk, and McNamara, supposedly our brightest and best.

We learned that our school mate Duane Likkel was killed, and then a college acquaintance Dave Buursma was also killed. That brings it closer to home, yet we escaped to comparatively quiet New Mexico, having more and more doubts about the war. Through the years, we were able to visit the Memorial Wall in D.C. at least three times, always finding the names of those two heroes.

Native people have always been unusually patriotic, thus many Native kids enlisted in the military, and too many lost their lives or were injured, some emotionally or physically for a lifetime. But like many Americans, we just watched TV and read the news—and believed what we were being fed.

The reception of those coming home from the war was outrageous. They were not honored for their service; rather, they were mocked and scorned. Just the other day, I ran into an old classmate Ted Lautenbach, who served in Vietnam; in fact was wearing a cap signaling such. We had coffee and talked about his experience. In his 6th month of service, he learned his mother had cancer, and thus was sent home for a visit. As he arrived in the LA airport, he was spit upon by six protestors. Can you imagine?

At some point in our Wingate years, we had a community talent program directed by our friend Martha Hurst. Nana and I were asked to sing "Cruel War," a protest song of Peter, Paul and Mary—"the cruel war is raging and Johnny has to fight…." But Ronnie didn't have to fight! The song got a warm response from the audience, but it served to imprint a little more guilt on my soul.

The war at last ended sometime in the 70's, and the U.S. essentially got beat. Before long, movies about certain aspects of the war were coming to the big screen. Given my dislike for violent movies, I did not take them in until the movie "Platoon" came out. A bunch of LC teachers and I went to see the movie in Bellingham. The main character was a young man from small town America, like me. Ten minutes into the movie, I was so troubled I wanted to leave. But I couldn't, given the company I was with, so I suffered through it, and watch how this innocent kid deteriorated in every way. Again I asked, "Why not me?"

The Way to Fort Wingate

When Nana and I were students at Calvin College, we began to understand the idea of calling and serving the Kingdom. We learned about a big world with its misery and pain. And it was the time of the Peace Corps, though we wanted to bring our Christian testimony to the task. Further, we wanted to do something "different," not settling back into middle America.

One mid-winter Sunday afternoon, we were invited by our friend Jim Hofman to his parents' home, the Reverend and Mrs. Walter Hofman. Pastor asked us around the dinner table what our plans were for the next year, generating a response something like the above paragraph. He promptly told us about his brother John, a missionary pastor in Fort Wingate, NM. He described the big government (Bureau of Indian Affairs) school with a thousand kids in the high school and 700 in the elementary school, all boarding students and all Navajo. Further, those schools allowed for "religious instruction," but they were always short of help to do the teaching after normal hours. He assured us that a young couple like us would be significant help in the ministry, while working for the BIA.

We took note, talked it over and began to search it out further. We discovered a recruiter would be in Grand Rapids at Aquinas College in February. I visited with the gentleman and it sounded intriguing. If we applied, we could only be assured that we would have a job with the BIA, but our exact placement would not come until summer. Applied we did, and before long we were hired. We did indicate our choice of placement was the Wingate schools.

But we made a serious mistake in the application, indicating that it was in "Western" Navajo Agency. Little did we know we were supposed to put "Eastern" Navajo Agency.

The months wore on and finally we got in the mail our assignment, to Shonto, AZ in Western Navajo Agency. Oh my, where was that? We read the material they sent which indicated there was a K-8 school, and a Presbyterian church in Shonto. Evidently, the Lord was calling us to Shonto.

Nana was not at all so sure, so one day while I was at my summer job at Darigold, she took it upon herself to call the personnel office in Gallup, New Mexico. Little did we know that the personnel office in Gallup is a large building, two stories, loaded with a hundred bureaucrats, and quite impossible for a stranger from Lynden, WA to penetrate. What happened next was a mighty act of God.

Nana went through a couple of different clerks to get to a desk more familiar with the assignment process. She explained in detail that we wanted to go to Ft. Wingate, that her husband was a Social Studies teacher, and she was a music teacher. Incredibly, the Superintendent Eastern Navajo, Mrs. McClure, whose office was 60 miles away in Crownpoint, happened to be in the personnel office and overheard the conversation. She knew that the Wingate schools needed both a Social Studies teacher and a Music teacher. She proceeded to make all the right moves for us to have a lateral transfer to Eastern Navajo, and Ft. Wingate.

To jump ahead, after arriving at Wingate we learned from our supervisors that it was almost impossible to get lateral transfers—they described that series of events as a miracle.

Back in Lynden, Nana eagerly told me about the phone call when arriving home from work. My heart was set on Shonto, but I admired her courage in calling and getting through to the right people. Surely this was of the Lord.

We called John Hofman who was elated to hear that help was on the way. Little did we know that he was being called by Bethel Church in Lynden, and when we arrived in August, he shared the news that he had accepted the call. We were crushed—Hofman was such a lively, fun-filled fella, and a really good preacher. Nevertheless, we had a couple of months with them, good preparation for what we faced in our work and in the church. We were ready to roll up our sleeves, confident the Lord had called and "made straight" the way (Isaiah 40:3) to this obscure little community in Western New Mexico.

Teaching at Wingate: An Adventure and Privilege

We packed our meager belongings into our '59 Ford in early August. We decided to drive through California to visit Uncle Bob and Auntie Eleanor, our first of what would be many trips to Bellflower. We did catch a baseball game in Oakland, but then south where we had some wonderful days California. Auntie Eleanor, always a gracious hostess, showed us the sights—surely we went to Disneyland and likely a Dodger game. Nana and Auntie Eleanor had a warm relationship, as she did with all my sisters.

When it was time to leave, Eleanor wisely warned us to leave in the afternoon and thus miss the desert heat as we drove east. We did so, but the desert at midnight is still unbearable. I think we drove all night, maybe with a nap along the way. Remember, no air conditioning in a '59 Ford, but we finally found the higher elevations of Arizona, and then to Gallup, New Mexico. Of course, neither of us had ever been there. I remember seeing Earl's Restaurant and saying, "At least we can go out to eat once in a while."

We drove on to Ft. Wingate, at least we thought so, driving into an active fort with guards at the gate. I proudly announced that we were new teachers and were moving in. I can only imagine what those Native guards thought: "Dumb Bellaganas" (the Navajo word for white folks). They directed us down the road to old Ft. Wingate, which was built in the 1840's and then became a school sometime in the early 1900's. Our first sight was a new school building, built in 1965.

Would you believe the first person we met was the school nurse, whose office was close to the entrance and lobby. We introduced ourselves, indicating that we were fresh out of Calvin College. Her name was Cecelia Begay, a Rehoboth grad, who also went to Calvin, at least for a year or two. We eventually became friends with the Begays, her husband Ed T. and daughters Shar and Sandra.

On to the main office to meet Supt. Jaeger who took us to meet my supervisor, Mr. Ernie Hurst, a large man with a warm personality. We soon learned that he was quite familiar with the CRC, was himself a Methodist at the time, though became CRC with his wife Martha and son Don. He was clearly a Christian man, which naturally calmed us.

From there we went to Nana's building, which was hardly a new building. The office was a portable building, where we found Nana's supervisor, Martha Hurst. In a short time, this husband-and-wife team became like second parents to us, another gift from God. They previously lived Brigham City, Utah, where they first worked for their church, and then at Intermountain School, likewise a large boarding school for Native kids. We learned so much about how to relate to Native students, and the do's and don'ts, and the culture of the BIA.

Yet we were pathetically naïve and unprepared. I don't even recall if there was an orientation. But we had good supervision, and I soon enjoyed my colleagues, all veteran teachers, who were willing to help the new kid. Nana was less fortunate. Her music room was isolated in the "Plant Management" area, some distance from the office. It was a stone building that had been a shop of some kind, and dirty. But it wasn't long and she had that room looking sharp, as you would expect from Nana.

But truthfully, we were poorly prepared for the cultural differences. We had not really studied Native cultures like we should have. We had no idea that our students all spoke Navajo as their first language, and their facility in English was in most cases substandard. We learned they were quiet, and thus hard to engage in discussion, which makes it more challenging to teach Social Studies. And who knows how many insults we perpetrated without even knowing it. Of course, our students were familiar with insensitive white people coming to their reservation to "educate" them. We often thought we learned more from them than they did from us.

The first day of high school, we had about 300 students, the next day about 500, by the end of the week maybe 900, but the end of September, after the Shiprock Fair, we had over a 1000. Attendance was all too sporadic, sometimes kids going home for religious ceremonies that could last a week or more. Students lived in remote areas of the Rez—maybe a hundred, even two hundred miles from school.

After school the first day, I walked out to football practice. Not having football when I was in high school, I thought this would be pretty cool. Bad mistake! They were so desperate for coaches that the next day they asked if I would help coach the Freshmen. And I was dumb enough to agree to it, having never played a down in anything but sandlot intramurals. I had a good partner in Pat Graham—he did the offense and I did the defense (kinda). These kids had never played before, and most of the opposition had played middle school football. They did not know how to put on uniforms; of course neither did I. They did love it when at game time I came around with the black paste to put under their eyes. At least, they could look like football players.

Most of our kids were outsized, as Natives tend to be of shorter stature. We played overage kids, illegally, some of them 17 years old. Lots of Navajo kids did not start school until they were nine or ten. We had a few really good players, but not nearly enough. Most really didn't have their heart in it and were not by nature competitive. We ended the year 0-6.

Then another bad mistake—I agreed to do it a second year, and even took a football course in the summer at WWU. This was dangerous because now I actually thought I knew something. I didn't; we ended another season 0-6. Thus I ended my football coaching experience with a perfect record: 0-12.

The teaching experience was largely positive, though I always wanted more discussion. I had some wonderfully bright students, and of course, and lots of students who really struggled, often because of language deficiencies. But my memories are essentially positive of those Wingate kids—very few discipline problems in the classroom. Once you got to know them, and they you, the relationships were warm.

There was also a lot of pain in that student body. Often the morning report on Monday morning included a list of students in jail in Gallup. They had gone AWOL, hitched a ride to Gallup, and as is the pattern too often amongst Native people, they drank to get drunk. There were also unwanted pregnancies, another sad pattern in the Native community.

Attendance was always spotty. We had a strange scheduling pattern called modular scheduling, which meant that kids had unscheduled periods, where they could walk the halls. It was easy to skip class. It was one of those "innovations" that did not make an ounce of sense, thus many students had horrible attendance records, even though they were in the school. One girl never registered for any classes but was caught in November just roaming the halls and hanging out in the bathrooms.

During the second year, a group of teachers started meeting to create a new attendance policy, determined to get kids in the classrooms. Further, they chose me to become the attendance officer, so the next year I taught only four of six classes, roamed the halls for delinquents and created a detention hall after school. It was quite successful—my first administrative role. But I also paid a price with students that didn't much appreciate my policing posture. Yet, when student council created a Teacher of the Month, I was the first to be awarded the honor, I think because students recognized that our attendance policy was better for the school.

Meanwhile, Nana was teaching music to middle school kids, most of whom had not sung much in their lives, save at religious instruction that the BIA mandated. She loved those kids, and they her. She was something of an anomaly, this tall, gorgeous white woman, sometimes walking through the mud to get to her classroom.

But she did it only one year, as she was moved to the High School to teach piano in a fancy, new piano lab that enabled her to have twelve students. With headphones she could tune in and talk to each student. She enjoyed the role—I wonder if any of those kids kept it up and play today.

She was also the accompanist for the High School choir, where the teacher could best be described as a fool. Nana suffered through it, though many of the students admired her in the process.

As I will explain below, she eventually became the school registrar, which meant that she had the onerous task of keeping track of who was in school and who was absent for the day. Thus our third year found Nana in charge of who was actually on campus, and me trying to get them to class. But she was so good at record-keeping and detail, it actually showed her how much she enjoyed clerical work. Thereafter, that became her preferred line of work.

Our four years at Ft. Wingate were marvelous—hard at times, but we learned so much, and we met terrific kids. They were more traditional kids, often first generation educated. We learned a lot about the culture, learned how to relate to the instinctive quietness of Navajo youth. We very rarely ever met the parents, but some of those kids became lifelong friends. While we would move to Rehoboth in year five, we were always thankful that we started at Wingate. A rich adventure indeed.

12 Wingate students, professions of faith

Youth Group and More

You will recall that a primary purpose in Nana and I coming to New Mexico was to be off help in the little Wingate CRC church. It did not take us long to get in the thick of it. After the Hofman family left, it was early October that Stan and Nelvy Siebersma came to pastor the church. Their eight kids helped fill up the church, and our youth group.

We had about five steady families that attended beside the Siebersmas—the Pintos, the Dobbs, the Toledos, the Polinders and eventually the Hursts. We were a committed crew and threw ourselves into the life of the church. If you can imagine, early on Pastor Stan came down sick on Saturday morning in the first fall. And he called on me to preach, having just turned 22. I still have the sermon in my files, but I don't dare to read it.

On Wednesday nights, the middle school kids came to church for religious instruction. Mrs. Den Bleyker from Rehoboth and Nana took turns playing the piano, both of whom where excellent players, and I was the song leader. The church was full of kids, I think about 200, and they loved to sing, especially the old gospel songs in our red book—"When the Roll is Called up Yonder," "Sound the Battle Cry," "When We All Get to Heaven," "Heavenly Sunshine." Those kids could raise the roof—it was a joy.

But our biggest challenge was forming a youth group, which met on Sunday afternoons at 4:00. Rather quickly it caught on, and for the next four years we averaged between 25-30 kids. There were those who never missed and also a variety that would come sporadically. Nana and I took the lead, planning lessons and activities, while the other church families joined us in taking turns providing supper. Supper was a big attraction.

One of the patterns of Native people is that they will eat a meal, but if there are any leftovers, they will gather them up, wrap in a napkin or two and take it home with them. This made a couple of our families so ticked off—how dare those kids? This was a good example of white people not adapting to the culture. Nana and I took it as a compliment.

It was in this Youth Group where our richest relationships developed, and kids came to Christ. One year we had a dozen professions of faith. Not only did we see these students in school and church, but they would often come by our house to just "hang out." And it wasn't just the church-goers— others did as well. In those days, Nana and I were "cool," at least those kids thought so, and it was quite a steady stream that would stop by.

Thankfully, the Hursts taught us that you did not always have to feed them or make conversation. Even if they came during supper, they would sit in the living room, page through Time magazine for a while and then we would hear "*te eh*," which means "let's go." Even though we did not engage them in conversation, or feed them, they had a perfectly good time, and may well come again the next night. Our place was a diversion from dorm life, and we were honored to have them come.

In the spring, we always borrowed the Rehoboth bus and took our group to Wheatfields Lake, about 80 miles away. The bus was old, the conditions primitive, but we always had a terrific time—again, a wholesome diversion from the dorms. Nana and the girls would make frybread over the open fire, and the church provided enough food for a feast.

It may seem odd, but Nana and I often looked back and thought those were our best "missionary" years, teaching at Ft. Wingate. Sometimes toward the end of my career, I often wished I could go back and start over as a Wingate teacher, given the experience we had gained. We made plenty of mistakes with our cultural insensitivity, but there was something simple and pure about those four years. In hindsight, we know a solid number of kids who remained faithful to the Lord, and we know some who fell away. But we earnestly sought to serve the Lord, along with others at that little Wingate church—what a privilege it was to be called to Ft. Wingate.

Shawn Mitchell Polinder

That was the name of our first baby, stillborn on October 16, 1970. Nana became pregnant the previous winter, and of course, we entered the new school year with great anticipation. She had given up her piano teacher job at school to be a full-time mom. As only she could do, a nursery was perfectly prepared.

As the due date approached, the doctors were concerned about toxemia and high blood pressure. In hindsight, we were so naïve that we did not take her condition seriously enough. As I recall, they finally induced labor, which did not seem to work very well. Nana had occasional contractions, but nothing steady. The doctor in the old, old Rehoboth hospital (the one that was still on campus) was from out of town, taking the place of Dr. Stam who was away taking his "boards" for licensure.

The labor went all day and all night. I recall trying to sleep a bit on a long bench, one still used in the main office at school. I still remember what I was wearing that fateful and sleepless night. The next morning, maybe mid-morning, the nurses indicated that they were not getting a heartbeat, but that could be just the position of the baby. Nana could not dilate beyond seven, even as the contractions became more intense.

We could sense some alarm from the staff now, and finally Dr. Jack Kamps was called in from Gallup. Mid-afternoon, over 24 hours after labor was induced, Nana was rolled into the delivery room. I followed behind, standing at the head of the bed holding her hands and rubbing her face. I could not see what was happening, but I knew they finally used a forceps to pull the baby out.

Shawn's grave, Rehoboth cemetery

At long last—there he was. *But no cry!* My precious Colleen looked at me fearfully, and I could only say, "He is not crying." The doctor and nurses worked feverishly to bring about some life. After several minutes, they told us the painful truth—he was not alive.

What happened next is a blur. Nana, of course, was exhausted. I remember Rev. Veenstra, who we did not yet know very well, coming to pray with us. I remember calling Rev. Hofman in Lynden to ask him to tell our parents. I remember him saying, "Remember the promises…." He in turn called Rev. Negan, pastor at Third Church, to talk to my Dad and Mom.

Again, this is a blur—I know that Nana had horrible headaches, resulting from the anesthesia. I know we were stunned! I am sure we cried, which was always easy for Nana and me to do. I don't remember how long she stayed in the hospital, but I suspect she came home the next day—still with bad headaches.

Here we were—24 years old, in a strange community called Ft. Wingate, with Rehoboth down the road a dozen miles—scared, broken-hearted, shaken to our roots. I recall the love from the Wingate church and community—the Siebersmas and the Hursts surely took the lead. Grandpa and Grandma Haak flew quickly from Washington. Uncle Bob and Auntie Eleanor drove from California.

Unlike what they do today, we never again saw our baby. We didn't hold him, look into his face, cry over him—that was not the custom in those days. Grandpa and Grandma Haak and Uncle Bob and Auntie Eleanor went to the funeral home to see his body. They described him as best they could.

We had picked out a name—he would be Shawn Mitchell Polinder, and now we had to bury him. Rehoboth cemetery was the natural place, though we had never been there. We decided to only have a graveside service, with Pastor Siebersma sharing a short message. Rev. Al Mulder from Bethany church in Gallup sang, "Children of the Heavenly Father," a song sung at every one of our baptisms and weddings thereafter. Staff members from Wingate came, new friends from Rehoboth, and of course, John and Ruth Hartog and Ken and Nancy Faber, both of those ladies themselves pregnant. They would deliver Jeff Hartog and Katie Faber Veening within the month. And the Wingate school took a bus for the students who wanted to come—I believe there was 20 or 30 kids that stood around that graveside.

Good news: Stacia's baptism

In New Mexico, they have a custom that was new to us. We saw off to the side a dozen or so shovels. To our amazement, when the little casket was lowered into the grave, one of the students, our friend Notah Benally, picked up one of the shovels and started to throw dirt on the grave. He was a junior and took the lead. Nana and I were honored by that, and deeply touched. And others joined, passing the shovels so everyone could take part. In New Mexico, they create a mound, using the dirt dug from the grave.

How to process all of this? Let it be said first that so many people were so good to us. But what were we to say to God? God, why this? I recall a week or so later that Ken and Kay Koeman came to see us from Albuquerque. We had already become friends with them. Pastor Ken used a passage from Hebrews 12:6—"that the Lord disciplines the one he loves." At first that seemed harsh, but the verses following became words of great comfort.

It was a couple of months later, around Christmas, that Nana and I went to American Furniture in Albuquerque and bought a brand-new, expensive Magnavox stereo, the one we kept throughout our married life and beyond. We bought records to go with it, of course. I remember us weeping together listening to George Beverly Shea. There was much comfort and joy that came from that stereo.

After about a month, the high school principal, Mr. Hoover, called to ask Nana if she wanted to go back to work, and if so, he had a job for her. It was then that she took on the Registrar job at the high school, a good diversion. She found her niche.

It is fair to say that I was more able to accept the will of God than Nana was. More often, I would be the doubter, but this time it was Nana, the grieving mother. We were advised to wait a few months before trying to get pregnant again. A few months became longer that we had hoped. The following August, we took our youth group to the Young Calvinist Convention in Montana. One night, the leaders were up into the early morning hours praying for the hearts of the couple thousand young people. Unbeknownst to me, Nana had come down from our room to join in, sitting in a different part of the room. It was that event that prompted Nana to surrender Shawn, and his death, to God. It was like a burden was lifted—she was ready and able to move on with a refreshed heart.

The next month, September, Nana became pregnant. We always declared the timing was God. On May 17, 1972, God gave us Stacia Lin, but that is another story—a really good one!

Raymond and Notah

I think it was the first Saturday that we were in Ft. Wingate—we headed for Gallup to buy some supplies and groceries. Wingate was about three miles from I-40. On the side road were two boys hitchhiking to Gallup. We decided to pick them up, moving away the boxes to make room for these two fellas. Later we learned we were not supposed to pick up students, because most often they were headed for a drinking spree in Gallup.

We got to know those boys, Raymond Daw and Notah Benally. I recall Notah, within the next week or two, walking the couple miles to church—alone. Notah was quite faithful at church. His relatives in Church Rock where students at Rehoboth, and Uncle Harry was an elder at Church Rock CRC. Though his nuclear family was more traditional, Notah clearly had Christian instincts.

Raymond on the other hand attended church more sporadically. One could sense he was more of a doubter. I recall a particular Sunday eve service led by Rev. Sampson Yazzie in which he made a serious alter call. After a few minutes, Notah went forward. Raymond did not—he could not! Sitting with us, we could feel his anguish.

Raymond and Notah hung out at our house a lot. I can still smell the wet cowboy boots, wrapped in duct tape to cover holes in the soles. We loved those guys—had much fun together. Our second year, we took Raymond to California with us for Thanksgiving—Auntie Eleanor showed us the sights, including finding the elementary school that Raymond attended for a couple of years. Raymond was the smartest student I had at Wingate and was student body president his senior year.

Thus, we were a bit puzzled Raymond did not take the bus with Notah to Shawn's graveside service. A few days passed, but then one night, there was a knock at the door. Nana and I were both laying on the bed—Nana still suffering from headaches. Visiting friends let him in—he walked into the bedroom. Seeing us, he threw himself on our bed between us, weeping profusely. And then he asked, "Why would God do this to you?"

I don't recall our answer—likely because we did not have one. But obviously we have never forgotten his affection for us, and his absence from the graveside was understandable—in his own way he was grieving.

Notah was a fine athlete. He was a starter in both football and basketball--a good Wingate basketball team. We went to a lot of his games. He too was a good student. Notah regularly attended church or youth group and made profession of faith after his Junior year. And he had a girlfriend, Maggie Wiley, likewise an excellent student and basketball player. She and her two sisters also were faithful at church. For two summers, Notah twice came home with us to Lynden in the summer, working on the farm, or painting houses with our friend Ken Faber.

Our friends Raymond and Notah

After high school, Raymond joined the Marines. Notah went to MacPhearson College in Kansas. Of course, we stayed in touch, but much harder to do during post-high years. Both would visit us.

And so it was through the years—occasional visits when we lived in or visited New Mexico. On one of those visits, I asked Raymond, "How did we ever get to know each other?" He quickly responded, "Don't you remember—you picked us when we were walking to Gallup—you still had boxes in the back seat."

We've all had disappointments in our lives and in our families, none of which need be rehearsed here. But always respect and friendship. Recently, I wrote a message on Facebook to Raymond reminding him of the comfort he shared with us when we lost Shawn as noted above. This was his response:

> *Those memories return to me now and then, my dear friend. My belief is that if not for you and Colleen, I would not be where I am today. You've been my love always. Thank you for sharing with me and continuing to be a friend, mentor and teacher of living life.*

It is hard to explain as to why cross-cultural friendships are so special. Maybe it's because they are all too rare. To my great joy, our three children have often become friends with people different from themselves—in culture, or race, or religion. I hope and pray the pattern continues in my grandchildren. Remember the story of Raymond and Notah—the gift is rich!

Arthur and Emma

Our relationship goes back 50 years, to our first years in Ft. Wingate. Somewhere in those early years, a "couple" named Arthur Kee and Emma Sandoval started coming to our youth group at the Wingate church. Their relationship started with an argument over a pencil which Arthur had stolen, but strangely it developed into a romance. By the time they were Seniors the romance was serious, even one of commitment.

It was not until recently that we learned more of their background, their growing up years. They are stories that need to be told, ones that will cause you to marvel at the good providence of God.

Arthur grew up in Cross Canyon, AZ which lies between Window Rock and Ganajo. He was the fourth child of an even dozen. His father was a medicine man, which in his case did not bring much income. They never owned a vehicle in Art's school years. They had a team of horses and wagon, which Arthur was expected to use for trips to the trading post. On rare occasions, they borrowed an uncle's pick-up.

Arthur is a gentle soul. He was submissive to his parents and siblings, and thus taken advantage of consistently. But it was not in his spirit to fight back. Not knowing the specifics, Emma would say that he was abused emotionally and physically. He was not the family slave, but close. It no doubt shaped Arthur to this day, yet Arthur has a wholesome view of life and a servant heart that is unmatchable.

Emma, on the other hand, is not so submissive. Her feisty spirit showed up early and often. In fact, you could say that it outright saved her life, and contributes to this day to her forthright conversation and her willingness to lead. Her story is equally remarkable.

Emma was born and raised in Pueblo Pintado, which is 90+ miles northeast of Gallup. She too was from a family of 12 and was also the 4th child. More ironically, while Arthur had seven sisters, Emma had seven brothers. Her story is maybe more painful still than Arthur's.

Emma was a sickly child, and her parents thought she was going to die. It was Navajo tradition to place the dying person outside the Hogan lest an evil spirit forever invade their living space. Thus, the pattern was to burn the Hogan if there had been a death therein. When discovered, Emma's grandparents thought it wrong, and took Emma into their dwelling. Needless to say, she survived and has since flourished. But not without further challenges.

At age 12, her parents wanted her back in their home. Emma would say they wanted her servitude—babysitting, cooking, cleaning. Far worse, as she was coming of age, she would become subject to sexual overtures and abuse from (let's just say) family members. With her thoughtful and more aggressive nature, she fought back. Emma found a key to an old, unused car in the camp, and began sleeping in the car for her own safety. Later, she made curtains to provide even more privacy. In short, Emma would describe her teen years as essentially miserable when she was home.

"When she was home" is a key distinction. In a more broad-based discussion, the Boarding School reality that most Native young people lived with, has been under much scrutiny by a percentage of the residents and most of the scholars that write about it. It is surely a mixed bag—for some the boarding school was a painful experience given their separation from parents. For others, they came to like the boarding school—three square meals a day, warm showers, recreational activity. And they thereby managed to avoid herding sheep and chopping wood while at school.

Our friends, Arthur and Emma Kee

For Emma, it was an escape from the range of abuses that threatened her. Do you think she wanted to go home on weekends, or even go home at Thanksgiving or Christmas? As hard as it is to acknowledge, there was and is a level of abuse that happens in all too many Native families, what Emma would call "the dirty little secret" on the Rez. But again, I also want to defend the countless Native families I know who love their children and families and who do "walk in beauty." The legacy of the boarding school is about balance, and who really knows the truth that will stand the test of time?

Thus far, very little has been told of Arthur and Emma's spiritual journey. Both of their families were deeply involved with traditional Navajo religion. Only in the Boarding school might they have heard of references to the Christian faith. But they did start to walk up to the Wingate church, or catch the church van. They would tease me that they merely came for the good lunch/supper that we served at youth group.

But the Holy Spirit was blowing where He wills, and steadily they both began to respond to the Christian faith. During their Senior year, they made public profession of their faith in the Ft. Wingate CRC, under the leadership of Pastor Stan Siebersma.

Shortly after graduation, the Wingate youth leader, Marilyn Baker (who became Marilyn Begay upon her marriage to Pastor Tony) was inclined to help them proceed toward marriage. She took them to Emma's home in Pueblo Pintado to seek the blessing of her father to marry Arthur. They came upon a father who was under the influence of alcohol, and who became very angry and threatened to harm Arthur. Arthur and Emma quickly ran back to the church van where Marilyn was waiting. She began to circle her way away from the camp while the father was shooting in their direction with his shotgun. The influence of alcohol no doubt affected his aim.

Arthur and Emma had spent a brief time at Cook Christian Training School before the incident with her parents. But after that, Marilyn took them to the census office in Window Rock for a marriage license, where thereafter they promptly were married right there in the office. Within the week, they both had jobs. Arthur started in construction but eventually worked in maintenance for the Window Rock School District. Emma held various assignments, including driving the Rehoboth bus from Window Rock. She had to remind me that I hired her for that job. That allowed her during the day to take courses in finance and accounting. Subsequently, she began to work for the Indian Health Service in which she held highly placed roles in hospital finance.

The Kees were blessed with two children Titus and Tara, who now are best known as Arthur (Redcloud) and Emily. As diligent parents, they soon began saving money to pay for tuition for the kids to attend Rehoboth Christian School. Arthur Redcloud is a truck driver living in Dallas, where he a couple of decades ago went to church with Auntie Marge and Uncle Jim. But he is also an occasional actor who had a key role in the movie Revenant, working alongside Leonard DiCaprio. Emily has a master's degree and has held various counseling or social work roles. Both are believers.

Art and Emma mostly, and currently attend the Window Rock CRC. Both have served as elders; in fact, they are best described as pillars of that congregation. Arthur is the first to help with maintenance issues. Emma is the de facto church administrator. They steadily bear witness to their faith to their neighbors and friends. And they are people of prayer—how I admire their devotion!

Arthur and Emma have been our friends through the decades. They thrice visited us here in Lynden in the 90's, and this past summer (2019) they visited Judy and me. Art always asks about the farm and the fair, wanting to work, and Emma is always ready to make frybread for family and friends. Whenever we visit New Mexico, we have dinner at Jerry's in Gallup, and refresh our friendship.

In closing, how blest Nana and I, and now Grandma Judy, have been to know this special couple. Our friendship has been deep and rich. Emma would occasionally call us, usually when we were still in bed, given the hour time difference between Arizona and Washington. There is treasure in cross-cultural friendship—one can learn so much by spending time together.

But surpassing it all, was the oneness we have in Christ with Art and Emma Kee—a 50+ year blessing, and until death do us part!

Jimmy Horton

Jim Horton was my colleague in the Social Studies department at Wingate. He was a dozen years older than me, born and raised in Texas, about 5'7, a good mentor and friend. I cherished his advice, loved his Texas humor, and joined him in being a Dallas Cowboy football fan—along with lots of other Texans on the staff.

Jimmy was not a Christian. Though raised in the church, somewhere he turned against it. I think it had something to do with a horrible accident that crippled his wife, Marge, for the rest of her life, who interestingly often came to our Wingate church. He would say she was excellent at the piano, but after the accident, she would only become frustrated when trying to play. Finally, they sold their piano, and that is the piano that became ours, at modest price, for virtually our entire married life. The Hortons would be so pleased to know how much it was used and blest our family.

Christmas of '68, we were working together at school—government teachers were required to work 8-5 unless you took annual leave. I don't recall the nature of our conversation, but I will never forget one sentence. Jim said, "The Indians would be a helluva lot better off if those god damn missionaries had never showed up."

Oh my, I was speechless. Where I came from, missionaries were honored. I soon realized my sheltered life in Lynden and even at Calvin College had protected me from the assault that would increase in the coming years and decades. Missionaries would be accused of all manner of evil for disrupting the "pristine" culture of Native communities.

I didn't buy it and still don't. No culture is pristine, though some are more wholesome than others. I had already heard enough about Navajo culture to know it had some ugly, devilish elements. I believed that our church, through the work of the Holy Spirit, had done much good, establishing churches, schools, and a hospital. It was many years later when a scholar and researcher Robert Woodbury produced an exhaustive study proving that those countries and communities where missionaries came where more prosperous, better educated, and healthier than their counterparts.

But Jim Horton and I remained good friends throughout our Wingate years. He taught a course called "Modern Indian Psychology" based on a book by that name written by a Father John Bryde. Bryde identified five great values that were universal to all Native tribes—respect for creation, sharing, individual freedom, bravery, and respect for Indian wisdom (or elders). I found this to be true in the Navajo communities, and among other Native people that I had met. I was grateful to Jim for helping me understand that.

It was two years after I left for Rehoboth that the students asked me to come back to deliver a Baccalaureate speech. In those days, a "religious event" prior to graduation was standard practice. Of course, I was honored and worked very hard to prepare a good speech. I used a Leighton Ford outline to guide my speech, "Burn baby burn, Learn baby learn, Earn baby earn, and Turn baby turn." As I prepared, I thought of former colleagues, many of whom were not Christians, who would likely not respond kindly to my remarks. Yet, a Baccalaureate speaker is free to give testimony to what he or she believes to be the essence of life. So I labored on.

For some reason, I had not included Jim Horton in the list of colleagues that I was reflecting on—a mere oversight? But as I drove on to the Wingate campus, who did I meet but Jim Horton in his familiar blue pick-up. I froze—I said to Nana something like "I never considered that Jimmy Horton would also be in the audience." But what are you to do—I surely didn't have another speech in my back pocket. So I would have to trust God to make this work.

It was a full house, 250 grads, parents and staff in the large (1000 +) Wingate auditorium, by far the largest crowd I had ever spoken to, and a mere 27 years of age. I felt overmatched, but again prayed from Psalm 19:14 that God would use the "words of my mouth and the meditations of my heart." So I gave it my best shot!

As the speech ended, I saw someone briskly walking down the center aisle toward the stage. Oh no--it was Jim Horton—he met me at the steps coming off the stage. I was sure he was going to chide me. But with a warm smile he said, "That was a great speech." Not unlike the long-remembered statement from our first year, I will always remember that statement as well.

Respect is an important concept—Jimmy Horton and I respected each other, and he was my friend.

Be open to what others have to offer

This is an article I wrote for the Bellingham Herald in 1988. I used it extensively to help people begin to understand cross-cultural differences. It speaks directly to cultural issues and values we needed to learn and adapt our behavior accordingly.

Recently I received a visit from a Japanese teacher interested in developing a relationship between our respective private schools. We cordially exchanged ideas, I worrying that American students can be narrow, ethnocentric, provincial.

With a broad smile he observed that "some people are trilingual, some people are bilingual, and some people are American."

While Americans are inclined to declared themselves the greatest nation on earth, the fact is we display and alarming combination of arrogance and ignorance toward other people, nations, languages and cultures. Most people I know become "ugly Americans" by their attitude that they, their community, their nations are the measure by which all other people are to be judged.

Traces of the paternalism, combined with the Peace Corps mentality of the '60s, prompted my wife and me to start our professional careers teaching native Americans in New Mexico. A year or two with the Navajos would fulfill our altruism. Certainly these people would be thrilled that we came to teach them. Thereafter we could take up our place in "middle America." But two years became 14. While I hope we were worthy of our calling as educators, it is increasingly clear that we learned more from them than they did from us.

What did we learn from the Navajos? We began to see culture beyond textbook definitions. We experienced culture, not so much in some romantic viewing of a traditional dance, but in grappling with the deepest issues and values of life. By living in a different culture, you begin to understand your own.

Although we had been taught the importance of sharing, it was our Navajo friends who gave that concept new meaning. If a student did not have money to pay admission to a ballgame, collectively they came up with the money. When resources were scarce for funeral expenses, the extended family helped out. The banana splits were always shared with those who did not have one.

Whereas I learned about earth-keeping in my own religious tradition, it was an elderly Indian basket weaver who demonstrated and confirmed reverence for the earth by asking permission of the Great Spirit for each reed selected.

While I was taught to honor my grandparents, it wasn't until I sensed the respect my students had for their grandparents that I realized how deficient mine was. Indian wisdom came from the old people. Gray hair was a badge of honor, something our disposable culture would do well to recapture.

The idols of Western culture are materialism, technology and recreation. The biblical question in Mark 8:36, "What good is it for someone to gain the whole world, yet forfeit their soul?" was answered for me by traditional Navajo people who lived in hogans, chopped wood, carried water and herded sheep. I saw people who were happy with the simple things of life, for whom a worship service and a church potluck were enough to keep life in perspective.

My point is simple: We Americans badly need cross-cultural experiences to cope with our ethnocentrism.

I'm not for a minute trying to idealize Indian culture like some blurry-eyed anthropologist. I lived too long by the broken glass capital of the world (Gallup, NM), saw too many dirty diapers left in the parking lot at Safeway. I've seen too much jealousy over cows, sheep, horses and jewelry, and heard too much about witchcraft to believe any culture is pristine.

While I reject cultural relativism because of the inevitable moral bankruptcy that follows, we should not reject cultural pluralism.

Ours is a pluralistic society, and our world is a crazy quilt. God designed it that way. Down with theories of melting pots.

Let's learn from each other, white people and Indians, young and old, east and west, Soviets and Americans, pro-life and pro-choice, evangelicals and mainliners, Catholics and Protestants, male and female. Every nation, tribe and tongue has its contribution to make.

The gift is rich – if our minds and eyes are open to receive it.

Gary and Carol: Such Friends

We were newlyweds moving back to Grand Rapids for our Senior year at Calvin. We heard about this church, Eastern Avenue CRC, that had a "Young Couples" club, which back in the 60's was not unusual. Nana and I instinctively decided to check it out. To our surprise, between 20 and 30 couples were in attendance, many of the guys enrolled at Calvin seminary.

One of the couples, Gary and Carol DeVelder, native to South Dakota, seemed warm toward us, and we became friends. Their initial invitation to their apartment was the first of many, and our friendship flourished. It is still a mystery to me as to why and how this happened, save the good providence of God.

We discovered much in common—Gary grew up around the dairy industry, and Carol's maiden name was Kredit, relatives to the Lynden gang. And they were fun—in spite of our workloads, many weekends we would be back and forth visiting. But we were serious too, exploring our thoughts about our Christian faith.

After nine months of friendship, we said our good-byes, wondering how we would ever see each other again. We made our move to New Mexico, and they had another year in Grand Rapids. Gary, more inclined toward church education than the pastorate, snooped around at Home Missions, only to find out that they were considering the creation of a position on the "Indian field" in church education. Who would have "thunk?"

So it was that we were reunited—Gary with an office in Rehoboth and Carol ready to give birth to their second child. Our friendship picked up where it left off. We spent hours together, often talking about the challenges of cross-cultural ministry and the issues surrou

I'm recalling this lasted about four years, and the Gary was offered a similar position in Scottsdale more affiliated with Presbyterian churches. They had a formula for teaching that was very impressive prompting us to take our student teachers (a program we had with Calvin) to Phoenix for a long weekend.

Beyond that, Nana and I and kids would often go to Phoenix on breaks from school. They had a swimming pool, and Carol taught me how to swim at age 26. They had two boys, and with that pool, there was great fun in the sun of Arizona. Of course, all this changed when we moved back to Washington. Our visits were all too infrequent, though when we had contact, it was like we never parted.

Carol became a superb PE teacher, working for many years at Grace Christian School. Gary more recently started a ministry for refugees, helping them learn English and their way around a new country. Carol, in her retirement, was a faithful helper, her dynamism enriching their important ministry.

But then came Carol's cancer, of the uterus, nasty, not responding to treatment. And she passed away, all too quickly.

Gary has remarried, to Cindy, happily so. But a cancer is now afflicting him, colon cancer. It has responded to treatment, at least holding it down. The ministry is now under the leadership of son Derek.

So it is with friendship, such friends. It must come to an end, but not really, for even now we wonder if Nana and Carol are reunited in the heavenly places.

CHAPTER 5

REHOBOTH (1972-1982)

Our new challenge 1972

Our high school girls—28 plus little sister

Frieda Norris and Gerry Skeet came
with us to live in our basement

School board meeting; Frances Bates,
Peter Borgdorff, Jim DeKorne

The Road to Rehoboth

The road to Rehoboth from Fort Wingate is about a dozen miles, but our road was much more circuitous. Actually it happened by way of the Grand Canyon. But first some further background.

Of course, we knew something of Rehoboth—we were Christian Reformed, and if you grew up Christian Reformed, you would have heard about the mission to Natives in the Southwest. But neither Nana nor I had any direct knowledge of Rehoboth Mission. But in moving to Ft. Wingate, it was natural for us to begin to have relationships with Rehoboth and Rehoboth people.

One soon picked that there was discontent on that campus. And we could sense it when Rehoboth students would occasionally come to church at Wingate on Sunday eves—they seemed to have a chip on their shoulders, even angry. In contrast, the Wingate kids seemed perfectly content.

There were other stories that came to our attention—it was hard to hear that about "our" school. It seemed oppressive. Dare I say that the 60's were not the best years at Rehoboth—it was the 60's and the campus seemed tone deaf to the changes in the air. Red Power was on the rise, and Native people started to use their voice. They wanted a say about the issues and direction of Rehoboth Mission School, and for that matter their churches also.

At some point in our third year, I decided to write a letter to Home Missions reporting our concern for the vibes we were picking up. I shared it with Rev. Al Mulder who suggested that I get a couple more signatures. Both Ed T. Begay and Ray Pinto agreed to sign it as well. We got quite a surprising response from Home Mission Field Secretary, Nelson Vander Zee, saying it was the "most intelligent letter he had received from the field in years."

But what came of it? I have no idea if there was a relationship, but the controversial high school dorm parents resigned at the end of that school year. To our utter amazement, we heard over the summer that a young couple by the name of Gary and Pat Nederveld were coming to take the job. Goodness sakes—we knew them from our Calvin days. Pat and Nana were both on the Homecoming Court the same year, the winter of '65. We didn't know them well, but in our minds, they were classy and capable people.

Though we continued at Wingate, we soon became fast friends with the Nedervelds. They quickly made adjustments to dorm life, steps in the right direction, but they soon were overwhelmed with working six days a week, managing nearly 60 students. One long weekend in February, we decided to go together to the Grand Canyon, Pat and Nana both pregnant that winter of '72. They were exhausted and did not think they could come back for another year. We could not let that happen!

We stayed up late on that Saturday night, wondering what could make the job tolerable. It dawned on us that the 1st through 8th grade dorms were divided into boys' side and girls' side, with dorm parents for both girls and boys, 1-4, and the same for grades 5-8. Each dorm had roughly 30 kids. Why shouldn't the high school dorm have a similar division?

That night, Nana and I pledged that if Home Mission would approve the division of the dorm, with two sets of dorm parents, and would build an apartment onto the north end of the girl's side, then we would apply for the newly created position. Miraculously, all that happened within a few months (though when we returned in August, there was only a new slab of cement where there was supposed to be an apartment). In hindsight, it was quite bold of us, even arrogant, to make such a proposal—us young couples in their 20's. But the Lord blessed it!

We left Wingate with sadness, leaving the church, the youth group, good colleagues at school. But we left also with joyful hearts because Stacia Lin was born on May 17, our last month. (That story will be told elsewhere.) Given all the circumstances, we felt called to Rehoboth. We hoped to make a difference in the culture of the dorm, and maybe even the whole campus.

Gary and Pat were every bit as capable as we expected. First semester, we lived in an apartment in the middle of campus, but we spent most waking hours living communally with the Nedervelds, sharing meals and babies and dorm responsibilities. Second semester, our apartment was ready, and now we were on our own, with 28 high school girls. We were probably too young for such a task, though the Nedervelds, two years older, were our "wise" neighbors.

Gary Nederveld was a visionary guy who dared to rock the boat. That year, we proposed that the students should be going home every weekend, rather than once a month. It happened by second semester, with Gary and I taking turns driving a bus to Shiprock, 90 miles, full of kids and luggage, dropping kids off along the way. It met with some resistance from both parents and students, but it was the right thing to do. We never wavered.

Further, Nederveld proposed to Calvin College that they send student teachers to Rehoboth. And that too was approved. Since I had just completed my Masters the previous summer, I was asked to supervise the program. We had six student teachers that first year. It was wonderfully successful and continued all the years we were at Rehoboth. Incidentally, I was also teaching three classes each morning, Social Studies and Bible. Our lives were full—maybe too full.

I said it was a circuitous route—including the Grand Canyon. Now you know the fuller story, one that only God could have executed. It was not a straight path, but surely he made the crooked path straight, as is his pattern. What we thought would be a couple years in the Southwest and then back to middle America, now appeared to be even a longer stretch. God was in it—in the midst of our coming decade of adventure.

Dorm Parenting

As noted above, when we arrived in Rehoboth in August, there was a mere slab of cement waiting for an apartment to be build thereon. We were told to move into one of the apartments central to campus and walk back and forth to the HS Dorm to share duties with the Nedervelds. While seeming less than ideal initially, it turned out to be a blessing, because we learned a lot from Gary and Pat as their apprentices. Further, a rich relationship developed between us that has lasted to this day.

One of the most memorable developments was a spiritual revival within the first couple of weeks. One of the girls was the daughter of Rev. Scott Redhouse, who by this time had left the CRC in favor of a more charismatic expression of the faith. Caroline and a couple of her friends were the leaders and soon most of the students on both sides of the dorm were participants. The Nedervelds and Polinders were in over our heads—there was much that was wholesome, but also behavior that concerned us.

As too often accompanies such revival events, they tend to be short-lived. Such was the case, and after a month life returned to normal. Yet I would claim that lives were influenced, even changed. We claimed the verse; "Greater is he that is in you than he that is in the world" (I John 4:4).

We had 28 girls on our side of the dorm, who then became our full responsibility in January of '73. We had many good times and good support from parents, though they did not often come in to visit. There was a definite routine, up at 6:00, off to do "detail" (work around campus for 45 minutes to an hour). Breakfast at 7:30, and to school by 8:30. After school, most kids were out for sports, devotions, and supper at 5:30, study hall from 8:00 to 9:00, lights out at 10:00. It was not nearly as rigid as it appears—we had plenty of free time and fun time through it all.

Stacia was by now crawling, and the girls treated her so well. She would sneak up to 2nd floor unbeknownst to us—never was there a problem in our three years.

One of the challenges that Colleen took on was to teach some sex education. She had good book in that regard, and the girls took to it nicely. Well, maybe too nicely—it seemed our pregnancy rate increased, somewhat to our embarrassment. But who's to know—Colleen had a wholesome approach, and the girls respected her.

There was the occasional discipline problem, most often alcohol-related, but we had a good three years with those girls, and still hear about them and have occasional contact. By year three, Colleen was with child with Shawna, actually born in February of '75. Again, the students were excited to have another little sister. But by this time, my work at the school was intensifying, and we decided it was time to give up the job, though we did quite enjoy that assignment.

Elementary Principal

In 1974, what would be our third year at Rehoboth, I was named Elementary Principal, thus giving up my part-time teaching role. This would be my first real administrative job. We had quite a young staff along with two veteran teachers. It was a good experience, one class per grade and a cooperative, creative staff. We had a dandy little school!

As noted elsewhere, it was here that we started to send home a monthly parent bulletin, and the next year making it weekly. We got lots of good feedback from parents, and though I didn't realize it at the time, I was getting some good practice in writing. I believe my first article was "Christian Education Begins at Home," which led to other thoughtful articles about the education we were trying to make happen at Rehoboth.

Parent-Teacher Conferences

Our little staff was concerned that we had so little contact with parents, so we decided to have Parent Teacher Conferences. This had never been done at Rehoboth and some of the campus veterans were quick to offer their skepticism. These were the days when most of the kids were still boarding students, and Native parents were reluctant to even come into the school—that was white man's territory.

But we conspired with the kids, promising an afternoon off to watch a movie, if we got 50% of the parents. Further, if we got 60%, we would have popcorn, and if we got 70%, we would have Coke. The students bought into it. But given the hesitancy of some parents to come into the school building, I told the teachers that if we saw parents sitting in their pick-ups, not coming into the school, that I wanted them to go out and knock on the window, hand them the report card and try to engage them in conversation. They were reluctant but they did it!

Sure enough—the very first effort yielded a 70% turnout. We were thrilled, and of course the students were as well. The bigger issue here is we began a pattern of involving parents in the education of their children. As I recall, we did the same "reward system" for a few years, but the parents began to feel comfortable coming into the school. It wasn't long and we had 90%, and then a 100%. The high school also started the pattern, never getting quite the high percentages, but still very worthwhile.

There was one other part to those conferences: the Navajo Taco Suppers. I don't recall if we did it on that first time, but it became long-standing pattern. One must understand that Native people were intimidated about coming into the school buildings and the dining hall kitchen. Again, that was white man's territory. But we began to break that down. The white folks couldn't make frybread—we needed Native moms and grandmas. The white ladies would cut up the lettuce and tomatoes. But the beauty was they were all working together in the kitchen, laughing, sharing, becoming friends. Today that campus is full of parents, interacting, volunteering, participating in their children's education.

Miss Helland

My first administrative role was as principal of Rehoboth Elementary. I was not that secure about the elementary assignment, having never taught in the elementary, nor having a self-contained classroom. But we had a fine staff of six teachers, and they were grateful to have a principal who showed up every day as compared to a 1-12 principal who simply did not have the time.

A most precious moment came in my first year. Already I had come to appreciate Luella Helland enormously. She was a single woman from Minnesota in her 50's who had the worst case of diabetes (type 1) that I had ever witnessed. But nothing could deter her from teaching. She was outstanding—maybe the best teacher I ever worked with. She loved her kids and was particularly committed to teaching Native Americans.

She had to watch her blood sugar very carefully—eating the right food at just the right time. But one day she forgot something, though I don't recall the specifics. And she began to show tiredness as she sat by her desk, and then put her head down on the desk. Her 3rd graders were obviously concerned and assumed that she had a poor night of sleep and just needed a nap. So, they pushed some desks up against the wall by the black board hoping to create a comfortable place for Miss Helland to lay.

It was at that point that one of the students was concerned about the safety of all of this, and figured they better get some adult advice. A couple of kids went across the hall to tell Miss Vander Woude, much to their credit. Miss Vander Woude knew exactly what to do—Miss Helland needed a drink of orange juice, which was quickly retrieved from the fridge. And just as quickly, Miss Helland was fully awake, completely embarrassed, and very tired. I sent her home, but as I recall she was back by noon.

Miss Helland, of Lutheran Brethren roots, was one of my heroes—so determined, so devoted and so devout. But those sweet 3rd graders are also to be honored, for caring for their tired teacher and trying to make her comfortable. That was precious!

Formation of the Rehoboth Christian School Board

I learned a lot in those first years, which included going to meetings of the newly formed School Board. I believe it was '74, that the day-to-day operation of the school was transferred from Christian Reformed Home Missions to the local school board. These were exciting times, with an inexperienced Board who had a few things to get off their chest. Remember, the Native folks had had very little input for 75 years into how the school was run, and now they were the ultimate authority.

There was some pettiness to be sure, but it was absolutely the proper thing to do, to move from being church-controlled to parent-controlled. And of course, we administrators had some things to learn also. I shall always be grateful for Rev. Al Mulder who schooled me, noting that boards are not likely to lead, but that administrators needed to bring forth the new ideas and lead, but always respect the Board who had the right to respond either negatively or positively. Further, Rev. Al taught me to write a monthly report, which I then did for the full span of my career.

There was one meeting where representatives from Home Missions were present—Rev. Peter Borgdorff and Rev. Duane VanderBrug. During the finance report, delivered by my friend Elaine Stam. I objected to her aggressive attitude about tuition collection. In short, we got into a peeing match, in the presence of these honorable leaders.

They were not pleased, and the next morning they took me to the woodshed, so to speak. They told me I was out of line, and that the Board was the Board, and I best learn to respect them. It was a valuable lesson, and I am forever grateful that they had the courage to confront me. Borgdorff was actually my immediate contact/authority at Home Missions. I often claimed him to be the best guy I ever worked for.

Peter continued to mentor me, eventually along with the School Board making me Superintendent (age 32). We remained close friends until his untimely death a couple of years ago. And he was always fond of Nana—I teased him that he liked her more than me, and with good reason.

The moral? Don't be afraid to take advantage of the wisdom of your elder colleagues. Peter subsequently was Executive Director of the CRC for many years—I still miss him!

Native Preference

One of the policies of Home Missions was to replace an Anglo teacher if a Native teacher became available. Evelyn Begay was about to graduate from Reformed Bible College, and with some extra courses at neighboring Calvin, she would be qualified. Thus, the decision was made to replace our 2nd grade Anglo teacher, a decision that was not particularly popular around campus. Yet, we had the necessary support, and we pulled the trigger—the first time in RCS history. It would not be the last.

It was not easy for Evie, being one of the very few Natives on campus. I felt badly that she spent too much time in her room, rarely coming to the staff room. And there were a couple of Anglo families were not so sure a Native teacher was up to the task. Yet, I think it was a good experience for Evie, and she came to know Willie Benally who worked on the maintenance staff, and whom she eventually married.

Securing Title I Support

The hiring of a Title I teacher came about because we pursued our right for federal funds for remedial reading. But it took a little guile to get the position, and the help of my friend John Hartog, who taught in the Gallup schools. He told me to take the lead Title I lady in the district our for lunch and further to buy her a martini. I followed John's instructions, and we got our Title I position and more, to this day. I charged the lunch to the Board of Home Missions.

Long-range Planning

After my first year as principal, we decided to leave our role as dorm parents, but then were asked to take up a novel project at Rehoboth; that is, a two-year long-range planning assignment for Christian Reformed Home Missions. My agenda included some analysis of the current Rehoboth

Christian School program, the potential for Satellites Schools, and need for some version of Post-High education or Pastoral education.

The first big project was to have a long-range planning conference. We invited leading pastors from the REZ, new school board members, some random parents, and Home Missions leaders. As I recall, about 50 people gathered in the basement of the Rehoboth church. We invited Calvin Seminary professor, Dr. Eugene Rubingh, to be the primary speaker. Rubingh was mission's professor and had experience in Nigeria. We asked him to present on the history and success of mission boarding schools. He was the right choice, giving us a broad overview and noting these schools had mixed success.

The discussion was lively and generally positive. I was responsible for writing a substantial report on the two-day event, which was well-received and became my agenda for the next two years. The idea of a satellite school in Crownpoint drew immediate favor, leading to a steering committee of church members. Subsequently, we hired one teacher the first year, and a second teacher the next for grades 1-6. The school had a 25-year run but closed in 2000 given financial stress.

Such were the life and times of that three-year experience. It was a time of learning and growing and creative effort. The next chapter of Rehoboth administration would be far more challenging.

High School Principal/Superintendent

Change in administrative assignments again was underway, with my appointment in '77 as Academic Principal 1-12. At the same time, there were other changes in personnel which led to some very important hires, most of whom were in their 20's. I don't recall the exact years, but most were the 77/78 school year. Allow me to list them:

- Elmer Yazzie—Art
- Joel Jasperse—HS English
- Mike DeYoung—HS Science
- Gail DeYoung—Home Ec and Reading
- Jim DeKorne—HS Math and Science
- Glen Hendricks—Mid school Science and Math
- Doug Hart—Bible
- Keith Vander Laan (came a year later)

John Vant Land returned from Hamilton, ON to take up Math and Science, we retained Tom Weeda, Stan Pikaart and Ken Faber.

This was an outstanding crew—I remember seeing the lights on at the High School late into the night. We worked hard, held strategic staff meetings, and had good times together. One of the best decisions was to surprise the kids with a day off. After chapel, I simply announced that the buses were outside the church and they were to load up. The students were wonderfully surprised and up to McGaffey we went. Games and food filled the day.

After doing it that first year, it became a game with the student body as to how we pull off a surprise—we always thought of some way to confound them.

These were also the days of some excellent boys' basketball teams, under the leadership of Coach Kuipers and Coach Faber. We won a state championship and a couple 2nd places. The games were in Albuquerque and we would load up the high school students for the 2 ½ hour drive and turn around and come home the same night—what else could you do with a dorm full of boarding students? And the next days we would repeat it.

Rehoboth fans were loyal, many driving a couple hundred miles one way to attend the games. The final games were played in 'The Pit" of UNM. We were a 1A school, followed by the 4A schools. We yelled our hearts out, thinking we were making some serious noise in this cavernous arena. But when the 4A student bodies responded to their teams coming on the floor, we learned how small we were. Their cheers—sometimes vulgar—humbled us, yet we were proud to be there.

School Culture

Despite some positive efforts on the part of a quality staff, the culture of the high school was not what we desired. Even as known in other Christian high schools, there was a time in the 70's when drug issues were painfully prevalent. So it was at RCS, along with the usual incidents of alcohol use. Sadly, too much of my time was taken up with these infractions, and it always takes all too many hours to get to the bottom of the facts of the case, plus follow-up with parents.

A couple of examples:

A new sophomore student from seemingly a fine family one day took used some drugs of some kind and was completely overtaken, to the point of roaming around behind campus, and eventually threatening staff members with a knife. Somehow, we managed to corral him, and turn him over to his father. We never saw him or his dad again. What failures we felt like, and how embarrassing for a Christian school.

One of our junior girls, a member of the basketball team, had been drinking before the game and smelled of alcohol while playing. It was a second offense, and our policy at that time was expulsion for a repeat offense. I had to deliver the news to her parents, who were friends of ours—and the father was a school board member. As we expected, they appealed to the School Board, a situation where I knew full well the Board would readmit the young lady. In such cases, several of the extended family often would show up, for what was a Saturday morning Board Meeting.

It was here that Pastor Rolf Veenstra saved me the risk if I would not be supported by the Board. He reminded me of a case at Calvin College decades past where the President had to discipline a professor based on Board policy. But he said to the Calvin Board, "I enforced your policy, but if you want to make an exception, I will not take it as a vote of no confidence." Calvin made the exception. I used the exact same line, and another exception was made. We all left the meeting in good spirits, and my rapport with the family was restored. Further, in hindsight, the policy was too harsh, and the next year we changed it.

School Years 79-82

Keith Kuipers had been Superintendent since the mid 60's and was at the stage of his career when he was burned out on administrative duties. Given some staff turnover, he decided to return to the classroom. He always had a good relationship with students, and this afforded him the opportunity to reengage with them.

In turn, I became then the Superintendent and High School Principal, though I was able to pass on some part-time administrative tasks to some very able colleagues:

- Mike DeYoung—H.S Head Teacher
- Glen Hendricks—J.H. Head Teacher
- Denny VanAndel—Elem. Head Teacher
- Jim DeKorne—Business Manager
- Tom Weeda—Dean of Students

Each of these men performed ably. I was still left with a pile of work, much of it related the High School, but also the work with both the School Board and the Board of Home Missions, on whom we were very dependent financially. I was now 32 years old, which is young for leadership in Navajo country. No doubt I made youthful mistakes.

My recollection is the culture of the school remained not as wholesome as we hoped. Yet, there were so many terrific kids, and families. So, one had to keep a balance. One of the nagging problems was racial or ethnic—it was too often the case the Anglo kids hung out together as did the Native kids. The book title *Why Do All the Black Students Sit Together in the Cafeteria?* likewise applied to Rehoboth. That is not to say there were not times of camaraderie and friendship—clearly there was.

It wasn't until a couple decades later that I came to understand institutional racism, and in hindsight there was plenty.

1. The staff was almost exclusively Anglo. Teachers Elmer Yazzie and Evelyn Begay were the exceptions. John and Emily Lee and Jim and Fern Gonzales were Native dorm parents. The was one maintenance employee, one secretary, one food service worker after we invoked the Native preference policy.

    Imagine, given all the schools in the region, loaded with Native people working in the kitchens, we could not find a Native Christian to join our food service staff. My hunch was there was little effort to do so. In short, the white folks dominated, though there was a required Native majority on the School Board.

2. Additionally, most of the Native students lived in the dorms. I recall having a birthday party for 1st grader Stacia and we invited her classmates from the dorm to our house—that was a big deal. But never could Staci go play with her friends in the dorm. The same was true at the High School dorm—it was rare for an Anglo student to walk through the door. It was strangely a segregated campus. Why?

3. The curriculum was all too Eurocentric. There was some, but not enough Southwest Studies, Navajo History and Culture. It would be nearly two decades before Navajo language was routinely taught (though John and Mae Charles would teach the elementary students' Navajo songs and words in my elementary principal days—dear people). We were negligent—our student body, Native and Anglo, needed a fuller understanding of the Native context.

4. There was an event the Spring of '82 that captures some of the angst we were feeling regarding the school climate. One of our staff members, when asked to sign one of the student's yearbooks, happened to read some of the comments some of the students were writing to each other. Though not the majority, there were a handful using horribly vulgar language, indeed shameful. I asked the teacher to make copies of some of the yearbooks

for the rest of the staff, who in turn agreed these students at the very least needed to be suspended, if not expelled. Such was our recommendation to the School Board who readily agreed upon seeing the evidence.

A Stalemate, and Winter Trip Home

Nana and I had been giving serious thought to moving back to Lynden. The task of administering Rehoboth was enormously demanding. While we had a good staff and board, the culture of the high school in the late 70's and early 80's was not as healthy as it should have been. Further, we had a couple lead Native pastors who were not supportive of the School. They had a critical spirit and were not shy about sharing their opinions.

I had decided the previous summer that this needed to be confronted. We could not do good work if churches and pastors were not with us. Our constant refrain was, "Home, Church and School must work together—then the School can do its best work." I had talked to Board Chair, Ed Carlisle, Pastors Earl Dykema and Al Mulder indicating that I was going to call a meeting with these two prominent pastors, Rev. Paul Redhouse and Rev. Charlie Grey. Dykema and Mulder were wary, but they agreed to attend.

My letter to Redhouse was rebuffed with a phone call claiming that he really did support Rehoboth and saw no need to meet. Charlie Grey did agree to come to a meeting, set for the morning of the last day of school before Christmas vacation. I don't recall any specifics, but we made absolutely no headway. Charlie bowed his neck, and we just talked past each other. It was a difficult session and outcome!

I went home for noon lunch and said to Nana, "Let's go home for Christmas, and look for a new job." She was all for it and started packing. We knew that first grade teacher, Janet Kaemingk, was also eager to spend Christmas at home in Lynden. She quickly agreed to join us. I believe, we were ready to go by 4:00 and headed NW on a cold, winter day, hoping to drive straight through. We decided to make it a surprise, though Nana would only call Grandma Haak.

A glorious surprise it was—I can see my Mom yet, sitting at the kitchen cove she used as a desk. She was thrilled! And then on to Grandpa and Grandma Haak, where we would stay for the next couple of weeks. One of the grand parts of the holiday was that Auntie Eleanor's Valley Christian basketball team was coming to play Lynden Christian. Thus the Polinders were quite tied up with housing and feeding Eleanor's team. It was a fabulous vacation, including a VC win over LC. Polinders like to win!

During that time, I had a promising interview with the Chair of the Concerned Christian Citizens Board. We also talked with Dad and Uncle Sherm about the Abbott Road place, wondering if I could actually start milking some of the older cows that needed a little more space in their stalls. I was not afraid to become a part-time farmer.

CHAPTER 6

HOMEWARD

Family picture, Summer '81

The Lynden Tribune

Home town picture newspaper for Lynden, Everson, Sumas, Nooksack, Laurel, Deming and Acme

VOL. 94 NO. 38   WEDNESDAY, February 2, 1983   LYNDEN, WASHINGTON 98264   30¢

Farm accident takes Mina Polinder's life

Wilhelmina Polinder, lifetime Lynden resident, was killed Friday in a tragic farm accident. She was 62.

Polinder died of injuries she received when a calving Holstein cow apparently turned and attacked her. Polinder was checking on the cow for her brother-in-law, Fred Polinder, Jr., on his farm at 1090 Polinder Rd.

Mina Polinder is survived by her husband Henry, two sons, three daughters, 11 grandchildren and numerous other relatives. See Obituaries for more details.

Funeral services were held Monday in the Third Christian Reformed Church of Lynden.

According to Chief Criminal Deputy Doug Gill of the Whatcom County Sheriff's Department, Polinder was apparently mauled and trampled by the 1,300-pound, three-year-old cow. She died of head and internal injuries.

Gill said Polinder died up to two hours before an ambulance crew arrived on the scene at 3:40 p.m. A family member discovered the body and notified officials.

Polinder had been asked by her brother- and sister-in-law to check on the cow—and to call a veterinarian if any problems arose—while they were gone to a convention.

It is believed that Polinder entered the pen to check the cow for milk fever or to help the newborn calf nurse.

Mina Polinder was active in the Sharon Ladies Aid Society of her church and served as a volunteer for Project Hope. She was also a member of the Whatcom County Dairy Wives.

Henry Polinder is president of the Northwest Dairymen's Association and is a prominent representative of the local dairy industry. He and his son Sherm operate Ronelee Farms of Lynden.

MINA POLINDER

Mom's picture in newspaper

Dad's surprise at our farewell

Our family—moved to Lynden

Devastation

On January 29, 1982, I had a meeting in Albuquerque with NMANS, (New Mexico Association of Non-Public Schools) of which I was a board member. I always enjoyed meeting with this diverse group of people. That afternoon, a strange nauseous feeling overcame me—it felt like was getting the flu. I worried that Nana would have to drive home with a miserably sick passenger.

I would say it lasted about an hour, then I started to feel better again. Strange! I was feeling normal when Nana picked me up from our meeting. We had to drive to the airport to pick-up our friend, Dr. Jay Dykstra, who then rode home with us. The 2 ½ hour drive brought us home around 8:00.

Oddly, when we arrived at our house on the Rehoboth campus, there were some cars around, and lights on in the house. My long-time friend Denny Van Andel stood outside. We greeted him, and then he said he had some bad news for us: "Your Mom went to be with the Lord this afternoon." He had scanty details, but we knew it was a farm accident of some kind. We were devastated.

We called home to learn more about what happened. I don't even recall to whom I talked. We learned that Uncle Fred had asked Mom to check his maternity pen where he expected a cow to give birth. My Dad, Brother Sherm and Uncle Fred had a Holstein meeting in Everett that day. It was not an unusual task for my Mom—she was a farm woman who was not averse to being around the birthing process. Our best guess it that she went inside the pen to check if the newborn calf was a heifer or a bull—common practice for farmers.

What happened next is most uncommon—the cow attacked Mom, no doubt being protective of her calf. Evidently, with her head she knocked Mom to the ground and continued battering her. It is hard to imagine to this day. Auntie Phyllis was the one who found her. From the phone call, at least we had accurate information, which of course flooded our minds for the next 24 hours.

After our initial weeping, we had to collect ourselves to make plans to go home. Thankfully, we decided to take our kids. Plane tickets were purchased. Packing began. A restless night followed. We would leave quite early to catch our plane in Albuquerque—a long, agonizing trip.

The plane trip was equally awful. I do remember a man sitting across the aisle who was reading his Bible. He was from Bellevue and his kids went to Bellevue Christian. He offered comforting words. And then off the plane to see Uncle Gary and Auntie Gloria waiting to take us home, another long trip. I remember so clearly seeing those two signs on the Samish highway—Bellingham: 9 miles, and then Bellingham: 6 miles. All those years coming home from GR or NM, those signs were a greeting—you are almost home. This time—I didn't want to go home, my Mom would not be there.

But we did arrive, the extended family gathered. As I walked in, I actually collapsed from sheer grief. I then recall particularly my embrace with Uncle Fred, who carried such pain about having asked Mom for the favor. Two big men holding each other up, wailing in anguish. We were the last family to arrive home—Auntie Marge and Uncle Jim, Auntie Eleanor and Uncle Bob, and of course, Auntie Karen, the youngest, a Calvin student, not yet married, had arrived earlier. The sorrow was bottomless.

We were most concerned for Dad, who lost his Mina after 42 years of marriage. And Auntie Phyllis, who saw the grisly sight of her mother-in-law, who had somehow crawled outside of the pen, under the gate. She would have nightmares for years. It was the next night I was walking to the barn with my Dad to get some milk, and he said, "Mom never said anything, but she wanted you to move home so bad" (which we had been considering). Dad wept on the way to the barn, like I had never seen before.

More details emerged. Mom was supposed to bring a birthday cake to the Rest Home for my Grandpa Polinder's birthday. When Auntie Phyllis arrived, my Aunt Anna, who worked there, ask her, "Where's Mina—she is never late! There is something wrong." Auntie Phyllis had heard Uncle Fred ask her to check up on the birthing cow. She immediately headed for Polinder Road. Coming over the bridge, looking to the left, she saw Mom's red pick-up. She knew it would be trouble but did not anticipate what she was about to see. As noted above—a ghastly sight.

All the painful phone calls would follow, to family and relatives and friends. The community was in shock. While Dad was a more public figure, Mom was a behind-the-scenes worker. She had lots of friends in church and with her "Dairy Wives" pals. In the 80's there were still 500 dairies in Whatcom County, thus a very active group of ladies that promoted dairy products. Both the Herald and the Tribune wrote stories, along with the Hoard's Dairyman. Even Paul Harvey reported it in his national noon hour radio program.

I don't recall much about the funeral except Third Church was packed. Of course, lots of locals were in attendance, but also Darigold and Holstein friends of my Dad and Sherm. I believe Mom's cousin Dewey Bajema sang and Rev. Sheeres presented the Word. I do recall the outpouring of Lynden love. I think Dad and family got 500 cards.

I remember sleepless nights. I was missing my Mom, and would for many days to come. So it was for everyone, each in their own way. Auntie Karen had to head back to Calvin, so alone. Waiting for her in the mail was a letter from her Mom. My kids suffered, but there were many more. I remember particularly nephew Jason who had such a close relationship with his grandma. I remember a moment at the Fair in August, six months later while untying a cow, I realized how much I missed Mom at the Fair. I stood by the head of that cow and bawled like a baby.

Naturally, one asks all the difficult questions of God. I don't believe I, or Nana, were ever angry. We rested in his sovereignty—"The LORD gave and the LORD has taken away; may the name of the LORD be praised" (Job 1:21) We tried to lean into the positive—that I was blessed with a good mother for 35 years, that my kids remember a loving grandma. But I miss her—still do! I believe we will meet again.

Moving Home (1982)

Our trip back to Rehoboth after our Christmas at home would be another straight-through drive, with a bad weather report. In fact, I believe we left in the snow, and had snow most of the way. I recall Mom, standing in the garage waving good-bye—it would be the last time we saw her alive.

The next month went by uneventfully, though we were considering options that may develop in Lynden. Then on January 29, the devastating phone call, as described in the previous story. This would change everything in terms of our future.

Our loyalty to Rehoboth was deep, and if we left, who might come to take my place as Superintendent? Nevertheless, in early February, Nana and I decided to move back home. In no small part it related to my Dad, who now was so very alone. I was particularly unsettled about calling my supervisor and friend Peter Borgdorff at Home Missions. But I made the call through tears, and then also announced to the Rehoboth Board and staff. All this with no assurance of a job, and a wife and three kids to support. But such was our faith—we believed God would provide.

The departure from Rehoboth was difficult. To say farewell to friends and parents was excruciating. They had a wonderful farewell event for us—almost too much. The staff surprised us by having Dad, Sister's Eleanor and Karen come out for the event. In the back of the Fellowship Hall were three big refrigerator boxes, and at the start of the program out popped my Dad and sisters. Thus the tone was set, but I am still embarrassed by the emotion of the evening.

A couple of weeks later, we headed off campus, but not before stopping at the post office where I mailed the letters that would suspend the students describe earlier—the vulgar ones. The Board supported my request to not have me spend my last two weeks dealing with difficult students and parents.

Lynden was a four-day journey with a U-Haul. We ran out of gas outside of Twin Falls, Idaho—Nana was not pleased. One night, we stayed with the Trulls, Jim and Judy, in Sunnyside—the same Judy that one day would join our family. And then home—what a feeling of security that comes from being "home." The house at 1518 Abbott Road was still in the process of remodel, under the supervision of a generous Dad. We stayed in the guest house by the River House and moved into our new home around the first of August. What a thrill that was!

On the job front, things were also happening. The job with CCC was offered, halftime, in April, and we decided to sign on. We knew we could supplement our income with milking 20+ cows if no other job was on the horizon. We set September 1 as our deadline.

Concerned Christian Citizens, Politics, and More

One of the most interesting jobs I ever had was director of Concerned Christian Citizens (CCC). That story goes back a long way, even to my childhood. In the first grade, 1952, I recall making a sign on a piece of paper, tearing a hole so it fit over my shirt button, thereby declaring "I like Ike" (Ike short for Eisenhower).

My portion of the extended Polinder family was Republican. My Grandma would watch the political conventions with rapt attention. Before we had a TV we would go to Grandma's and watch with her. One soon picks up political values even at a young age.

Dad was more political than Mom, and I believed every political word he said. I tried to remember his points, his arguments, so I could use them on others. In High School, my friend Linda Pilon would debate me, she being a Democrat. Uncle Sherm would often claim it wasn't Linda and Ron arguing, it was John Pilon and Hank Polinder.

At Calvin, I got a double major, History and Political Science. Calvin has a way of opening one's mind. My favorite professor James De Borst, with whom I had five courses, was in fact a Democrat, as were many of my friends. This was during the Viet Nam war and the Civil Rights movement. The spring of our Senior year, both Martin Luther King and Bobby Kennedy were assassinated. A cherished memory was our Student Council, of which I was the Treasurer, participating and helping organize first a march on campus, and then on Sunday afternoon, marching with several thousand to downtown Grand Rapids. I remember Prof. DeBorst saying it was his proudest moment seeing his Calvin students engaged in those marches.

I was not a great student, even in Political Science. There were too many distractions, though I surely regretted my slothfulness later in life. DeBorst, in a conversation with some friends and me, encouraged us to subscribe to the *Reformed Journal*. Indeed, I did for as long as the magazine lasted, and it too helped me open my mind to a range of ideas, all from a Christian perspective.

Post college, in New Mexico, I was not all that active politically, though I did not vote for Richard Nixon. My Grandpa Polinder claimed the most important quality of a politician was honesty, and Nixon did not measure up. Thus I voted for Hubert Humphrey and George McGovern, both Democrats, both defeated by Nixon. Thereafter, I reverted to my Republican posture, voting for Ford, Reagan and the Bushes. I did not vote for Donald Trump, preferring to write in John Kasich, the moderate governor of Ohio in 2016 and Senator Ben Sasse in 2020.

Center for Public Justice

When I took the job with CCC in '82, having moved to Lynden, I was not all that qualified, but I suppose I had potential. Knowing my lack of depth and holistic thinking, within the first month of the job I wrote a careful, thoughtful letter to James Skillen, Executive Director of the Center for Public Justice, which had just opened an office in Washington D.C. I frankly stated that I, and our whole organization, needed mentorship. It proved to be one of the most strategic letters I ever wrote.

Skillen responded warmly and indicated he would be coming West the next spring. Indeed he did, and spent three days with me. We drove around the county, from sea to ski, all the while he was schooling me on a more Christian approach to politics. Perhaps most important, he introduced me to Abraham Kuyper, the brilliant Dutch pastor, journalist, politician. Of course, I knew of Kuyper from my Calvin days, but this went much deeper. I have often said that Jim Skillen may have been the smartest person I have ever known. And his teaching me about Kuyper shaped my thinking ever since.

We did some good stuff in the CCC movement. We wrote thoughtful newsletters, we sponsored public forums with good speakers and important topics every couple of months and I taught various church education classes on Faith and Politics. The most popular product of CCC was our Voter's Guide. We interviewed every candidate we possibly could and wrote up a forthright summary. By being forthright, we did not please everyone.

One favorite story was our interview with Pete Kremen who was running for the legislature against our friend Roger Van Dyken. We wrote that he "lacked a moral compass." Regardless, he won the election by the slimmest of margins, a bitter defeat for those of us close to Roger. Years later, Pete and I buried the hatchet and became quite friendly with each other. He appointed me to a couple of different commissions and urged me to run for County Council. One time he shared with me how hurt he was when we commented on his "moral compass." But then remarkably he said, "You were right—at that point in my life I did not have a moral compass, but I have become a Christian and have developed my moral posture." He thanked me for our honesty.

I should back up to say more about the Center for Public Justice. After that long visit from Director Skillen, I was soon asked to stand for election for the CPJ Board. I figured that was an honor and surely I would learn much—and I got elected. It was a fabulous experience, serving with mostly Ph.D.'s, all way smarter than me. But I had my role to play, reminding all those scholars that they needed to learn to talk and write in language that commoners could understand. They respected me for asking my simple questions, and I gained lifelong friends from that six-year experience. It also enabled me to fly to Chicago and Washington DC, which in turn allowed me to see the sights, attend the inauguration of George H.W. Bush, and twice participate in the March for Life.

The Bellingham Herald

My role with CCC enabled me to move around the County and meet some very interesting people, including reporters from the Bellingham Herald. I recall my first interview upon taking the position with Bob Partlow, from the Herald, who had a reputation of being quite cynical towards Lynden and life in general. I was a nervous wreck with this first big interview. He asked good questions and I did a decent job of answering them. His last question was a clincher—he asked, "What is the difference between CCC and GGG, the Glorious Guardians of Good?" which was featured on a popular TV program in those days. My first response was of sheer laughter, which he really appreciated. He could tell I had a sense of humor and didn't take myself, or our organization, too seriously. It made for a warm relationship thereafter.

Similarly, Dick Beardsley, who was the editor of the editorial page for the Herald, took a shine to my writing in the CCC newsletter. He asked if I would become one of twelve community columnist who would write one column each month for the Herald, an op-ed piece of about 750 words. I accepted and did it for four years, though it was a challenging assignment. This now was a county-wide audience with mostly secular readers. I wanted to represent my community and my faith honorably. Dick was the editor, but never did he challenge anything I wrote. To the contrary, we became very good friends, often going out to lunch and even going to Mariner games together.

We were both serious baseball fans and he was once a sports reporter in Boston—even interviewed Ted Williams at one point. Dick was not a Christian, but he loved to discuss serious matters. Our conversations would first be about the Mariners, then move to politics and finally to matters of faith and philosophy. Sadly, my good friend had a stroke when he was yet in his 50's. He would spend the rest of his life as an invalid on machines but had the presence to signal to his dear wife to unplug the machines—and he died. Nana and I were on the longest trip we had ever taken in '99, so we missed his memorial service, much to my regret.

Charter Review Commission: Running for Office

My involvement with CCC, my movement around the County, and the Polinder name led to good name recognition, which is helpful in running for office. I always had a desire to run, but avoided State office or National, knowing how disruptive that would be to our family. But in our County, every 10 years, a Charter Review Commission was elected to review the Charter or constitution of our County and recommend changes. I threw my hat in the ring to be one of 15 Commissioners, with over 50 people running for a position. To my great surprise, I was the leading vote-getter. Wow!

It was a very interesting experience and quickly taught me some of the lessons of politics. I learned that if you were the leading vote-getter, you would likely become the Chair of the Commission. That was not to be—the Democrats knew that I had Republican instincts and they dutifully went about gathering their votes to elect Marge Laidlaw, a well-known Democrat party partisan. As it turned out, I was fortunate not to be chair, given my workload as principal, and my modest knowledge of parliamentary procedure. Very soon, I discovered that the Republicans on the Commission were too far to the right, prompting me most often to join the Democrats with their more moderate and sensible proposals.

Nine years later, the process was repeated, this time coming in 2nd in the county-wide voting. Again, a similar phenomenon—the Republicans were far to the right, even obnoxious, causing me to most often caucus with the liberals. This time I was more confident in actually making some proposals, in particular to suggest some edits to the actual opening lines of the County Charter. I was able to propose a change in the language of the preamble to the Charter to "*advance justice, inspire confidence, and foster responsibility,*" the key addition being the advancement of justice. This had to be added to the ballot in 1995, and it passed. Further, the conservatives wanted to make all the offices partisan, like auditor, assessor and the council and executive. Happily, the voters turned that down.

These experiences did whet my appetite for running for the Council. I approached Supt. Kamps about it, along with the Education Committee. As I expected, they were not inclined to give their blessing; I had hoped with the help of a good assistant principal, I could make it work. And it would be a model to students to engage the world, get involved, move beyond our smallish town. But it was not to be, though now the late 90's, I was getting restless in my role as principal.

Parental Choice

I need to back up to my Senior year at Calvin during their first January Interim. I signed up for a course on the 1st Amendment Religion Clause with my favorite Prof. DeBorst. The genius of this statement calls for the balance between "free exercise" and "no establishment of religion." In large part, we focused on the injustice of private school parents paying taxes, but also substantial tuition for the free exercise of their conscience regarding their children's Christian training. This excellent course gave me the framework for subsequent board work throughout my career.

Early on in my principalship at Rehoboth I attended a first meeting of private school leaders regarding justice issues for private schools. This led to the formation of the New Mexico Association of Non-Public Schools (NMANS), and I was asked to serve on the Board. What a privilege as a young principal to meet with diverse leaders, particularly Roman Catholic!

In moving to Washington, I had a similar experience serving on committees with the Washington Federation of Independent Schools (WFIS). Likewise, the Catholic administrators were terrific co-workers. We never had as much success as we hoped, but the fight still goes on. I believe, given the ongoing failure of the public school monopoly particularly in inner cities and reservations, there could be a major shift in the education story in this country.

A Letter To My President

Author's note: I have not been in the habit of writing letters to the President. The last time I wrote was when President Ford was looking for a Vice-President, and I nominated Sen. Mark Hatfield (R-Or). He didn't listen. The chance of a President reading any letter is pretty slim, but just maybe this letter will wind its way to "W." Regardless, I feel better for having written it, and if he doesn't read it, maybe at least a few folks in McKinley County will.

Dear President Bush:

Congratulations on your November victory. As you gear up for your Inaugural Address, may I suggest some things to include, and to make them a priority in your next term. I had the good fortune of hearing in person your dad's address in 1988—the one about a "kinder, gentler nation," and "a thousand points of light." I think Peggy Noonan helped write that—it may be a good idea to bring her in for some advice—those phrases are now part of our vocabulary.

I am a Christian, though I am not a fundamentalist Christian. If you don't know the distinction, ask your pastor to explain it to you. It is important to understand the difference. I have appreciated your evangelical posture, though I realize you get a lot of heat for it.

Lots of Americans are hostile toward religious worldviews. They fail to comprehend that their secular worldview, tired though it may be, is every bit as much a faith as yours and mine. Secular faith and values motivate their politics just like Christian faith and values influences our political perspectives. Many secularists actually believe that their values are worthy of the public square but ours are not. It would be wise to explain to the nation that all citizens are driven by their values and vote accordingly. And we do well to show respect when we disagree with each other.

I can tell from your speeches that you understand the pluralistic nature of this country. Principled pluralism means that we hold fast to our worldview, debate it in the public square, let the democratic process work its way, though always protecting the minority and their right to actively participate in political life.

Mr. President, while I agreed with many of your positions (pro-life, pro faith-based initiatives, pro traditional marriage, pro an aggressive posture toward terrorism), many of us would ask you make your faith even more pivotal to your office. The Bible is a powerfully political book. Indeed it is the norm for how to do politics, and that norm or standard is the pursuit of justice. You tend to talk about freedom a lot—I wish I would hear more about justice.

- Before we went to war, how carefully did you weigh all the issues against the longstanding Christian tradition and theory of a "just war," first articulated by St. Augustine?
- When you consider public policy regarding poverty, will you please remember the biblical injunction to do justice to the poor, the widow, the fatherless? You are right to create opportunity rather than entitlement, but more of your compassionate conservative language helps us understand that.

- When considering our environmental policy, please consider what the Bible has to say about caring for the creation. To be sure, this requires balance and good sense, but show us that you want to do justice to the land.
- Will you do all within your power to nurture racial reconciliation? Please express your deep desire to bring people together. Spend a disproportionate amount of time in the African American, Hispanic and Native American communities—come and visit us here in Northwestern New Mexico.

Such priorities would do much to disarm your enemies. More importantly, it demonstrates your desire to be an obedient disciple of the One who has called you to do justice and serve the political community in America and the global community around the world.

Sincerely,
Ron Polinder
Rehoboth, New Mexico

Lynden Christian: Community Development

Our departure from New Mexico only yielded a part-time job with CCC. I would be looking for additional work, though I was assured that I could be taking over the milking for about 20 mature cows on the Abbott Road place, if another assignment did not present itself.

July and August of '82 led to considerable work on our little 14-acre farm—it was run-down, but we tackled it. Colleen and family worked to finish the remodeled house and I did a lot of yard work and farm work. We got a lot of work done, and the place soon looked respectable.

But another development was unfolding in that Lynden Christian was opening a part-time job in "community development." In short, the School Board saw the need for expanding the student body beyond the Lynden community into Bellingham. Having had considerable experience in NM in student admissions, this seemed a natural job to explore.

My paycheck from RCS ran through August, and this new job would start Sept 1. In God's amazing providence, I was offered the LC position on Sept 1. Along with CCC, I now had full-time work, and would not have to resort to milking cows. I would have some young stock to care for which I tackled along with my kids. But we were able to make a living—in part Colleen supplemented the income by selling Discovery Toys, a task she grew weary of quite quickly.

My work was likewise a positive experience. We have already addressed the CCC assignment, but the LC work was equally important. The school had never advertised—it was seen as a Dutch ethnic school with little diversity, accurately so. We first developed an application process which was new to the school. We expected all new families/ students to apply; after all, you could not expect just those new Bellingham folks to apply. Of course, some Lynden folks didn't think they needed to apply—they were entitled. But we worked our way through it.

Further, we started advertising on both radio and Bellingham Herald. Here too, there was resistance—it cost money, and some of our creative ads were challenged. Again, we worked our way and eventually our methods were accepted.

A third attempt at reaching out included a slide show that we used in churches—this too was useful in communicating that LC was open for business—the progress was slow, but steady. New names and faces began to appear, and over a four-year period that character of LC began to change. I had to outstanding partners, Gerrit Byeman and Donna VanderGriend. Now, four decades later, the Lord saw fit to bring numerous new families into the Lynden Christian community. It was an honor to be part of it, and to fulfill this first effort of the School Board.

Colleen: Church Secretary

Nana had numerous gifts that enabled her to be a good church secretary. Her experience as the Registrar at Wingate demonstrated her superb organizational skills. She was pleased to put those gifts to the test again.

Also, she knew the community, she knew names and relationships. Newborn babies or sicknesses or deaths were soon recognized and shared with the staff, passed on to the prayer chain and placed in the church bulletin. If she missed something, a call of apology followed.

She took pride in putting together a good packet for the Council. But she could scowl when the elders didn't bother to pick up their material until meeting time, prompting her to reflect, "I'm not sure what the Bible says about women in office, but if we want to get anything done around here, we better choose some women."

Colleen had a wholesome relationship with Pastor Ken—they were a team. She respected him wonderfully, but she could also challenge him if she thought he was off base. More than once she said, "If you send this letter out, you are going to get in so much trouble…" And the changes were made.

At morning coffee, she would not allow anyone to stay in their office. If need be, she would drag them out herself. She knew that the staff would often use that time to communicate, and thus avoid problems. Plus, she needed to hear what they were working on. That pattern has long disappeared.

In short, she was blessed with common sense—she knew how to deflect problems or answer questions with a sweet spirit.

As technology got more complicated, Colleen got more insecure about her capacity to do an efficient job. During year 16, she decided it was time for the church to look for someone else. At the same time, we were being pressured to return to New Mexico. The timing seemed right for us both to tackle new assignments.

I surely take too much pride in comments we hear to this day, "Sonlight was never the same after Colleen left—she knew the congregation, and kept the staff talking to each other." The Lord indeed "established the work of [her] hands" (Psalm 90:17, adapted).

Colleen Polinder: A Tribute

I would like to honor the spirit of Jesus in Colleen Polinder, who for over 16 years has served as Sonlight's Administrative Assistant.

If ever the prayer, "Let the beauty of Jesus be seen in me…" was answered, it was answered in her. Colleen is, simply, a beautiful person.

And why? Where does one even begin to sing the praises of the beauty of Jesus radiating out of her? I have had the privilege of working with her for all these 16 years, and a high privilege it has been. Thanks be to God for his indescribable gift in Colleen Polinder, and for that matter, in her supportive husband Ron who has been a team player with her and all of us all the way. May God bless them both in Rehoboth!

Think just of her warmth, her smile, her approachability, her genuine interest in every person she meets, and her eagerness to serve them. Who doesn't just plain like her? And you see this so beautifully in her composure when she is interrupted. That's been almost her whole life here these years: interruptions.

Colleen , Koeman, Huleatt, Miles on the job at Sonlight

Then there is her thoroughness blended with her wisdom. For Colleen, it must be not only correct; it has to be right. So in her we have that rare gift of a person who checks and rechecks, writes and rewrites, thinks and then rethinks, until "It is right!" She has spared us, spared me, from doing or saying something unwise so many times. Her wonderful question is, "Now just a minute here: are we so sure that's what we want to say, to do?" What a gift of the Spirit that has been to us all.

And then there is her sincere faith, her friendship with Jesus, her godliness. she is a woman of prayer. When Colleen prayed with us, it was so good to hear her pray because she prayed with such alertness, such earnestness, and such confidence.

She is not comfortable with a tribute like this, which itself speaks eloquently of her humility. But these things must be said, lest, like the couple on the road to Emmaus, our own preoccupation blind us to her Christlikeness, which sets so excellent a standard for us all. She is a true fashion model of the finest kind: a model of character.

So tonight we honor her in a special way.

For her countless acts of kindness to each and all
For her steady, uninterrupted reliability all these many years
For her cheerful spirit, her quick laugh
For her industriousness, many days barely stopping for lunch
For her memory of important lessons learned in the past, important for the present
For her effective way of finding and supporting a team of office volunteers

For her tact, correcting, but never condemning
For her quietness, her restraint in her speech
For her obvious loyalty to us all
For her impartial support of every staff member
And for her friendship in my life, a debt I will never be able to repay ...

For all these beauties of Jesus in you, Colleen, and so many more that I have no time to tell, I speak for this whole Sonlight family as we gratefully and joyfully heap an overflowing measure of honor upon you tonight.

Pastor Ken Koeman, 2000

Part-time Farmer, the Kids and their Chores

The work associated with Concerned Christian Citizens and Lynden Christian was certainly a full load, but we lived on a 14-acre small farm, 1518 Abbott Road, and that added to our collective workload, thus three half-time jobs. In Northwest Washington, the grass grows fast. Animals need to be fed, and in turn leave their mess, all too often.

Early on the kids had their chores, especially from October to April, when the cattle were inside. We took care of 25+ unbred heifers and 15+ bulls of my brother. The girls would go out in the morning before school and Rusty and I would go out after supper for what was 30-45 minutes of chores (often followed by evening school meetings or ballgame supervision). In the 18 years, there were different "kid" combinations and as our kids left home, we hired neighborhood kids.

The kids were most often diligent, and thus made a nice contribution to our "making a living." But not always—when Shawna and Rusty teamed up, Shawna was an unwelcomed supervisor. Brother Sherm used to say, "When you have one kid working, you have a kid. When you have two, you have half a kid. When you have three, you have no kids at all."

Then there was the Saturday work when the manure needed to be dispensed with, when the bedding needed spreading and hay and grain for the week needed to come out of the haymow. Most often, Rusty and I were on that duty, often using our old equipment—we were farming in the 50's. Sundays I did the chores, cheerfully, in a clean barn. Occasionally, I would sneak the animal's extra grain, a Sabbath blessing.

Intermittently we had to give shots, which took an extra kid to catch the heifers. Once when my brother was helping, Shawna had the audacity to ask, "Uncle Sherm, how much older is my dad than you?" Sherm, 4 ½ years the elder, enjoys quoting Shawna.

The workload changed in the summer—Nana and the girls would tackle the flower beds, and I would do the lawn until Rusty was a bit older. We often had a garden which provided some extra work. There were some rocks that needed picking, providing discipline for slothful kids.

All three kids learned how to prepare a calf/heifer for the fair in August. Given our extended family took seriously "showing" cattle, our kids had some advantage in learning the process. They worked hard to prepare, and it paid off in the show ring. They all did well, and each won at least one Fitting and Showing event. Of course, their parents watched with plenty of pride, and now the same with a couple of grandkids.

Summer also brought with it pasture that needed trimming, fences that needed tightening, and wood from the trees that needed to be picked up. Our land was located right along the Nooksack River which occasionally would rise to the top of the dike. To walk that dike at flood stage spoke to the power of God—it could make you tremble. And thankfully, it never flooded our house or barn. Dad would say, "The old-timers knew where to build, always on the highest spot."

It was not all work—we always had a horse or two. All three kids were at least intermediate riders, taking trail rides on Saturdays or Sunday afternoons. Mac, HoneyBabe, and horses borrowed from Uncle Sherm were used as needed. Each of the kids still have affection for horses, and now some of the grandkids are taking lessons, which I should have provided for my kids.

Now all these years later, we look back fondly on our 18 years on Abbott Road. Our house was altogether adequate, though chilly upstairs in winter. It is music to my ears to hear them give thanks for it, and gratitude for their most basic education—learning how to work.

CHAPTER 7

FULL TIME PRINCIPAL (1986 – 2000)

The First Day of School

Of course, I lived through dozens of first days of school. But there is one that is particularly memorable: my first day as Lynden Christian High School principal. It first should be noted that Nana and I had discussed before our move back to Lynden whether I should pursue a principalship at my alma mater. We thought it unwise to become a principal, given that I would oversee innumerable kids whose parents were my schoolmates. I had not been a model student, as they would well remember.

However, in March of 1986, H.S Principal Len Stob took a new job for the next school year. Administrative hiring in the Christian School world usually happened in January or February, so to begin an administrative search in March would be too late. Thus when asked, I agreed to fill in for a year.

When you start a new job, there is natural excitement, so when the first day of school came, I was eager to start--until the first hour of the first day. We concluded opening exercises, after which I made some comments just to the high schoolers, and then sent them off to their classes. As I walked back to the front office, Mrs. Honcoop indicated someone was on the phone for me. I innocently walked into my office.

The call was certainly not what a new principal wants to hear. A disgruntled parent felt it their obligation to tell me that many our football players and cheerleaders were at a party a couple of weeks previous. Oh my!! Lynden Christian had long had a code of conduct that athletes were to sign before they could participate in their sport. It particularly highlighted drinking alcohol, using drugs or tobacco, and other negative behaviors. Further, you were considered a participant if even if you were present and did not immediately depart the event. Punishment included a four-week suspension from athletic participation for the first offense and an eight-week suspension for the second.

On the job—Lynden Christian

Surely, I must have sat in my chair stunned, even frightened. Is this how I must start a new job, a new school year? I still had scars from dealing with way too many alcohol-related violations at Rehoboth—I could not bear to start at Lynden Christian where I left off at Rehoboth. I pondered and prayed, I am sure. What would this mean for our school and our football program, which had already been weak for several years? It could mean the end of the season before it even started. But as important, it cast me in the role of investigator and judge, a task that would likely take two weeks—and then you still may not have it all figured out as to who was guilty or innocent. My experience told me how intense and painful this would be.

Thus, I decided that I could not and should not open the year up with this kind of scene, even upheaval. Thus, I informed Athletic Director Harlan Kredit and Superintendent Ben Boxum that I needed to meet with them at lunch hour. I shared the substance of the phone call, and then plainly said, "I don't want to start the school year, or my principalship this way—with a discipline case that could take two weeks to unravel." I recommended that we gather in the chapel all the juniors and seniors who had signed the athletic code—and offer them a gift of grace—with proper warning that if they were caught again, we would "throw the book" at them. After careful deliberation, Mr. Boxum and Mr. Kredit agreed with that approach.

Word had gotten out that the administration was aware of the party. Some of those kids were quaking, imagining their season going down the drain. I believe it was the afternoon of the next day that I gathered the students in the chapel—counting both classes, I'm guessing 60-70 athletes. Then I made my remarks—I wish I had a copy. Surely, I told them we knew about the party. I'm sure I said I did not want to start the school year this way—to put our relationships in jeopardy before we even knew each other. I know I then set before them a position of grace, the kind of grace that God offers all of us. (I have long wondered if those students have connected the grace of that event as a symbol of the grace of God—did they take that with them?) And I noted that if they thought this was an act of weakness, that maybe I did not have the courage to do the tough work, I told them I could give them some New Mexican phone numbers to check me out.

Naturally, there was a collective sigh of relief as the students left the chapel. One student recently described it as our "get out of jail free" card. Even as I believed then, I believe still that it was the right thing to do. In God's good providence, he blessed the football team with a marvelous season, tying for first in the league, and then into the playoffs where they won four games. Coach Van Hulzen and his staff did a fabulous job of motivating his boys. We lost the last game to Ephrata in the Kingdome. But we did not feel like losers—it was an outstanding season, which led to many winning years for Lyncs football.

The class of '87 was a fun-loving class, respectful to me, even to this day. I enjoyed the year so much that I decided to stay on, if the Board would have me. They did, which led to a total of 14 years as Principal. I am thankful for the experience—good colleagues, good School Boards, supportive parents, and hundreds of wonderful kids.

Mr. Boxum

My first year as principal at LC was the last year of Mr. Ben Boxum's tenure as Superintendent. Mr. Boxum had been my principal in High School, and as noted elsewhere, we had occasion to have wonderful conversation.

Mr. Boxum was a native of Kansas, a great story-teller, and despite his quite serious persona, he loved a good laugh. We had many of them together. He was a dedicated Republican, very conservative, and made regular gifts to the party. Until the mailings started coming to him with his name spelled wrong—suddenly he had become "Mr. Ben Borum." He didn't appreciate the new label and claimed to stop giving to the Party. He kept the envelope close, so he could get a laugh from others who visited his office. And I doubt he stopped giving to the Party.

My office was next to his, and there would be this one unforgettable day. Some parents came into his office to discuss a problem they were having with the bus driver of their youngest son. Mr. Boxum, as was his custom, piously started the conversation with prayer. He barely got "Amen" out of his mouth, and the Dad erupted in the loudest possible voice, demanding, "I want .... fired." Of course the entire office could hear the explosion and wondered if ...., or even Boxum would survive.

Of course they did, and somehow the problems were solved and life moved on. But if I would see Mr. Boxum in subsequent years, all I would need to do was say that certain name, and he would burst into laughter.

Then there was the family that attended Lynden Christian who thought all three of their children were gifted. They would too quickly come into Boxum's office and make demands about a developing a Gifted Program. Such innovation was not his strength. This went on for two or three years, and finally the family decided to move. Mr. Boxum's response, "I wonder if I could go help them pack?"

In his later years, Mr. Boxum got Parkinson's disease, which really slowed him down. He had that empty look in his eyes to make you wonder if he was with you. Well, he was not quick, but his wheels were still turning.

I believe it was on his 90th birthday, they had an event for him, and some former students came to greet him, not the least of which was Bill Kamphouse, a menace not only in school but the whole county. He was from Sumas, and somehow adopted all the worst traits of that legendary town.

Upon greeting Mr. Boxum, Bill introduced himself, not being sure he would be recognized after several decades. Long pause—and Boxum said, "You should be in jail!"

The earnest response of wife Kathy was, "If it wasn't for you and me, Mr. Boxum, he would be in jail." Of course, nobody enjoyed this exchange more than Kamphouse, who with great bluster told the story to anyone who would listen, especially in Sumas.

Bill grew up to be a fine fellow, even doing some preaching. I suspect Boxum and the Christian education all played a role in that maturity.

I close with a word of deep appreciation for Mr. Boxum. He may have been the most committed Christian educator that I have known. He never wavered. He would often say, "If every student at this school turned their back on the gospel, we would weep. But that would not be reason to close Lynden Christian School. The Creator God of the universe must have his story told."

He was not particularly creative, but he would let others try their hand at new methods and programs. Mr. Boxum's steady hand guided the school for nearly 30 years, and I give thanks for him.

Mr. Kamps: The Next Superintendent

Lynden Christian Schools has been blessed with a long line of Principal/Superintendents who inhabited the position for considerable time. Mr. Gary Kamps was one of these and was my supervisor for 13 years. Gary was the product of a Montana farm, all of 6'5" who stretched above almost all the students. Given my 6'2" stature, when we walked the campus or engaged in supervisory duties, I suppose we could be considered imposing. At a football game, a smallish high schooler came up, straining to catch our eyes and identified us as the "twin towers."

Gary graduated from Dordt in '67, married Jean, had three kids, two of whom were good friends with our kids. He started his career as teacher/principal at Monroe Christian School, and then on to Ontario Christian as elementary principal, and then to LC as Superintendent. Obviously, we spent many hours, days, months together if they were to be added up. Gary was a good-natured fellow, warm-hearted, wanting the best for kids and teachers. Yet he could get tough when needed and make the difficult decision.

I believe his greatest gift to the school was his managerial skills. In a school the size of LC, with over a 1000 students, the details are endless. Meetings, meetings, meetings—agendas, minutes, phone calls. If you do not take care of those details, failure will be close behind.

This was no more evident than in the building projects undertaken during Gary's tenure. Both the building of a new middle school and a major remodel of the high school building were tackled. These projects proceeded with efficiency and competence—and Gary's attention to logistics.

Gary and I had lots of good laughs through our years together, the following being our favorite:

A Dad and Mom, parents of four LC children, came into the office regarding their eldest who got himself in some mischief, though I don't recall the issue. He was disciplined—we were not in the habit of sweeping nonsense under the rug. But Dad did not think his son was guilty and came with Mom to make the case.

We met in Gary's office, he behind his desk and the parents across the table from me. Dad was waxing eloquent to Kamps and me, but oddly, every couple of minutes he would move his chair a couple of inches closer to Gary.

It was somewhat strange, and finally, he could not move his chair any further. Without missing a beat, he said, "The reason I keep moving my chair is because my wife keeps kicking me under the table."

The four us burst into laughter, which eased any tension in the room. I don't recall the outcome, but I doubt we changed our minds about the discipline matter. And the story provides a sample "administrative" life—every day has the potential for a surprise.

One of the hardest moments for me was when we had to call Gary to inform him that we would not be returning to LC after our one-year leave of absence. Gary was gracious, accepting the reality that we were being called back to New Mexico. I will always be grateful for that.

Detectives

It was some time in the 90's when we were noticing a strange pattern at school. Someone was putting a little rock in the southeast exit door by Mr. Kredit's room. There did not appear to be any damage or anything missing—yet as principal, you don't want to have vandals penetrating a locked building.

With my colleague, Harlan Kredit

One Friday night, after a football game, Harlan went to his classroom and there it was—a little rock in the door frame, preventing the door from locking. Harlan called me and suggested we wait inside the school to catch the culprits. It sounded good to me. Harlan suggested I come in the back way from Brookfield Drive and walk across the football field toward the school.

I was greeted by Harlan and his son Tim. We parked ourselves in the old chapel, now the library, sitting in the dark for a good while gabbing about the issues of life. There were several cars and kids outside in the parking lot as was their custom, harmlessly visiting with each other. I decided to take a walk through the building just to look out and see who the kids were.

Bad mistake! Those students were close enough to the school that they could see a figure moving inside the building through the big windows of the school lobby. From inside, I could hear it said, "There is someone inside the school." Not good—I hustled back to Harlan and Tim, bending low past those windows. Harlan figured I should have known better—that you can see through windows even in the dark.

We figured that the students would drop the issue and eventually head for home. Wrong again— they started walking toward the school to check it out—who might be snooping around in their school? In peaking around the corner, we could see their noses pressed against the lobby window. Maybe 20 students were out there discussing what they should do, and someone said, "We need to call the cops."

This was before cell phones, but using the old phone booth, they called 911. We by now know we are in deep weeds, and we are not going to escape. A few minutes later, we see a couple cops cars driving into the LC parking lot, red lights flashing. We're toast! And we know that we must surrender. By now there are students guarding each of the exit doors.

So we turn the lights on inside the school, each of us going to separate doors to let students in. I went to the back door facing north, and there stands a group of kids, big Jason Meenderinck and Chris Libolt, leading the way, one of them holding baseball bat. To this day, I can picture the incredulous looks on their faces as I opened the door and let them in.

Of course the two cops were close behind, and soon they and the whole gang of students were inside the building glowering at the wannabe detectives. The officers were not amused. I can only imagine how red we were in the face. The dutiful officers gave us a stiff lecture on the folly of being vigilantes. Our heads hanging, we accepted their admonishment, with the students enjoying the moment.

I will always be proud of that group of kids—they saw someone inside their school, and they quickly moved to protect it. What we were not so proud of is that in the next week's Tribune, our names were listed in the police report. Of course, the community had some good laughs over that, at our expense.

That night, the students and police were the teachers. Harlan, Tim, and Ron were the students—we learned a good lesson. And we never had another incident of students propping open a door.

Claudette

She lived a mile away on the Noon Road where she and her husband Jake ran a dairy farm. Claudette had six children, though she had an additional five from a previous marriage. So being the mother of 11 tells you she is not a typical mom.

In fact, Claudette Dykstra is one of the most wonderfully unique people that I have had the privilege of knowing. I'm told that she drove logging truck up in hill country around Deming. She was also a country-western singer, and a yodeler, even cutting a record or two. Later in life when she was driving bus for Lynden Christian, she taught the kids on her route how to yodel. Check YouTube "Bus Yodeling."

In our neighborhood, we would occasionally gather the whole gang at someone's house. Claudette and I decided we would prepare a song or two, one being a takeoff of John Denver's "Country Roads." She came to practice one evening where we discovered how low her voice actually was. Rusty, listening from his bedroom upstairs through a register that allow the heat to go upward, hollered down, "Dad, you are singing higher than Claudette." It was true, Claudette was a tenor like me, so her range enabled her get down a ways.

The Dykstras had those six kids at Lynden Christian, and when the oldest two were in High School, they were something of a handful. Travis and Troy were both quite social, which meant they would gab with friends during the 4-minute pass time between classes and stack up tardies as a result. That meant, if they got too many, they had to show up an hour before school for what we called Breakfast Club.

Singing with friend, Claudette Dykstra

Claudette got weary of getting those kids to school early, likely meaning they were missing chores at home. The boys insisted to Mom that it was impossible to make it to the next class in four minutes. Claudette would have nothing of it, so she decided to come to school, go to class with those boys, and walk the halls with them. True to her style, she wore the brightest yellow dress known to humankind—like a piece of the sun moving down the halls. She was hard to miss!

Of course, Troy and Travis were horrified, which is what Claudette intended. The yellow dress added to the drama. The teaching staff, on the other hand, was enjoying every minute of it. They would come into the staff lounge slapping their knees in delight. And the principal celebrated the most.

Claudette didn't go home at noon—she stayed past the 2:00 hour, and easily determined that it was quite possible to make it to the next class in four minutes. While I didn't keep record, I am sure those boys thereafter did not need to show up for Breakfast Club.

Claudette was a true friend. She "had my back" in her challenging home. We rode horse together. Her hearty laugh outdid mine. We enjoyed her singing whenever we could. While living what she would call a pretty rough life, when she met Jake, she started to go to church and became a vibrant Christian.

But then Jake died suddenly of a heart attack—she lost her dearest friend. That summer, home from New Mexico, I stopped by her home, now on Hampton Road. She was still grieving—we wept together. But Claudette is instinctively cheerful, and after a couple years, she married Gerrit Sterk, her fellow church member at Nooksack Reformed.

And a couple of years later, now in her mid-70's, she brought her guitar and sang and yodeled at Judy's and my wedding reception. With all her noise and laughter, the crowd cheered her on. Our friend Claudette, there will never be another like her.

Frank Steidl: An Unusual Letter

I got the strangest letter, handwritten, from a Frank Steidl out of Stony Brook, New York. Turns out that he was native to Spokane, WA and a teacher and dean at the Stony Brook School. He was looking to move his family back to the home state of both he and his wife Judy.

Frank had heard about Lynden Christian from some South African visitors who had come to Stony Brook, visitors who previously came to Lynden Christian to check us out on their tour of Christian Schools in North America. Frank asked them for names of some impressive schools, and Lynden Christian was high on their list. Thus the letter.

My work as H.S. Principal was becoming more taxing, and I had been appealing to Mr. Kamps and the Education Committee for more help. Further, I had in mind someone who was from a different kind of school tradition than L.C. Certainly, the storied Stony Brook School, a boarding school no less, qualified as "different."

The letters and calls back and forth continued, and I was warming up to this fellow. I don't recall how this passed the School Board, but a trip was approved for Frank to fly to Lynden from New York. My biggest concern was whether he would catch on to our philosophy of education and fit into the culture of our school.

On the Saturday of that weekend, we took the ferry to Friday Harbor, which afforded lots of time for conversation. I was able to dig deeper into his theology and worldview. All new to him was the jargon of the Reformed tradition. Finally I said, "Frank, you are Reformed, you just don't know it."

Frank claims to have quoted me dozens of times when people ask him how he came into our family of Christian schools. Thankfully, when I shared my confidence with Mr. Kamps and the School Board, they were ready to offer him a job, part-time assistant principal and part-time math teacher.

Obviously, the move all the way across country was a big deal, but Judy and four kids were ready. A house was rented and this new family to Lynden would have to adapt to its culture, find a new church, and pay lots of tuition with little more than a Christian schoolteacher's salary.

Frank caught on quickly to his administrative duties. His Stony Brook experience brought some fresh ideas and experiences that became helpful to us. For instance, a simple but profound concept was "truth-telling." We hope for that from our students, but Frank labeled it, and made it part of our lexicon and student handbook.

In most schools the vice-principal is assigned all the discipline cases. I never thought it was fair for one person to do it all, but since he was teaching halftime, some of those cases naturally came to me. Of course, the serious stuff we did together.

Sadly, we only had four years together, as he was offered a principalship in California. We trusted each other; he worked hard, had great instincts and a gentle spirit. I always say, "In four years, we never had a harsh word." What a blessing to have such a colleague and friend, who came to us by the circuitous providence of God.

Faculty Room at Lynden Christian

The faculty room was a wonderful gathering space. The staff would often show up early to school, but five or eight minutes before classes began, they would wind their way into that staff room. Likewise at morning and noon break, and after school. It was a time to share with each other, have a few laughs, needle and debate. It could be serious too, always devotions on Monday morning, prayer, even tears at times.

But most often it was light-hearted. The height of hilarity came at a morning break when we needed to choose a representative to serve on the Convention Planning Committee. Nobody volunteered or were even willing to be drafted. Thus, the decision was to pull a name out of the hat—I believe it was Gary Van Hulzen's idea. His buddy Bob VanderHaak agreed to prepare the ballots and place them in a paper bag.

With great fanfare, Van Hulzen prepared to reach in and pull the name of some poor sap to attend those committee meetings. Lifting his arm high in the air, he placed his hand in the bag, stirring the ballots, and then making the selection. He lifted it out, VanderHaak looking over Gary's shoulder, only to watch him pull out his own name. Bob quickly read the name 'Gary Van Hulzen.' The room erupted, Van Hulzen literally falling to his knees, the laughter reaching thunderous proportions.

It was some years later that VanderHaak admitted to writing Van Hulzen's name on each of the ballots.

The terrific staff at LCHS, one of my birthdays, put me in a wheelchair

Mariner Club

Early in my principalship at Lynden Christian, I overheard what I thought to be some potential rowdy students talking about the Seattle Mariners. Given my love for the Mariners, I stopped and ask, "Are you Mariner fans?" They sure were—and it immediately gave us a topic for ongoing conversation. They said there were more Mariner fans in school than I might think, even though they had never yet had a winning season. We decided we should form a Mariner Club.

The faculty and most students scoffed at the flimsy idea, but we were not to be denied. We called our first meeting during a noon hour around the time of spring training. As I recall, 30-40 students routinely showed up, most with opinions about the manager, who should be traded and where the team would place. There were even some optimists in the group, God bless 'em.

I announced this would not be a democracy, that I would be the dictator, and would appoint a chairman. We only had one meeting a year, so why bother with bureaucracy. I would choose a student who wasn't afraid to stand in the front of the room. One year, in a liberal move, I appointed Janelle Matter, the first woman to be so honored.

It was always light-hearted fun, and cause for banter in the hallway. A few times, we took a busload to Seattle, always arriving home after midnight.

The 1995 season deserves special mention as the Mariners came from 12 games back in mid-August to tie the Angels at regular season's end for a one-game playoff—the "refuse to lose" year that saved baseball in Seattle. The playoff game was on a school day and such an historic occasion should surely be part of the curriculum. The dictator informed the faculty that their classes could listen to the game if they so desired, though I would announce the score after each period.

What followed was the most spectacular inning in Mariner history when leading 1-0 in the 7th inning, journeyman Luis Sojo hit a broken bat ball just over first base for an inside the park home run with the bases loaded. Mariners win and go on to play the Yankees where they won their most dramatic playoff series, on Edgar's double and Griffey race home.

All this because of the Lynden Christian Mariner Club—well, maybe!

Bob Keller

Bob Keller is one of the most interesting people I have ever known. My first exposure to Bob was when he called me at school and asked me to write the chapter on Lynden for the book *Whatcom Places*, which the Whatcom Land Trust was going to produce. He had read my "community columns" in the Bellingham Herald and thought I was a decent writer—so he gave me a call.

I knew Bob only by name, but was under the impression he was a liberal, tree-hugging professor from WWU. So my defenses were up, I confess. But during the conversation, I was frank with him indicating I could not write such a piece unless I had the freedom to write about a theology underlying our view of the land. "That is exactly what I want you to do," was his quick reply.

The conversation continued and I asked him if he was aware of the origins of the Land Trust. He really didn't know, so I shared the story—that did not start at Huxley College at Western, or some place in liberal Fairhaven. That started in the basement of the Dutch Mothers restaurant with a meeting called by Concerned Christian Citizens during the time I was Director. I told him more of the story, including some notable participants. He insisted that story be included in the chapter.

This was probably the most challenging writing assignment I had ever been given, considering the likely broad distribution of this book. So I took it very seriously, spending an off day at school, writing in the solitude of my office. With trepidation, I sent it to Bob, thinking I was over my head.

To my complete surprise, he quickly sent me a note stating "I am delighted with your essay..."! I have kept that note all these years. A few days later, he sent me some edits which polished the piece. I had never had a "professional" editor. The rest of this "book" story will be told in another chapter--for now I want to concentrate on the honorable Bob Keller.

Bob and I became friends. I suspect in part because he "never knew quite what to expect from Polinder"—I did not fit his stereotype of Lynden folks. He would periodically send me notes or cards or a bibliography on a particular topic we had discussed. We would occasionally go out for lunch, though in hindsight, not nearly often enough.

Bob was an environmentalist in the best sense of the term. He loved nature and wanted to be the best possible steward. He had heard about the salmon hatchery on Lynden Christian, so one day he came to see it. It happened to be the Monday in March of '99 after winning two state basketball championships, girls and boys, on the same floor back-to-back, the previous Saturday.

To his surprise, "no bands played, no banners flew." The school was attending to their "primary purpose of sound education on the day after their astonishing sports victory," he wrote in the Bellingham Herald as a community columnist. What follows is the full article, which I still find to be brilliant in insight and expression.

Because of Bob's perplexity of what he observed at school, I gave him a copy of "Lynden Christian Athletics: By What Standard." He took that 16-page document home and actually read it. What he wrote in the attached article astounded me—he captured the Reformed essence of how we view athletics in succinct paragraphs and insight that I could never match.

There is a reason for that. Bob held a PhD from the University of Chicago in Church History, studying under the renowned Lutheran scholar, Martin Marty. Though Bob had since become a Unitarian, he understood our Reformed theology maybe better than I did. And his fair-minded character enabled him to respect our view of athletics, and for that matter the Lynden community.

Bob passed away a recently and his memorial service was a Saturday thereafter. I had never been to a Unitarian service of any kind, so what to expect? The name of Jesus, or God was never used, that I heard. It included a list of talented speakers, friends and family, honoring this good man. His sense of justice, his love of nature, his insistence upon walking, rather than driving, his intentional simplicity, his respect for those different than himself, even Ron Polinder, humbled me. Would that I claim those qualities, his character, his gifts?

The closing song was Woody Guthrie's "This Land is Your Land." That may seem odd, at least it was for me. But then I realized this was not a cheap, patriotic expression. This was a spiritual statement of how we should view and respect the beautiful land we have been given.

Bob Keller's Article

Lynden Christian Keeps Sports in Perspective, Bellingham Herald (1999)

SOCIAL ISSUES: Principal Ron Polinder correctly assesses the role of athletics in life.

Monday, March 8, seemed no difference than most other days on the Lynden Christian High School campus. The morning had begun with the usual devotions, classes met as scheduled, students strolled calmly through the halls.

No bands played. No banners flew. Quiet reigned. Below the school grounds two teenagers inspected Fishtrap Creek, surveying stream conditions for recent graduates of the school's salmon hatchery. One of the young men was Lance Vander Giessen, who also happened to be a forward on the Lyncs Basketball squad.

During the previous two days that team from a school of 395 students, along with the Lynden Christian girls team, had won state basketball championships.

That the Lyncs student body and faculty could attend to the school's primary purpose of sound education on the day after astonishing sports victories was no accident. It resulted from LCHS leadership having carefully, and theologically, assessed the role of athletics in education – and in life.

Their conclusions may be found in a 10-page "Statement of Philosophy" (authored by Ron Polinder) on sports at a Reformed school where policy stems from three basic beliefs: in divine creation, in the fall of humanity and in religious redemption.

Athletic ability, for LCHS, is a natural gift from the Creator who honors human competition, playfulness, excellence and teamwork – all part of a divine plan. We are expected to use gifts that include body awareness and movement, plus "disciplines of the heart." Sports can do this.

But humans are fallen (prone to sin), which means we often err, lose sight of God's will, and can slip into depraved ways. In sports this happens if winning becomes an obsession, if amassing wealth becomes the major goal, or when play becomes an end in itself. In modern America, says the LCHS document, sports have "gotten out of whack." College athletic departments can exploit students, threaten academic pursuits and bury the arts. (Today the document could cite the University of Washington paying $1 million a year to its head football coach.)

From a Reformed perspective, Americans engage in an "incredible distortion of sports" which Christians must resist by keeping games and athletics in proper perspective. If fans feel more passion about the Mariners than about work, politics, family or religion, we have reached a point bordering on idolatry. A Lynden poet wrote that no one bothers to cheer the nurse's aid in a rest home, but when we hand a football, baseball or basketball to young athletes, "millions join the senseless stampede to screens and stadiums."

Redemption (getting back on the right track) involves self-discipline and self-sacrifice, keeping things in balance by setting priorities; it involves families and the entire community practicing decent behavior (sportsmanship), and being thankful for physical skills regardless of winning or losing. Redemptive faith involves moving far beyond superficial "locker-room religion" with its "hodge-podge of biblical truths" that proclaim God favoring one team over another, stars over ordinary players, winners over losers.

"We thank God," says the LCHS document, "for the gift of healthy bodies, physical skills, and emotional discipline that gives our community something to celebrate … may we participate with a spirit that respects the participants, and opponents. May the quality of our play and support be an attractive signpost that entices others to the richness of God's kingdom."

Piety and lofty words remain empty until embodied in people. Fortunately for LCHS, its athletic director, Harlan Kredit, believes in and acts on these principles.

Kredit has been an outstanding classroom instructor for 37 years, a naturalist park ranger, mountaineer and recipient of the Whatcom Land Trust's 1999 Land Steward of the Year Award to go along with the two 1999 basketball titles.

He is the biology teacher who built a fish hatchery, requiring Lance Vander Giessen and another student to wade in Fishtrap Creek on behalf of salmon fry during the team's first day back after winning a state basketball championship.

That's perspective and solid priorities.

Bellingham Herald Community Columnist, Bob Keller is a Western Washington University professor emeritus.

Two State Championships on the same night

CHAPTER 8

THOUGHTS ABOUT EDUCATION

Christian Education I

Christian education is one of the biggest influences in my life. Starting at age five, I started at Lynden Christian School. Nana moved to Lynden in 3rd grade and joined our class. Their move to Lynden from North Dakota was in part for Christian education. We went all the way through LC, and then to Calvin College—Christian education shaped us, no doubt about it.

Though we started our teaching career at Wingate, a government school, there was considerable freedom to share our opinions, and we witnessed often to our students. Teaching in a public institution enabled us to compare it to the Christian education, where I would spend the rest of my career.

One must realize it is a different kind of calling to teach in public/government schools, though very much a calling from God and an opportunity to serve Him and his Kingdom. We often looked back at our Wingate experience and believed that our Christian witness there was every bit as important and blessed as our years in Christian education.

Our move to Rehoboth enabled me to teach halftime in addition to our role as dorm parents. As I look back on it, I don't think I was a particularly good "Christian" educator. I recall teaching Civics to mid-school students, with a great opportunity to infuse my teaching with themes of "justice," and I don't recall ever using the word. This provided an important touchstone for me as I grew to understand Christian education more fully as the years progressed—remembering how poorly I had started.

It was a couple of years later that I became the Elementary Principal at Rehoboth, and I recall for the first time sitting down at my desk that first day and thinking deeply about what had just happened here—that these parents gave their kids to Rehoboth to teach their children the Christian way. For the first time, the weight of this descended on me—and it would never leave. I began a journey for the rest of my life to understand, define, and implement Christian education.

I began reading more; I looked for good speakers; I participated in good conversation. The annual CSI conventions were very helpful, six years on the Center of Public Justice Board, my eight years on the Calvin College Board of Trustees and a couple of years on the Board of Christian Schools International—always listening, learning, asking questions.

I'm still embarrassed that I did not come out of Calvin College with a better grasp of Christian education. I did catch on to some key themes—"world and life view," and a sense of the "Kingdom." But I don't know that I got a Christian view of history and politics, which does not mean it was not taught—it was more likely my foggy mind, and a lack of diligence about too much of my college education. I still honor Calvin College for what they did teach me, and what became a solid foundation.

Maybe my best teacher was the writing process. I started a monthly Parent Bulletin my first year at Elementary Principal, which was warmly received (in spite of some of the old-timers who thought it would be a waste). The next year, we put it out weekly and included the grades 7-12. It continues to this day, 45 years later. Each issue I tried to address some relevant topic that would enrich our parents understanding of Christian schooling. I discovered when you write it yourself, it penetrates your own mind more deeply.

The move to Lynden and my job at LC as Community Relations Director put me in charge of the admissions process. Heretofore, the school had no application form—parents signed their kids up in early August at enrollment night. New parents would be expected to show up there, though there were very few "new" families, that is, new to the Christian school community. Much to the credit of the School Board, there was a commitment to reach out to this broader community. We began advertising and slowly but surely, new families came into the LC family. It was pleasure to talk to them about the essence of Christian education, which obviously helped me articulate our Christian philosophy more carefully.

Through the years of writing and articulating the essence of Christian education, one becomes more proficient and confident in one's writing skills. So it was that often I became the scribe, the writer of documents related to Christian education. Mission statements, goals, articles and essays would fall to me, or be initiated by me. One assignment was to write a philosophy of Christian athletics, a document called "Christian Athletics; By What Standard."

Slowly I became viewed as the philosopher on the staff, first at Rehoboth and then at Lynden Christian—quite an unlikely label for a quite ordinary student. It was unplanned and unintentional, but I have viewed it as a gift from God and have come to enjoy the writing process. Educational philosophy is very important—it is like buttoning your shirt: If you start wrong you will end wrong.

This is merely the metamorphosis of my conviction about the veracity of Christian education. I never viewed myself as a first-rate mind—there were so many people and professors so much brighter than me. But in the absence of other willing colleagues, I took up the task.

Now to the substance: first a statement of my everlasting conviction about the truth and beauty of Christian education. Finally, some frustrations and disappointments with Christian education.

Christian Education II: A Mission Statement & Philosophy

What follows is an expansion of the mission statement of Lynden Christian School, crafted in the 1990's. While we had a committee appointed to help draft this document, I served as the scribe and editor. Rather than start a new document, this one will serve that purpose. It remains my best and truest rendering of what I believe about education.

MISSION AMPLIFICATION:

Since inception, Lynden Christian Schools have served as an extension of the Christian home and as a partner of the Christian church in the nurturing of children and young people. The respective roles of these institutions in training and education can never be clearly differentiated, for the Holy Spirit "blows wherever it pleases" (John 3:8). Yet, God has ordained families, churches, and schools to perform certain tasks for the building of His Kingdom.

HEADS: Forming the Mind

The head is the symbolic center for knowledge, thinking, and rationality. This ability to reason, to process information, to discern and synthesize is a God-given gift that contributes to our humanity and equips students for what our mission statement describes as perceptive Christians.

At the core of our mission lies the pursuit of knowledge of our triune God as revealed in Scripture, in Christ, and in creation. It is not enough to know about God, rather we desire to know God personally, through Christ, and to love Him, indeed, to love Him with our whole mind. Moreover, knowledge of God and knowledge of self cannot be separated. St. Augustine prayed, "Let me know Thee, O God, let me know myself." Furthermore, the unspoken eloquence of Creation serves as the content and substance for our academic curriculum; we use the natural, cultural, and spiritual contexts in which we live.

Lynden Christian Schools' rigorous academic program provides its students with the cognitive skill and cultural literacy that will enable them to take up their place in society. It is the purpose of this institution to challenge and equip young people to be productive leaders and participants who discover and use their God-given talents to shape family, church, and cultural life.

Knowledge, along with logic and critical thinking, is a marvelous tool that contributes to our discernment of the cultural and social forces that shape our world. Romans 12:2 calls us to no longer be conformed to the "patterns of this world, but be transformed by the renewing of your mind." It is the goal of this school to teach young people to understand God and His creation; to use their minds in the service of God and neighbor; and to "test the spirits to see whether they are from God" (I John 4:1).

Indeed, the "patterns of this world" are profoundly influenced by secular humanism, materialism, individualism, technology, and ideology (both from the left and the right), all of which can be modern forms of idolatry. We desire that our students learn to identify God-lessness, whatever its origin. The formation of a worldview that is shaped by Scripture and influenced by Christian tradition will equip our students for insightful and creative participation in society.

HEARTS: Educating the Emotions

As vital as Christian thinking is, we must be reminded that Proverbs 4:23 claims, "everything you do flows from [the heart]." Thus, Lynden Christian Schools must be vigilant in educating students in such a way that enriches the head and the heart. Novelist Walker Percy describes one of his characters as "one who gets all A's, but flunks life."

The heart is the symbolic center of our emotions, feelings, and motivation. Values and character are issues of the heart, and Matthew 15:19 identifies the heart as the source of our "evil thoughts." The desires of the heart, good or evil, are powerful often beyond our rationality, thereby controlling our decisions and dictating our behavior. So too, encountering Christ as Savior is relational, and following Him with one's whole heart is an act of love. Thus, the school strives to nurture the heart and educate the emotions.

Because of the brokenness and sinfulness of our human condition, every student and teacher at Lynden Christian Schools is in some way wounded. Rather than seeking wholeness through a transforming relationship of love and friendship with God, we are inclined, and sometimes compelled, to pursue counterfeit forms of healing. Staff and students alike need to rediscover their hearts to expose false desires that are really idols and addictions. For children and young people, they appear in the forms of popularity, "coolness" and conformity. As a learning community, we must address these relational issues, which fundamentally underlie both thought and action.

Lynden Christian Schools strive to be a place that is safe, affirming, and loving. Christian education, both in content and method, must attend to the issues of the heart. Spirituality and character are to be addressed with instruction that respects the dignity and individuality of persons as image bearers of God, each with multiple gifts and intelligences.

Knowledge is not enough. To accompany this pursuit of knowledge, Lynden Christian Schools teach our students to be caring, vibrant Christians, who are taught to maintain the linkage between head and heart, just as our Creator intended.

HANDS: Preparing for Service

A Christian mind impassioned by a Christian heart inevitably results in Christian service. Thus, our use of "hands" is symbolic of action and service. For every dimension of education, we must always ask: "Education for what purpose and competence to what end?" Nicholas Wolterstorff in *Educating for Responsible Action* teaches us that "a world and life view is inadequate, for it puts too much emphasis on view… To be identified with the people of God and to share in this work does indeed require that we have a system of belief – but it requires more than that. It requires the Christian way of life."

Lynden Christian Schools, by adult example and through specific opportunities, must challenge students to be "in the world," active, productive, and fully engaged. We aspire to produce adults whose effort and work is competent, ethical, and just. In word and deed, we are compelled to share the gospel in all its fullness. In church and society, we live in community with one another. Thus, our mission statement expects graduates to have a transforming influence in the world. Unless teaching translates into action, we are a "resounding gong or a clanging cymbal" (I Corinthians 13:1). The stark words of St. James apply: "Faith without deeds is dead" (James 2:26b).

At Lynden Christian Schools, we do not view education as a passport to privilege; rather, with more knowledge comes greater responsibility. We strive to link desire with duty, belief with behavior, scholarship with service. Our communal search for truth bears meaning only when lives of virtue and integrity are presented as "living sacrifices, holy and pleasing to God" (Romans 12:1). We desire our students and graduates, in school and out, to practice their faith in ways that transform culture and build the kingdom of God.

We seek God's grace and wisdom to provide a balanced Christian education for the head, heart, and hands of His children. In these commingling mysteries of life and education, we acknowledge that the "Lord establishes the work of our hands" (Psalm 90:17b, paraphrased).

Christian Education III: My Disappointments

A way to begin this is to identify the very nature of mankind. As a serious Calvinist, I am convinced of the sinful tendency in all of us. We are born in sin, and it rears its head all too quickly in each of us, and at the earliest of age. Surely, all have sinned and fallen short of the glory of God.

So it is quite sensible to believe that even Christian schools are going to be far from perfect, and given 20+ years as a high school principal, I know of our imperfections better than most. Where should I begin—they come in no particular order.

1. Let's start with the lack of diversity in most Christian schools. There are exceptions such as the Potter's House in Grand Rapids and Rehoboth Christian School in New Mexico, both of which our family has benefited from. But in the tradition of the Calvinist Day School, by far the majority were white kids of Dutch-American heritage. For Nana and me at LC, our whole school was culturally the same, and we had little exposure to people different than ourselves. Three decades later, while we had some non-Dutch kids in school by the time our kids got there, we had very few minority kids.

    I recall a list of top ten needs we created on our Administrative staff, and when we prioritized them, diversity got the least votes. So too, on the School Board level—our community did not have the interest or the will to bring in people different than ourselves.

    Thus, many of the graduates from our family of Christian schools upon graduation, entered into a world in which they were uncomfortable with diversity. They preferred to "hang out" with their "own kind." To be sure, many learned to relate well to neighbors of a different culture or ethnicity. But many did not and were confined to their own cliques. This affected their ability to witness, or even to welcome church members from different backgrounds.

    I shall never forget my colleague Donna Vander Griend's observation in her years of leading community Bible studies. She would say that public school graduates were far better at reaching out to the newcomers, engaging in conversation, and forming relationships. To me, this remains an embarrassment.

Some of it relates to the lack of resources that it would take to help some Hispanic or Native kids to come to LC. If our country ever had enough sense to support Parental Choice, and School Vouchers, we could well see a difference in the makeup of a student body and the behavior of our graduates.

2. The limitation of resources also relates to the next concern. There is a certain elitism that accompanies private and Christian schools. Often, the neighbors view us private school folks as wealthy and elitist. And there can be some snootiness amongst students and parents who send their kids to Christian school. As I am writing this, Christian school tuition has become so expensive that it is quite difficult for a middle-class family to afford the cost. Thus, many parents are now upper middle-class. This, somewhat unfairly, contributes to an image of elitism.

    What has long been irritating to me is how the public-school community and those who are anti-school choice promote the stereotype that our schools are for the rich. In reality in our tradition most of our families were very middle class and sacrificed significantly to afford the tuition. Surely, this would also have been true for Catholic schools. My mom's parents were so poor during the Great Depression they took their kids out of the Christian school. And I have seen dozens of families, especially at Rehoboth, come into school so excited to have their kids admitted, but after a year or two, crawl out the back door, embarrassed they could not make their tuition payments. In short, there is much misunderstanding by the public about how Christian schools operate. But we ought never, if we have the privilege of Christian education, allow an ounce of arrogance to invade our spirit.

    So as I write this at the end of my career in education, it remains a disappointment that we have not made more progress to find justice in education. There are a few states that have made some good moves in that direction, but nothing as significant as they have done in British Columbia and Alberta, where they are now paying over half of the tuition. In Europe, school choice is even more available. I remain convinced that parental choice will be the only way to deliver many of our inner city and reservation kids from the lousy schools they attend. Until then I will be disappointed. Injustice prevails as parents pay substantial taxes for public schools, and then out of their conviction regarding education, pay enormous tuition besides.

3. My friend Jim DeKorne, a long-time Christian schoolteacher and administrator, later in his career worked in the charter school movement in Western Michigan and beyond, the National Heritage Academies. When asked about the differences between the charter schools and the Christian schools where he had worked, he quipped, "Well, we actually

have time in our staff meetings to work on educational issues—in the Christian schools, we were always talking about money." Ouch, it was painfully true—too often we did not have the time or resources to work creatively at new programs and methods to deliver a higher quality of education. To be sure, we still did a superb job of giving a quality education to the strong majority of our students, but we could have done better. Most of our teachers worked hard to challenge our students, but the culture could have been more rigorous. The research by the Cardus group out of Canada showed that the Catholic school tradition had a higher standard of academic excellence than our schools. That was a disappointment to see we were outdone, though we honor our Catholic colleagues for their quality work.

4. I have long been dissatisfied by the actual quality of truly Christian education. A primary purpose of Christian schooling is to recognize that our world belongs to God, and everything in it. Abraham Kuyper's line about "every square inch" is the bedrock of Christian education. Thus, every subject taught has a spiritual dimension and every subject is supposed to be taught from a Christian perspective. Yet, often our teachers neglect, overlook, understate this Christian perspective.

I noted above that in my early years of teaching, I was not very good at it myself. But it became my passion as I matured in my thinking. I have fretted that too many of our teachers have not progressed in the course of their careers in this regard. It doesn't seem to be their passion. I once gave a speech to the LC staff at the beginning of the school year about Reformed Education and the different levels at which this could be achieved. (see next article for CEJ)

I would also say that it is a lifelong quest to discover ever more effective ways to teach Christianly. Sometimes there is a lack of resources to stimulate careful thinking along these lines. I have found that math teachers may have struggled the most; yet, through the years I found some worthy books for teachers to study. I wish that Christian Schools International would continue to develop such resources for teachers.

Our Christian Colleges have done some work in this area and continue to do so. A series was published during the 70's, *Literature Through the Eyes of Faith* and *History Through the Eyes of Faith*, and there were a couple more. I believe Kuypers Center at Calvin College is doing some good work in this area as well.

We must recognize that the culture in which we live is increasingly secular, and thus our young people need to learn the essence of secular thinking and then develop a stiff Christian critique based on Biblical thinking.

5. Did too often "the culture" win? This is difficult territory, because I can tell stories for a long time of students who have lived out the mission of Lynden Christian in faithful, even dramatic ways. If I could not say that I should have looked for other work. Yet there were too often evidences that the materialism, the individualism, the racism, and the politics of our graduates too easily reflected "the world" rather than a distinctive and vibrant Christianity. In no small way, this has been the challenge of Christians throughout the ages, going back to the Old Testament people who constantly were attracted to the "gods" of the neighbors, finally prompting God to send his people into exile. The good news is that the aforementioned Cardus research shows that Christian school graduates do show wholesome lifestyle decisions that places them above most of their peers. And ultimately, this is the task of the Holy Spirit, who "blows wherever it pleases" (John 3:8).

These points get at some key issues, and I bring them up with a degree of humility because I have not able to effect the changes that I often hoped for. Yet, it is good for us to be honest about our weaknesses, hoping that leaders can more successfully address them in future generations.

In short, the Bible remains our source of truth. As someone has said, "The Bible remains the most important book in the library." We need to use it to transform our thinking by the renewing of our minds, often rejecting the patterns of this world, as Paul describes in Romans 12:2.

Reforming Christian Education: Christian Educator's Journal, April, 1998

Editor's Note: The following article originated as a speech to the high school faculty of Lynden Christian School in August of 1997 and has been edited for publication purposes. It's themes are particularly relevant to Christian day schools in the Dutch Calvinist tradition of Christian education, though they relate generally to the challenge of passing on a Reformed worldview to the next generation. To what extent do graduates and teachers of our schools understand and articulate the great biblical motifs that the Reformed tradition has emphasized? And without proper theological literacy, how can we expect our schools to honor their commitments and our churches to be vitally Reformed?

It has been my custom to present some thoughts and ideas as we come together for the first time in a new school year. I consider it a part of my responsibility as a leader of this faculty to challenge, stimulate, provoke, and maybe even inspire. I take on the task this year more compelled than ever, having pondered anew some ideas and carefully measured my words. May the Holy Spirit breath into them, for my topic is not one that immediately will bring a tingle to the spine. I fear these issues have become ho-hum, passé.

Last May I was asked to participate in a pilot project, a colloquium on the Internet, sponsored by Calvin College. Dean David Hoekema, theologian Tom Thompson, philosopher Lee Hardy, and I each wrote an essay and thereby lead the discussion around the question "What is a Reformed Worldview?" 15 participants from around the country, using our e-mail, proceeded to engage in a month of discussion. For me, at least three things happened:

1. I was challenged and deepened in my understanding of "Reformed" thinking.
2. I am again impressed by how hard it is to articulate.
3. I am intrigued by how difficult it is to pass on to a new generation.

This in turn prompts our topic for this morning, "Reforming Lynden Christian," one which I believe we need to collectively attend to in this coming year and beyond.

To be sure this is a dangerous title, for it hints that we are not presently Reformed. It may suggest to others that we have a list of deficiencies as long as American public education and are in need of a massive reform movement. To the contrary, we affirm our Reformed character, and the high quality of our education. So we use this title to remind us of an old Reformed concept, that we are called to constantly be reforming—we are to be reforming our minds, the church, all of society, and certainly our school—to be conformed to biblical teaching, to faithful Christian living, to the mind of Christ.

Given that title, with this audience, raises another set of issues. All of us have different experiences with the concept of Reformed. These categories include:

1. Those for whom this Reformed language and jargon, the talk of a Reformed perspective and tradition is all rather new. You have heard the term but are just beginning to understand it. You probably don't dare to use it, because you are not sure you are using it correctly.
2. Those who have heard plenty of this Reformed talk, maybe too much to suit you, and you are yet wondering what it all means, how it fits. You are not even sure that you are a Reformed Christian. You may prefer simply "Christian," and you frankly struggle to know how this "Reformed" stuff should affect your teaching. You have not yet made it an integral part of your identity.
3. Those who have heard it all, and who essentially believe it all. Of course, you are Reformed, you have been for a lifetime, you can do a reasonable job of defining it, and you bring some of those concepts into your teaching from time to time. But this vision is not something you are passionate about. Your ardor in education is elsewhere. You are more practical and would prefer to get to your lesson plans, even as we speak.

4. Those for whom this vision is their passion, people who claim this Reformed thinking as the core of their life and work. They get their satisfaction and joy out of seeing students catch glimpses of truth and meshing it with their worldview. Their spine does tingle when they get a fresh insight, that they may be able to pass it on to their students.

You decide where you presently lodge. Regardless, this is an important topic at the dawn of this school year because this institution is founded on and rooted in Reformed principles. The founding documents of this school are not mere opinions, but a theology that has huge implications for education. Each of us who has had the privilege of working here since become trustees and stewards of that vision. We better know and be able to articulate and pass on what that vision is. Our generation will need to have convictions for this place to stand. We owe that to our forefathers and mothers.

Additionally, there are substantial cultural conditions that militate against the Reformed vision. Let me identify two coming from diverse, but not necessarily opposite directions. The first is our secular society with its materialism, consumerism, relativism, multiculturalism, scientism, egoism, conservatism, and liberalism. These "isms" bombard us, our parents, our graduates, and our students. To think that we are not collectively influenced by that onslaught is to be horribly naïve.

Secondly, we are profoundly influenced by generic American evangelicalism, or of greater concern, fundamentalism. We are adopting their worship style, their evangelism style, their youth group style. Not all of this is negative; indeed, some of it is very positive. But it is also true that we are therefore tempted to indiscriminately buy their church membership and their theology. And the theology issue is particularly bothersome, for theology is like buttoning your shirt—if you start wrong, you will end wrong.

Further, there is this nagging historical reality. The Reformed community continues to do battle with itself, which so compromises our witness to prompt any discerning Christian, young or old, to seriously question whether they want to be part of such an outfit. So we have the unfortunate task of trying to teach a worldview and theology that for all of its richness, possesses a propensity to self-destruct. George Marsden notes that "too often Reformed people have been so totally confident of their own spiritual insights that they have been unable to accept or work with fellow Reformed Christians whose emphases may vary slightly."

In summary, we are trustees of a tradition. We can be easily waylaid from the left or the right. And if that doesn't get us, we are capable of "turning on ourselves."

Despite this touch of cynicism, I am declaring today with a boldness that heretofore I have not expressed, that at Lynden Christian School we must dig deeply to survey our Reformed roots and expound on our Reformed confession. I would caution though that such talk as we are engaged in can easily be interpreted as hinting that we have a corner on the truth. We don't! I hope you will remember previous opening school speeches in which we called you to consider the issues of the heart, issues or relationality which the Reformed tradition in my judgment has often neglected. So we have spoken of the Roman Catholics, Baptists, Wesleyans, Charismatics, Quakers, noting all of these traditions and more have a gift that God has given them and they each help us to more fully apprehend the truth. To our peril, we neglect what God in history has taught through these brothers and sisters.

Do we have a corner on the truth? Surely not, but most certainly we have a corner *of* the truth. Consider the difference that one preposition makes! The Reformed tradition has some insights, understandings, jewels that without, Christianity is impoverished, incomplete, unbiblical. Without our corner, a very substantial piece of the puzzle is missing.

Further, what do we call it? Do we use the "R" word? How strongly do we identify with the Reformed community at the risk of frightening others off? Can we teach the essence of Calvinism without calling it that, thereby being exclusive?

Yesterday a graduate indicated that he could not recall hearing the word "Reformed" at LC, though he acknowledged that possibly he wasn't listening. He says that he hears it all the time now, in his Reformed Christian college. And then he noted, "But nothing of what I learned at LC contradicts what I am learning in college—there is full agreement."

I am proposing that we become more willful in our use of Reformed language, that is if we know what we are talking about. (And by the way, I think TULIP is largely an inappropriate way to talk about being Reformed to high school students.) I think that we must find and use a "Reformed" lexicon that is clear, objective, and sensitive. We are a Christian school, but we are a Christian school in the Reformed tradition.

I close, then, with my articulation of what is Reformed, though others would use a different listing. In my judgment it is first a theological understanding. It is something huge, cosmic, awesome, holy, mysterious, paradoxical. The words to describe it do not come easily for the lay person.

Sovereignty—We begin with the sovereignty of God. This is where Reformed people often start. We declare that "our world belongs to God," that he loves it (John 3), he preserves it (Psalm 19), he sustains it (Colossians 1). We say, "God directs and bends to his will all that happens in the world.

As history unfolds in ways we only know in part, all things…are under his control. God is present in our world by his Word and Spirit. The faithfulness of our great provider gives sense to our days and hope to our years. The future is secure…..!" (Our World Belongs to God Article 12).

Creation—Reformed people take the creation seriously, though many of their fellow evangelicals have an "underdeveloped doctrine of creation" (John Stott in a TV interview). And the Reformed understanding is not limited to the physical realm, but includes culture. We figure that if God invested that much effort into making it and sustaining it, 'each little flower that opens, each little bird that sings," then creation must be important ("All Things Bright And Beautiful" by Cecil Frances Alexander). And if he gave Adam the marching orders to be fruitful, to cultivate, to subdue, it must be weighty and consequential. "If God does not give up on the work of his hands, we may not either" (*C reation Regained*, Al Wolters). And if he told Noah to build an ark and to bring in those pairs so they would not become extinct, those critters must be significant. So our students need to consider the Endangered Species Act in light of Noah's ark. Is Creation for our students "just a Bible story," do they get beyond the triteness to the awfulness?

Fall—Reformed people comprehend the Fall. But do students these days in this morally bankrupt culture know how great their sin and misery is—how badly they need a Savior? Do they know how the Fall extends to every area of life and culture? Do not our students need a healthy dose of Romans as well as Neal Plantinga's *Breviary* which explains how deadly those seven sins are?

Redemption—Even as Creation and Fall are cosmic, so too must redemption be viewed as such. "Redemption in Jesus Christ reaches just as far as the fall" (Wolters *Creation Regained* p71). If we are serious about teaching and applying sovereignty, creation, and fall (above), and other concepts (below), why would we not also pay careful attention to whether redemption is occurring in our schools. We are confused about redemption (and this paragraph may be a good example of it). At times we readily consigned it to "the task of the church," and ignore its implication for the individual and corporate life of a school. Other times we conceive of redemption in the "accepting Christ" sense, the task of the chaplain or the evangelist on staff. But Redemption needs to reach just as far as the Fall in our personal lives, in the communal life of the school, but even as fully as the grand biblical vision of shalom, the redeeming of life and culture.

Covenant—Do our students know that God has visited not only our planet but also our family and that He wants to be in relationship with us? What does it mean to be a "Covenant God?" I recall participating in the interview of a young history professor at Calvin College, from Baptist roots, who testified of sitting at the feet of a Reformed preacher and hearing for the first time a sermon on the covenant—and he wept. That is how much the understanding of the covenant meant to him! Does it mean anything to us anymore?

Kingdom—"Thy kingdom come, thy will be done, on earth as it is in heaven" (Matthew 6:10 KJV). Reformed people are fond of quoting Abraham Kuyper, who claimed, "There is not one square inch of creation about which Jesus Christ does not say 'This is mine!'" Clearly one of the greatest gifts we can give our students is that there is no room for dualism, no dichotomy between sacred and secular, public and private, fact and value. That suggests our students will take up their calling in a wide array of vocations, from accountancy to zoology.

Revelation—Sir Francis Bacon said that God has written two books, Scripture and nature. We ought to be reading them both all the time, and certainly do at this school. We have a high view of both, though we say Scripture is inspired and infallible. And we believe those two books are not intended to contradict each other, and when it appears they do, we must get to work to try to figure it out.

I am pleading for some passion about these concepts, that you would take them into yourself and allow them to penetrate your head and heart and hands and teach them to our children. None of us can do that by ourselves—I need some help in comprehending and applying this to my work. Do you?

Would you be willing to attend to some of these ideas beyond this hour, engage in some reflection? Or better yet, would you be willing to participate in an ongoing discussion, or a book study, maybe after school for an hour every couple of weeks? Do you want to understand this better, so that it might affect your teaching inch by inch, your goal setting, your curriculum outline, your classroom applications?

If your answer is no to all those questions, you really should be looking for other work!

If your answer is yes, we will trust the Holy Spirit to remove the dimness of our soul and give us utterance as we individually, corporately, and intentionally strive to ever more faithfully "reform Lynden Christian."

Ron Polinder
High School Principal
Lynden Christian School

A Long Obedience in the Same Direction

Such is the title of a book by Eugene Peterson, the prolific pastor and Bible scholar likely best known for *The Message*, his paraphrase of the Scriptures. "A long obedience..." is a phrase wonderfully useful to describe the story of Lynden Christian School, as it celebrates its 100th anniversary.

Like many of you reading this, Lynden Christian School has been integral to our entire life. Long before I was born, my parents attended, my Grandpa Otter was on the School Board, my Grandpa Polinder described volunteering in the building of the old Grover Street school. My wife Colleen and I are graduates of LC, as are our three children.

In 1982, I had the privilege of joining the staff, first as Community Relations Director and then High School Principal. One cannot help but ask, "What would my life be like without Lynden Christian School?" And so it is with hundreds, even thousands in our community and beyond. Those newer to the Lynden Christian family are merely in the earlier chapters of their LC story.

When one comes into the homestretch of a career or lifetime, one cannot help but be reflective about the shape of one's life. The decades will do that for you. We begin to recall relatives and teachers and coaches that influenced us, guided us, maybe even admonished us. We all could write pages about certain key people.

But I want to reflect on those anonymous souls whose names are written in the Book of Life but likely not in the chronicles of Lynden Christian School. One such person was my Uncle Case Van Diest, a meek and mild man, soft-spoken, never drawing attention to himself. My dad said about Uncle Case, "If we had more Caseys, we would not have so many wars."

Back in the 80's, Uncle Case drove a one-ton truck that I would see parked at the Paper Baler. It was curious to me. His three children graduated from LC, but at the time, he had no grandchildren attending. Yet, there he was, faithfully contributing to the well-being of Lynden Christian School. It was a strange inspiration—it became for me a symbol of faithfulness.

And so it is with the hundreds of other cars and pickups parked at the Paper Baler, Cash for Trash, and more recently the Second Chance Store. Since Colleen and I have moved back to Lynden, we stand amazed at the mere sight of all the vehicles around those buildings—all those faithful grandpas and grandmas, uncles and aunt, fellow church members, quietly blessing the next generations.

The theme of our Lynden Christian 100th Anniversary is appropriately "Great is Thy Faithfulness." Surely we can and should testify to God's faithfulness. But part of that faithfulness is his call, his invitation to a life of obedience. Happily, there have been hundreds of "saints who from their labor rest" who have participated in this long obedience.

Christian education must be seen over the long haul. Frankly, sometimes in the short-term it can be disappointing, as we see the foolishness of youth unfold before our very eyes, or worse, when we see young people turn their back on their Christian training. Parents and teachers may get discouraged. It's those faithful grandparents that have the best view—they have seen the results onto the 3rd and 4th generation. They understand and believe that Christian education is a long obedience in the same direction.

And thus they show up at the Paper Baler! Uncle Case did not live to see his granddaughters, Kasey and Taylor Finnson, enroll at Lynden Christian, and now his namesake, Kasey, graduate. He was blessing his grandchildren even before they were born—and did not even know it. Such is a life of obedience and faithfulness—and Lynden Christian is blessed to have thousands of similar stories.

I had the privilege recently to observe a Lynden Christian graduate beautifully address these issues in a different context. Glen Van Andel, Class of '61, is now a retiring Professor of Physical Education at Calvin College. He was asked to give the closing remarks at the dedication of a new Health Center on the Calvin Campus, and ended his comments by quoting a song that most of us have heard, but probably never carefully read. The chorus is as follows:

> *Oh may all who come behind us find us faithful*
> *May the fire of our devotion light their way*
> *May the footprints that we leave*
> *Lead them to believe*
> *And the lives we live inspire them to obey*
> *Oh may all who come behind us find us faithful*
> ("Find Us Faithful" performed by Steve Green, written by Jon Mohr (c) 1987 Birdwing Music)

Such is the story of Lynden Christian School—A long obedience in the same direction!

Ron Polinder
For the LC Home Bulletin, 2014

Athletics

Preface: Theology and Philosophy for Athletics at Lynden Christian School

Christian Athletics: By What Standard?

Given some issues surrounding athletics at Lynden Christian, the School Board gave me a summer assignment to prepare a statement that would help us apply our Christian faith more carefully to what was a substantial athletic program. The final product was 19 pages, too bulky to fit in this book. It will be included in with the appendices referred to at the end. However, this preface appropriately introduces the topic, and may prompt others to seek out the full piece.

An attempt to tackle a project like writing a statement of philosophy and perspective for athletics at Lynden Christian School must begin with some context and explanation. Such will shed light on the document itself, giving it some parameters and placing it in history. These five points of departure:

1. Whereas one could approach this task more broadly, i.e. writing a statement of philosophy for extra-curricular activities at Lynden Christian, it seems to me that the issues involving athletics present such unique and significant challenges that it seems prudent to narrow the focus. To be sure, this statement should flow from a more comprehensive attempt to look at all extra-curricular activity; we can only hope that such will soon be developed and that what is included herein will not be contradictory.

2. Heading up the mountain to a cabin with a briefcase of books and articles forces one to conclude rather early in the process that this attempt cannot be as exhaustive as one would like. Time does not permit it, and further unless such documents possess some brevity, nobody will read the miserable things. So, there is much left unsaid about an increasingly complex and influential part of our culture and school. Yet to many it will appear to be rather lengthy. But length is measured carefully. Mission statements and philosophical statements are better served by some accompanying commentary to put flesh on the framework to make application.

3. The following document should be dynamic, i.e. changing. This modest effort may address some of the issues of the 80's and 90's, but as the culture changes, our response and critique will need to change. We will raise profound questions in the course of this writing and subsequent discussion, and frankly we have far fewer answers than we have questions. But the task of Christians is to increasingly surrender our lives to the Lordship of Christ, so these discussions and our interpretation will need to extend into the future.

That is not to say in the face of this daunting and dynamic task that we end up with a relativistic, mealy-mouthed statement. Some questions will be open-ended; but we will declare some fundamentals that guide us in our effort "to play" at Lynden Christian.

4. By so doing, by saying what we believe and how we should live it out, we run the risk of alienating some of our friends and supporters. There will be a prophetic quality about this document, and it will likely ruffle a few feathers. But such a "stirring of the pot" will serve to even us out, blend us, temper us. Some of us need to feel a little heat. Not unlike competition itself, "as iron sharpens iron, so one person sharpens another" (Proverbs 27:17). So again, our only purpose can be to "spur one another on toward love and good deeds" so that God is better served in our Christian school community (Hebrews 10:24).

5. Finally, this document can on one level serve as a statement of the mind, a philosophy, an intellectual exercise. But I believe it will serve us better if it is also a statement of heart. Athletics by their very nature involve the whole child—mind, heart, body, spirit. So too, we must search our hearts and passions to get behind our "mindset" and our "behavior".

This writer has plenty of his own passion regarding sports, and I hereby share some of myself only to serve others in identifying these issues of the heart. And so it is that I confess that I have been ejected from games in my life, I sometimes hate the opposition, I have "booed" the officials, I have second-guessed the coaches, I have cheated, lied, and cursed.

I have been impatient with my own kids. I have wished that I could have been a better ball player, evidently searching for a greater love and acceptance. I confess that when my beloved Seattle Mariners are in a losing streak, I go to bed crabby. I am tempted to idolize Ken Griffey Jr., Steve Largent, and Jack Sikma, and if they came to my church, I would want to give them a place in the front row, and I would like to sit by them.

Such are the issues of heart. Do I have any company?

My pastor, Ken Koeman, has said it thus: "The passions raised by sports in our community are among the sharpest and strongest of all passions. More of us get more worked up, and more quickly, over sports than over any other aspect of life, including work, religion, or politics. This strongly suggests that the attachment we have to sports borders the idolatrous, because idols evoke passions. Show me a person's passion and you reveal his or her idol."

Rev. Clifford Bajema, 1959 graduate of Lynden Christian, himself a father of athletes and uncle of several Lynden Christian athletes, has penned a poem that gives us further perspective on our athletics pursuits:

Blasphemy

It maddens me some
to think that fans don't cheer
the nurses' aids
who dignify the lingering deaths
of medicates,
urinating and vegetating
in joyless geriatric units.

It maddens me more
that crowds don't mass around
ignoble bedsides
to roar the praises
of minimum-wage nurses
enduring the smell and hell
of fleshless specimens
fighting off the end.

But give a youthful athlete
an agile body
and a ball in hand
    to hike
    and heave
        or dribble
        and dunk
            or hit
        and chase
            or kick
        and spike,

and millions will join
the senseless stampede
to screens and stadiums,

where an afternoon's play
under silver domes
will secure multi-millions
of maximum pay,
and simultaneously engage
the fan's full praise.

God Almighty,
do you share my rage?

I think it is a helpful model to see ourselves as pilgrims on a journey, even regarding athletics. The image of a pilgrim suggests obstacles and setbacks and goals. Is that not where most of us are—in progress as pilgrims?

But by God's grace, we can see progress in our lives. We grow up, mature, mellow out and submit to Jesus. Toward that end, may what follows help us as a community to become the peculiar people we are called to be.

Ron Polinder
High School Principal
Summer, 1991

Basketball Lessons

This op-ed piece was first written for the Bellingham Herald, then Christian Home and School, and finally the Gallup Independent—it remains one of the most popular pieces I have ever written. rp

The smell is in the air—no this is not Christmas we're smelling. It is the sweat of the high school gym. It is basketball season, and in McKinley County and on the Rez, this is serious business.

Allow me some early season perspective, some balance, some words of comfort.

Nearly four decades ago, I had the privilege of being cut from the high school basketball team. Although it didn't feel very good at the time, I have since thanked the coach. Ability to play good basketball was not among my gifts, and I needed to face that reality.

It took some time for me to acknowledge that. Like any normal teen-ager, I had delusions of stardom—swishing 25 footers and sweeping down rebounds. Just two years earlier, I was on the starting five and thought I had some future.

But the coach did the right thing. And I had to understand that my self-worth was not dependent on whether I could play basketball. Because I was created in the image of God, my self-image ought first to be rooted in being His precious child. I would need to unwrap other gifts that He had given me.

Within the last month, dozens of kids around the community likewise had that the experience of getting cut. Some cried, some were angry, some feel cheated. There were parents who likely confronted the coach and maybe even accuse him or her of being a racist—which usually contributes to their kids carrying chip on their shoulder for decades.

But I want to encourage those who had this privilege of being cut. The hurt will go away, and you are learning some of the good lessons of life.

That leaves us with a couple groups of kids who will have to wait to experience this privilege. The day will come when they too reach the end of their athletic road.

Of those who make the team, some are going to have the privilege of riding the bench. You will not play much, even though you desperately want to. You will get to go to practice, run lines, wear a uniform and warm-up.

You will also learn some crucial lessons of about life. You want more playing time, but the coach will rarely call you over. You will learn patience and preparation, in case a teammate gets injured or in foul trouble. You are the one making the team better by competing and hustling in practice. The starters will be better for it, and so will you.

What a privilege to learn the lessons that only a benchwarmer can learn!

That leaves a final group—the kids that have to play! Think of it—fragile teen-agers on public display with hundreds, maybe thousands of noisy fan(atic)s looking on, some of them cursing if a player makes a mistake. You will have to walk the streets or go to grandma's house and run the risk of some old crab or relative wanting to talk about Friday's game. What a drag!

There is even a greater risk: thinking that your self-worth is measured by how good you are on the basketball court. That means if you had a bad game, you're not worth much, and if you had a good game, you're cool.

Worse yet, your parents' self-image may be determined by how well you play. What pressure!

I used to think it tragic when parents didn't come to see their kids play. Now I am concerned when parents never miss seeing their kids play. By chasing all over the state to watch a ballgame, we are communicating that this is awfully important stuff.

Have I overstated my case? A bit perhaps!

But let's all remember that these kids are children of God, and that basketball is a wonderful game to help their learning process. We would do well to explore our motives and values this week and this season. Our kids will be better for it!

Ron Polinder
Executive Director
Rehoboth Christian School

Uncommon Decency

Such is the title of a book by Richard Mouw, President of Fuller Theological Seminary. The book's subtitle is *Christian Civility in an Uncivil World*. This title came to mind while watching the wonderful basketball game between Lynden and Lynden Christian on the night of Jan 11.

Anyone who has spent time in Lynden will know that the rivalry between the two schools has often been intense, at times even unruly. But not so in the latest athletic match-up! Indeed, it could only be described as downright decent—an uncommon decency. What we beheld that splendid evening should not go unnoticed. It calls for celebration.

Athletic contests between our two schools began in the Spring of 1960, when Lynden and Lynden Christian played their first baseball game. Lynden Christian won that first contest, though Lynden came back to even the record a few days later. Through the years, especially in basketball, the rivalry grew. And the Lynden boys dominated, though LC from time to time would surprise their neighbors. There were even legendary games with four overtimes still rehashed in Lynden coffee shops.

To be sure, there are lots of communities that have these passionate high school rivalries, but there was something about this rivalry that made it more painful—we are such a small town, and we have relatives in the "other" school, and ultimately, we disagree about the nature of education and that can all lead to name-calling and most of us claim to be Christians.

How could a ballgame take on such weight, such meaning? No doubt there is a lot of psychology surrounding that. As the former principal at LC, I would often quip that we only needed to beat Lynden once a decade for me to retain some measure of self-esteem. Too many of us placed the worth of our school and even ourselves on how some high school kids performed in a ballgame.

There was more—this upstart, isolationist move way back in 1910 by Dutch immigrants could only be considered by most "Americans" as something between odd and arrogant. "Our school isn't good enough for them?" public school supporters questioned out loud. This division in the community widened in the 40's when it was decided to add a Christian high school. And when LC students misbehaved, which happened aplenty, there were the natural sneers: "I guess they are not as good as they think they are."

The rivalry lessened somewhat when Lynden outgrew Lynden Christian and was elevated to a higher classification. That made all of us behave a little better, but the feelings were still there. And a victory was a big deal when we played. In Girls' Basketball, LC tended to dominate, which was always the fallback excuse when the LC boys got clobbered by a talented Lynden boys' team. Suddenly, we LC folks were serious about gender equality.

But God in his good providence is guiding an evolution we can endorse—we are learning civility. And it was on full display at that recent ballgame. Consider again what all happened that night! A packed gymnasium of 3000 fans at Lynden High School watching this interesting blend of athletes. Three dads of the Lynden Christian team were grads of Lynden. And playing for Lynden, were three terrific athletes who had roots at Lynden Christian. Go figure!

There were two sets of first cousins playing on opposite teams, prompting Grandpa Hommes to say, "I always go home a winner." As this intense game moved into the 4th quarter, one of the cousins missed two free throws. As if he wanted to keep it even, his first cousin, a minute later, goes to the other end of the court and misses his two free throws.

There were some poignant moments—to see Lynden Christian boys run to the corner of the gym where sat the legendary Jake Maberry, long the outstanding coach for Lynden and after whom the gym is named. In a wheelchair, suffering from Parkinson's, it was a fitting gesture to honor this community icon. And then there was a moment when the lesser-used Hornstra entered the game for LC. His stroke-victim father watched his son drain two free throws. How sweet was that! Too, the Lynden and Lynden Christian cheerleaders choose to do their half-time dance routines together, as neighbors, not opponents.

The pattern continued—LC girls won the first game quite handily, but the scrappy LC boys gave #1 ranked Lynden a whale of a good ballgame, into overtime no less, with Lynden finally winning. It was a ballgame where everyone played well. One wonders if there was ever a finer group of Lynden/Lynden Christian athletes together on the same floor.

I found myself smiling a lot—and as I looked around, so were most of the spectators. Gone were the angry looks and gestures of yesteryear. It felt like civility had descended over our community. We have come to respect each other, and actually "play"—the way it is supposed to be. Surely, this did not just happen in one night—this evidence of maturity has been coming on through the years. But when it climaxes in such a beautiful way, we ought to note it, and give thanks.

Yet, underlying all these good feelings remains a deep and fundamental difference in our view our philosophy of education--two very different views in the same community, not unimportant, and worthy of debate.

While civility is hard to come by in all too many corners of our country, there was an uncommon decency that prevailed on the night of Jan 11 in Lynden, WA. By God's grace, may it multiply around our nation and world--that we may learn to love across our differences.

Ron Polinder, January, 2013

Lynden/Lynden Christian BB—Lynden Gym, picture of one side

CHAPTER 9

FAMILY

Mina: Our Mom

What follows is a glimpse of her personality and character—what was particularly precious about Mina Polinder? I was 35, now 75. I have added to it, with my siblings' helpful insights.

1. While we often think of her work ethic, I love to remember those times when we laughed together. There were special moments—around the kitchen table at night, likely not all of us there, but reflections on the day, on certain people or events with her comedic spin. She knew how to analyze, and then chuckle and laugh. She really did have a good sense of humor. I might wish we saw it more, but I sure do miss it. All of us enjoy a good laugh—in no small part that comes from mom/grandma.

2. We do have to talk about her obsession with work, and we were not always very pleased with it. She had things for us to do, and we often resisted, sometimes with a big mouth. I'm sorry for that, though thankful that we got the message that our work was essential for success in life. She could not stand the slothful person, and if it was her kids, she tried to do something about it. But consider her pleasure when we got the job done well, when we swept up, cleaned the calf pens, finished the yard work. So too, each of us enjoys the feeling of accomplishment when a job is well done.

Mina, age 16 (circa)

Mom with Jesse and Lady

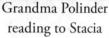

Grandma Polinder
reading to Stacia

Grandma Polinder, Rick and Cindy in
Model T, owned with Aunt Dort

4. Mom loved the farm—she thought she had the best life imaginable as compared to those "city slickers." She actually preferred working outside, even in the barn, though she never continued "milking" after we got the milking parlor in 1954. Prior to that, we helped dad in the flat barn. And she wasn't afraid to harness up and drive a team of horses. She wanted things neat and was quick to tidy up outside. She loved it when we would wash the equipment, and pitched in even with the manure spreader. Already in the mid-60's, she had her own Honda 50-cycle . She loved to fly around the farm and fields with her Honda, and make sure the guys had enough water on a hot day. And grandkids riding on the back was all the better. I loved the observation of my/our friend Donna VanderGriend, who during her high school years hoed corn with her cousin Bev and my sister Eleanor. She once told me how she admired mom for the way she could manage the farm and wasn't limited to housework. Long before that was a part of our vocabulary, she considered her a "liberated woman," even though mom would not have much liked that designation.

5. Mom enjoyed athletics. She rooted for Lynden Christian's teams, and loved to go to the State Basketball Tournament, often taking some widowed friends with her. And Mom was a ballplayer, a member of the Farmer's Equipment Woman's softball team, their first baseman. Some years later, she would play catch with us kids, and hit us grounders. Later still, when Cousin Shari was in high school, Dad and Mom became the managers for their summer league softball team. Those girls loved them, calling them Grandpa and Grandma. I remember how sad they were when "Grandma" was killed, and how they came to the funeral wearing the shirts of their uniforms.

6. Mom was a good student. Part of her education was at Lynden Christian, but there were the depression years where they could not afford the tuition payments at LC. She lived in the Northwood district, thus attended that country school. Her report cards were stellar. And she always had some interesting stories about her classmates.

   I never heard why she did not go to high school. She would have flourished there, but I suspect they were too poor. And in her day, sadly, girls/women were not expected or encouraged to attend high school. Instead, she worked at the Co-op working with chickens and eggs. Mom was always good at math and a good speller, gifts that were not passed on to all her children. Her skills in math enabled her to keep the financial records for the farm.

7. This is about church—Mom/grandma loved her church! I suspect that started with her parent's example—Grandpa Otter the elder, grandma storing up all the old bulletins. I think mom kept the church bulletins for a many years also.

   She was not averse to hanging out in the church basement which often represented church work. I most remember the quilt-making that happened there with several other Third church ladies, often making quilts for Rehoboth. The last I checked; those quilts still grace the beds in the dorms now occupied by volunteers.

But my favorite lesson comes from the day Rev VanHouten preached his farewell sermon and Mom walked directly to the car, skipping her chat with friend Minner and that circle of lady friends. I watched from my circle—my mom crying at church. In those days, that didn't happen, that I recall. But our Mom was crying over her pastor's departure—wow, this must be important. Church is worth crying over. I believe that. I'm thankful for the example.

Remembering Dad

Darigold tribute to Dad

My Dad, Henry F. Polinder

Dad and Lois's wedding day

Commentary

Wednesday, May 27, 1998

Polinder's guiding hand helped build Darigold

Lynden lost a special man in the passing of Henry Polinder on Saturday.

Simple and soft-spoken, Polinder nonetheless wielded enormous influence in the dairy industry, both regionally and nationally. He was respected for his wisdom, his generosity, his intregrity.

He was elected a leader of Whatcom County dairy farmers in the 1960s, then served 23 consecutive years as the chairman of the board of directors of the Darigold company. He took his responsibilities seriously, but he wore his distinction lightly.

When Henry retired from Darigold in the spring of 1991, I had the opportunity to interview him about his years in the industry. We talked as he drove tractor on the family farm on Polinder Road.

In Focus
Calvin Bratt
Tribune news editor

Building a strong industry started with running a good farm, which Henry did with son Sherm on Polinder Road south of Lynden right up to the end. While striving for cooperation among dairy farmers, he also wanted quality Holstein cattle and efficient milk production on the family farm.

Farmers can sometimes be a contrary bunch, and I can remember some general Darigold membership meetings on contentious issues when Polinder's patient leadership was severely tested.

Yet he persisted in his common-sense goals of what he felt was right for the industry and he helped to unify dairy farmers across the Pacific Northwest.

After all he did to build Darigold over the years, I think it was particularly painful for Henry to see an insurgent movement surface within the ranks last fall. He sympathized with the plight of farmers struggling to survive on low milk prices, but he disagreed with any idea that threatened to dismantle the farmers' own company.

He came to me at my workplace to tell me if he thought my reporting had missed the mark. He was honest and direct.

In the 1980s and 1990s, Polinder donated much time to the local community, serving on the governing boards of the Lynden YMCA, Lynden Pioneer Museum, Queen Juliana Theater, and United Way. Even when he seemed out of his natural element, it was clear he was involved out of love for the town he lived in all his life.

For his volunteer community leadership, the Tribune chose Polinder its Man of the Year for 1983.

He experienced personal tragedy in the sudden accidental death of his first wife, Mina, in 1982. Even two years later, as we sat in Henry's kitchen and talked about the things that had earned him the Man of the Year honor, he was still clearly deeply grieved. Five years later, his marriage to Lois Kleinhuizen gave him a treasured companion and a new zest for life.

One of Polinder's last accomplishments, though the legal ends need to be tied yet, was to secure the acquisition of the Queen Juliana Theatre for the Lynden community through his old friend and classmate Hank Jansen. Polinder's influence made the deal happen.

I also knew Henry as a fellow church member who was firm in his Christian faith, yet often surprising in his progressive ideas. He had a way of seeing the big things that matter, not the little things that don't.

About four weeks ago, I had the opportunity to drive Henry home from church after a Sunday morning service. He was using a cane, but I never heard any complaint about pain. As I helped him to the back door of his house, he turned and said "thanks." I had a feeling it might be my last time seeing him, and instinctively I responded with a "thanks" to him – for all he had been and done over the years. I'm glad I said it.

Funeral Remarks: Dad's Eulogy

Before I pay tribute to my father, on behalf of Lois and our families I would like to express our deep gratitude to this community of friends and family that have supported us and loved us through what has been a long month. Lois' former pastor and friend Rev. VanOostenburg used to refer to "Lynden Love," which truly our family experienced again.

On behalf of my brother and sisters, I also want to express publicly our thankfulness to our stepmother Lois, whose relationship with our dad was unique and precious. Her love and respect for him in sickness and in health, and her affection for us, his family, motivates the designation, Saint Lois. We will long remember and forever be enriched by the enormous heart of this good woman.

To Lois's four sons, we also want to say thank you for the way you honored and esteemed, who to you was Henry. I think you know how much he grew to love you and your families. What a blessed thing to consider all the grace and goodness that has come our way since that first time our Dad and your Mom gathered us in the upstairs of the Dutch Mothers to talk to us and blend us together. What an event, and eventuality. Truly, God is Good.

And finally, a word for all the grandchildren: we have been so thankful for your affection toward your grandpa. Some of you had the privilege—and I say privilege—to participate in his dying, to serve him in the most menial way. Others were not granted that gift. Those who had the opportunity to serve and know well your grandpa, would you please share the stories with your cousins, especially the little ones. Polinders, and I'm guessing the Kleinhuizens, like to tell stories. Good stories have a hero, and for the purposes of our families, it is just fine to believe your grandpa had the stuff of a hero.

And now a eulogy for Henry Polinder, one that I have titled "A Good Eye."

A GOOD EYE

It was a high compliment when dad said to us kids, "Good eye!"

He would pitch to us in the evening, after milking. When we laid off a ball just out of the strike zone, he would declare "Good eye!"

Or we would go count the heifers at Northwood, always hoping that since the last visit a couple would have matured into show ring prospects. We would judge this one's size or that one's breeding, and dad would say, "Good eye."

His affirmations were not dispensed cheaply. When they came, they felt good.

A good eye requires training, experience, judgment. The eye of the artist or the athlete, the forester or farmer winnows and weighs, divides and digests.

Henry Polinder had a good eye, though he would blink at the suggestion. His response? "I'm overrated!"

But we persist, wondering what light gave him such sight?

    I.   *A good eye demands hindsight.*

As we forked silage to the cows, Dad would quiz us on our history facts. We figured history must be important. He was intrigued by the movements of history—famines and wars and depressions. How could a Stalin be so cruel to those good Mennonite farmers—the fool!

He was fond of the Old Testament stories. He didn't think there was a thing minor about any of the prophets. All were lessons.

> To understand price supports, you needed a history lesson

> To understand the river, you needed some experience

> To understand that family, you needed to know their story

The human condition, distorted and fallen, described in Scripture and proven in history, made him wonder, "Who will rescue me from this body that is subject to death?" (Romans 7:24)

    II.   *A good eye requires foresight.*

Henry Polinder did not live in the past. He was looking to the future. There was a progressive streak in him. Grandpa often did things the hard way, but Dad wanted to get past the horses. There was the milking parlor already in 1954. And he cast his lot with Holsteins and purebreds and Darigold.

> The fields had to be planed and drained to make them productive

> The merger of local dairy cooperatives had to occur for the future of the industry

> The nation needed to protect and honor agriculture to be healthy

It is that framing of the big picture that we will miss. For Sherm to see that white pick-up moseying down the road, for the girls to receive those comfortable calls on the phone, for me to stop in after school and share commentary about politics, the church, the community—with only a few words he could help us find a simplicity on the other side of complexity.

III. A good eye has broad-sight.

Henry Polinder made room for people, was not quick to judge, was open to new ideas. Generous, tolerant, catholic!

Not so open minded that his brains fell out, he could get hot at the democrats, the aristocrats, the bureaucrats, but in person he would become gracious. As kids, we would be tempered if we got too narrow or critical.

Our dad, like his dad, moved comfortably in circles beyond the Dutch community.

His friends included young and old, commoners and lords, sinners and saints

Worship experiences outside of his own tradition were respected

Friend Bill said: "Hank is the only person at the golfing table who will listen to a non-Republican idea."

IV. A good eye needs insight.

Henry Polinder could look into the hearts of people, and often with one cogent phrase, he could size someone up. In analyzing the spouses of his children he noted that we all married better than we deserved.

He came close to pride when he observed that he picked not one, but two good wives. Nobody would disagree.

Of Mina he would muse:

"In 42 years of marriage, she never had an overdraft."

"Each month she would first pay the church budget, and then the school tuition, and we lived on what we had left.

"Our entertainment was going for a ride, and if the kids were good, 'a big, fat ride.'"

Dad and Mom were in partnership. When they were younger, they both played softball—we think there were times when those cows got milked "pretty fast." And then the Darigold meetings started, and Dad knew that he could not be gone without Mom in charge of the farm. In teaming to raise five ornery kids, never did they disagree with the teacher or the preacher in front of us or allow us to drive a wedge between them over matters of discipline.

Dad admired Mom's service to the church, her love for Lynden Christian, her work with the Dairy Wives, her visits to the Rest Home.

And then, the devastation! Mina was taken! A bitter cup, a painful season, though not empty of comfort or the Comforter. The man who emerged was refined with emotion, affection, expression.

God in his providence did not hide his face from him, the affliction relented, and his days were again made glad. Lois, like a tender shoot, a root out of dry ground, ascended! Henry saw right through her, and liked what he saw. Surprised by joy, a decade of delight was planned for them. It was precious to see these two lovebirds at work. Lois giggled, "We had a pact."

> They went to work on that house on the corner, building fence, planting shrubs, decorating.

> They kept their respective church memberships, sometimes going together, sometimes separately, and we think occasionally they skipped.

> They did some traveling, even took a cruise. Dad had to buy shorts, which caused sister Marge to wonder "if those white legs had ever seen the light of day."

But something else was happening. Lois was nurturing a spirituality that heretofore Dad found difficult to express. Mealtime devotions and regular coffee times became the sharing of two hearts. Their love for each other, for their families, for their community, for God, deepened. We saw it more than heard it. And what we beheld in this past month was simply amazing, amazing grace, a perfect love, a love which knows no ending.

V. *Hindsight, foresight, broad-sight, insight*—it adds up to a good eye, or what Parker Palmer called "whole-sight."

Many of us live one-eyed lives, relying largely on the eye of the mind, or the eye of their heart. Either eye alone is not enough. Robert Frost observed in his poem "Two Tramps in Mud Time," "As two eyes make one in sight," and we would add, so let us our head and heart unite. Henry Polinder lived out of his head and his heart, and it gave him a fuller vision of the world.

By now Dad is terribly embarrassed if he is apprehending these proceedings. He would be quick to note that whatever ability he had was a gift from God, that he saw through a glass dimly, and that I should have gotten to "Amen" a long time ago. Besides, they tell a lot of lies at funerals.

But Dad, "Let me finish? I wish there was more of you in us!"

Sherm got his eye for a good cow.

Eleanor got the eye for a good ballplayer.

Ron got an eye for a meeting, though not always good ones.

Marge got the eye for good comedy.

Karen got his eye for efficiency of word and deed.

Dad may give us a little more credit, but not to our face. He was proud of his kids, but he was quick to make sure we didn't get "the big head."

And that may have been his greatest gift, his own humility, his inward eye, understanding his shortcomings, his fallenness, his need of redemption.

It was in this very room where Henry Polinder would come to get his bearings, to know his only comfort in life and in death. Friend Rube would say, "Hank was all around the country during the week, but on Sunday he was here, sitting in the pew."

He loved this church, grateful for your goodness, troubled if people left, heartened by the gospel in word and song, always reassured of his hope as a Christian.

It is fitting that we end it here, grateful to God for a husband, father, grandfather, a friend, a leader, with a good eye, an eye of love and hope and faith.

"Oh Lord, haste the day when our faith shall be sight!" (From "It Is Well With My Soul" by P. Bliss)

For our father, on behalf of brother Sherm and sisters Eleanor, Marge and Karen

Ron Polinder, May 1998

Sherm: The Farmer

Brother Sherm braiding horse's mane
Grandpa Polinder assisting

My brother was called to be a farmer, a calling that seemingly he received at an early age. I have wondered if he ever considered any other profession. My Dad seemed to have received Sherm's call also because he always seemed to have come to that conclusion.

Sherm was a good student. I don't recall much debate about him going to college—all agreed that Washington State with its strong Agriculture program would be the right match for Sherm. As the oldest child, it was a big deal to send him off to Pullman, WA. We looked forward to his stories when he came home from college.

Sherm started to date Phyllis in his senior year of high school. By the time he left for college, that seemed to be a match made in heaven. Phyllis stayed back and worked for a dentist. We all came to love her and knew that marriage would be in the works, which was then planned for the completion of Sherm's junior year.

But an intruding development came along at the same time as our close neighbor, Ward Vander Griend, decided to sell his farm, at least his cows, and offered them to Sherm. As hard as it is to imagine, Sherm got the necessary loan while still a college student and bought the 60 Jerseys. He proceeded to hire a man who he had to fire at Thanksgiving vacation for incompetence. He patched with other help, until finally he settled for me and another fellow in February of '64. I was yet a high school senior, which did not help my grades, or my ability to stay awake in class. Plus, I was dating Colleen, and most often challenging the curfew.

Sherm graduated that Spring and he and Phyllis settled back in Lynden with the eventual plan to partner with my parents on Ronelee farm. That transaction happened a few years later. Given my Dad's heavy involvement with Darigold and other board work, Sherm soon became the primary manager, which included herd management and the further genetic development of Ronelee Holsteins.

Through the decades, Sherm and Phyllis had four children, all of whom learned how to work on the farm. The youngest, Jeff Henry, in recent years took the lead in herd management and breeding. Phyllis was the steady behind the scenes manager of the books and endless details that fall to a farm wife. And she always seemed to have time to serve at church or the extended family or someone in need.

Sherm too, not unlike Dad, took up roles on the National Holstein Board, the Darigold Board, the Church Council, the Christian School Board and other assignments. The farm grew steadily but remained a family farm with good help along the way. Finally, in 2019, Sherm being past his mid-70's, sold the cows and farm to the Plagerman family.

It is not easily understood by most how hard it is for a farm to be sold, and the emotional stress and strain that comes along with it. To give up of those generations of cow families, to give up the land that has been worked and harvested, to give up the decision-making that naturally comes with it, is not an easy transition. As siblings, we were so thankful to hear Sherm testify, "The earth is the Lord's, and not Sherm's"—so it is that Sherm and Phyllis, husband and wife, move into retirement (mostly) and give thanks for God's care and provision.

Eleanor: The Coach

Remarks at her retirement event:

To my big sister, from her little brother:

She was the oldest daughter of Hank and Mina Polinder, with brother Sherm a year older, then me, and two younger sisters, Marge and Karen. We called her Babe—Eleanor was barely in our vocabulary. That was true for the entire extended family—I don't think grandpa ever made the transfer from Babe to Eleanor. Once he asked some years after marrying Bob, "No babies yet, Babe?"

We grew up in Lynden, WA on a dairy farm, along the river—it was our life. We learned how to work—"vacation" was another word not in our vocabulary. We went to Third CRC—never missed.

Our entertainment consisted of going to the Northwest Washington Fair for a week in August, though we worked hard in preparation. The world and competition of registered Holsteins was serious business, and Eleanor did her share, grooming and showing and judging. She was a first-rate cattle judge, at least twice making the county judging team, and narrowly missing the state team. She had a good eye for physical attributes—would that help her judge other talents later in life?

But even more fun were the ballgames—Hank and Mina both players in the 40's and 50's. Mom played first base for Farmer's Equipment; Aunt Dort was the catcher. We all remember her hitting a homerun when she was pregnant with Marge.

So sports were a big deal for the Polinder's, and Eleanor caught the fever. Dad would instruct Sherm and me to throw like Eleanor. Of course, in the 50's and 60's, there was not much outlet for girls in sports. When in High School, Eleanor set out to do something about. She created an intramural program—single-handedly, and got girls playing basketball and softball at noon hour and after school. Her teachers honored her by making her Senior of the Month.

And then to far off Calvin College, a big step for our family. We had to grow up—Babe finally became Eleanor. Brother Sherm was at WSU, but Eleanor all the way to MI? She set the pace—her three younger siblings followed, all grateful for her courage to show us the way. Women PE majors in 1965 were unheard of at Calvin, but as I recall, Eleanor and a classmate were the first women PE majors at Calvin College. Eleanor told us the story of beating all the guys in accuracy in a football throwing contest.

Bob, Eleanor, Jeff, Cindy and their ballplayers

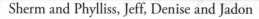

Sherm and Phylliss, Jeff, Denise and Jadon

Grandpa with Ethan
and Colin

It was in her bones—she was destined, no, more accurately, she was called, called by God to be a teacher and coach, though she herself had never played. Would that stop her from taking up the challenge? Not a bit—she was used to playing with the boys, which would come in handy in this man's world of gyms and locker rooms. The Babe was not about to be pushed around.

Others will recall this evening her accomplishments, but brother Sherm and I were around to watch her formation. God gifted Eleanor in a particular and unique way to bless others, mostly young women, and often women of color. She grew up overcoming obstacles and empathized with others who did the same. Eleanor recently had a heart check-up. I asked her how that went. I could feel her smile over the phone as she said, "The only thing they found was love." I think it is true.

Eleanor is a daughter of her mom in looks and temperament and work ethic, though even work was delayed for a good ballgame. And she is a daughter of her Dad, not given to a lot of public statements or self-proclaimed achievement. But ultimately, she is a child of God who in the midst of this messed up American sports culture, tried to do athletics the way it is supposed to be—the way of the Kingdom.

Big sister, you have honored our family, and more importantly tried to honor God—we are proud of you and we love you!

Ron Polinder
May 2009

My versatile sister Eleanor

Eleanor and Marge with nieces Staci and Shawna

Sister Marge—love that smile

Five siblings, offspring of Henry and Mina

Marge: The Comedian

It is this simple—when I need an emotional lift, I call my sister Marge. She lives in Plano, TX, but they hope to move to Chicago. We have great visits via the telephone, punctuated by laughter, even hilarity. She is the comedian of our family.

This is an inherited gift. We had an Aunt Gert VanderWall who lived in Grangeville, Idaho. She, and now her daughter Kristi, along with Marge, have this way about them, bringing out enough laughter to fill the room. Facial expressions and hyperbole are abundant.

Marge came upon this gift rather early in life. She could entertain visitors or workers on the farm. Around age five she announced she was "the lazy type." She also told a family friend that her mom was going to have an "Indian baby." This was because she was fascinated with Roy Rogers and such shows. She prayed nightly.

In her middle school years, Marge and I teamed up at haying season. I mowed, she raked, and together we baled and loaded, she on the tractor, I on the wagon rack. One or two of my friends would stop to chat, and I would motion to her to stop the tractor. This was a Case 400, best known for how hard they shifted gears, so I ordered her to hold her foot on the clutch. This way, I wouldn't have to get off the wagon and put it in gear for her when I was finished talking. Her short legs made that quite a stretch, and she tired all too quickly, but didn't dare to let the clutch out lest I yell at her.

Years later, suffering from a sore back, her therapist asked if she had an old injury from her youth. Well, she knew exactly what that was—it was that long stretch with her foot on the clutch. She now expects me to pay her surgery bills.

Marge had lots of challenges with her hair during her Junior High years. Her habit was to have it behind her ears, causing her "loving and sensitive brother" to offer free advice. She claims my critique left her with emotional scars.

Marge married Jim Bos, whom she met at Calvin. Jim trained as an engineer and later also got an MBA. This good man was in the line of in-laws who my Dad claimed were better than we deserved. As Mom would say, "He knows he's married. "

They lived in Fulton, Illinois for a couple of decades with Marge teaching at the Christian school, giving her lots of material for story-telling—none better than when one of the board members came to blows with another guy after one of their meetings.

Fulton, with its Dutch dominance, drew Marge into their annual Dutch Days which created a knowledge and loyalty to her Dutch heritage remaining to this day. Before they left town, she was selected as the parade's Grand Marshall.

Upon Jim's transfer to Texas, the family was in for major adjustments. From small town and small Christian school to the Dallas metroplex, it was a tough transition. Marge however was hired at Trinity Christian Academy where she taught until her retirement.

Marge has a superb reputation as a teacher. All her teaching was done in the primary grades, mostly 1st. Former parents and students alike sing her praises. Put her in a classroom, and life springs forth—she is a natural.

At Trinity, she teamed up with her Presbyterian friend Didi. This was double trouble, with those two critiquing the fundamentalist tendencies of Dallas evangelicalism. They would imitate the singing in chapel: "The mighty river is going to take you away…." The Elementary children of course knew not where they would be taken, or on which river. One of them speculated the Mississippi. In despair, Marge and Didi would often muse: "Poor God." He got blamed for a lot.

A painful crisis came upon the family when Jim suffered a major heart attack, at age 48, in a hotel in Baltimore, MD. We nearly lost him. I happened to be in Grand Rapids at the time, and the extended family thought I should fly to Baltimore to support the family. Marge was a pillar through this ordeal—sensible, steady, strong. Though Jim has suffered side effects, we rejoice that God spared him and their family remained whole.

At one of Jim's most precarious hours, he had a vision, which included his walking Erin "down the aisle" the coming summer—by God's grace he did just that. And a couple of summers later, his daughter Sarah. Recently, they celebrated son Alex's marriage to Aziza—Marge, joyful to the core!

I always wanted Marge to write more, hoping that some of that humor would ooze out, but also her depth regarding Christian education and the role of the church. She denies she is a writer, proven wrong when she offered up a description on Caring Bridge of spending a week with her sister-in-law, my Colleen, toward the end of her life. The windows she opened for others to see through drew raves from family and friends.

Well, this has become quite serious—where are the jokes? There is something about humor that makes it indescribable. I have no further language to borrow to portray my sister Margie.

Karen: Our Little Sister, on her 40th

Sister Karen and Mike with their two newlywed sons and brides

My Dear Sister Karen,

I regret very much that I cannot be with you this weekend. I know we would have had a grand time, though we will try to make up for it later this month.

But I want to share some thoughts and words with you. My first thought is that I cannot believe that my little sister is 40 years old. You will always be my little sister if that is OK. I want that perceived in the best sense of the term—that we all wanted to protect you and nurture you, maybe even parent you. And of course, when Mom died, that did not diminish.

But now you are only a little sister in chronology. You are a woman in your own right, and have been for years—a wife, a mother, a sister. You fulfill all those tasks with responsibility and diligence and Christian faith, the latter of course being the foundation for your life. That is where your strength lies, where your help comes from (Psalm 121). Colleen and I and, to be sure, your whole family are so grateful for the Christian commitment that you and Mike have made in your personal and family life. The blessings to you have been many, and they will be sustained as long as the Lord gives your breath. May you continue to participate in the "divine conspiracy," which is the title of the most important book that I have read in the last 10 years, and which I will hand to you in person, Lord willing.

Karen, you are entering wonderful years with Mike and your boys. May you make the most of them, enjoy them, invest in them. It will produce fruit, indeed the fruit of the Spirit. And the Spirit has shown over and over that He works through Christian homes, Christian churches, and Christian schools. It is this "long obedience in the same direction" that Eugene Peterson speaks of that is such a critical part of your, and Mike's, heritage. That is maybe the greatest gift we have all been given by our parents and grandparents and may be the greatest gift of the Reformed tradition.

There will be adversity and trial. Rarely do we sail through life without major challenge, which of course is hardly new to you, having lost your parents when you were way too young. But our "trials come to only make us strong, "as Andraé Crouch sang in "Through It All," which I believe that you have exemplified in response to pain that has come your way. Through it all, you have been courageous, solid, sensible. We commend you for it.

We sure hope that you have a whale of a good time. Have some good Polinder laughs. Enjoy your family and friends, make some "creative memories" and give us a report in a few weeks.

We love you,
Ron and Colleen

P.S. Added later: I write this note on her 60th birthday—how dare I call her my little sister?

155

Fred Polinder Sr and Cora Spaan
Polinder, Ron's grandparents

U.J. Otter and Dena VanMersbergen Otter,
Ron's grandparents of his mom's side

Dorothy Otter: Our Aunt (Mom's sister)

Precious Aunt Dort Otter, Mom's sister

On behalf of Colleen and our kids, I want to pay tribute to you, our beloved Aunt. You will recall the song by Andraé Crouch that bears the title, "My Tribute," and its opening line: "How can I say thanks for all the things you have done for me…?" While the writer is addressing his question to God, it is equally fitting, in that same Spirit, to address this question to one of God's children, in this case our Auntie, in whom Christ lives, and who has been working for Him for many decades.

I sense in our disposable and selfish culture that paying tribute is too seldom done. We can so easily pass over those who have deeply influenced and blessed us. It seems that thoughtlessness prevails—pastors and parents, aunts and uncles, teachers and even institutions are summarily dismissed, forgotten, cast aside. While final rewards are heaven's business, we need to get some heaven into us and pronounce more often "well done, good and faithful servant" (Matthew 25:21).

For what do we give tribute?

1. For caring about us, from our earliest days—in 2nd grade when I cut my nose open, it was Aunt Dort who came with candy and paid me some attention. All that attention made the accident almost worth it. And you have cared about me, and Colleen and our kids ever since.

2. For all those Christmas gifts—you made even better choices than Mom did. She was so practical—a flannel shirt or a pair of gloves. Aunt Dort bought us games, stuff out of the catalog from which we carefully crafted our Christmas lists.

3. For telling stories at Grandma's house on Sunday—I remember hearing about work, about going early to work to meet the farmers, about what you thought was appropriate and what was not—our ears were wide open.

4. For the TV in the basement—that was our introduction to a bigger world. We would have been even more "out of it" if we had not had some exposure to *Lassie* and *The Lone Ranger*.

5. For going to college—that was a surprise at your age, and suggested that college must be an important thing to do. And the stories that came with it, and then going to Calvin for the summer, and the positive report that came home.

6. For becoming a friend and roommate with Ad. That brought another set of stories, opinions, perspective to the family conversation—and she treated us with interest and respect.

7. For your loyalty to Third church and Lynden Christian—many qualities come to mind about Aunt Dort, but loyalty is high on the list. And loyalty to Kingdom causes and institutions that have had an enormous effect on our lives.

8. For loving music—your years of singing in the choir, attending concerts, enjoying music— even my music. Thanks for the encouragement and for sharing your alto voice with the rest of us. We always wished for more guitar and harmonica.

9. For loving ballgames—from my earliest days, I knew they were important. Farmer's Equipment, Lynden Christian, Otter's Trotters—what fun conversation flowed from all those experiences and memories.

10. For loving the Mariners especially—through thick and thin, I knew that Aunt Dort gave a hoot. She was loyal, she would not bad mouth our M's, or merely ride with the winners— and she knew the game!

11. For loving Lynden—you have shown us how to become immersed in a community, to serve and give, defend and critique. Surely Lynden is a much better place because Aunt Dort is one of its citizens.

12. For knowing how to make a buck—we have all marveled at your business acumen. What good sense, good judgment! And the willingness to not just make decisions and give orders, but to follow up with your own work and diligence.

13. For your generosity—to sooooo many—to individuals and institutions. And to a nephew who from time to time needed a lift and a gift at school for a project or support—and for recently encouraging Rusty (who shares your March 19th birth date J).

14. For your laughter—robust and plentiful. Your ability to come out on the brighter side, and to see the humor even in the pathetic. One could always plan on a good time if Dort and Ad were in the room.

15. For enjoying a good restaurant – we will not forget you taking us to a fancy Vancouver restaurant, now many years ago, and the bill came to over $100. We were in awe – you didn't bat an eye. And for all the good food prepared at your house, mostly by Ad, while you worried whether the yard was manicured.

16. For living hopefully—I think that you always hoped for your students, your friends, your customers, even your relatives. You did not think the worst of us, rather the best—you ended up on the positive side of people.

17. For living faithfully—faithful to God, to His people, to your calling, your family, your parents, your siblings, to Ad, to nieces and nephews. And many, many folks would call you a faithful friend.

18. For living lovingly—loving God, loving life, even loving work. It was not mere duty, rather so often it flowed naturally from an oversized heart. We all knew that you loved us—thank you for loving us, Aunt Dort!

Four generations: Grandma Otter, Mom, Marge, Erin

Grandma Polinder with Princess and cart

And now you come to what is called four score—80 years! Facing your coming days with courage, and with faith, hope and love. What a blessing to have you as Aunt, a surrogate mother really, to whom all this tribute is due!

Ron Polinder, 2005

Nebraska Polinder home, 1890's

Genera tions. Great grandpa, Jan, Grandpa
Fred Sr., Dad Henry, Brother Sherm

Sketch of Grandpa Polinder

Four Siblings, Fred, Joanne, Henry and Anna

Grandpa Polinder: One of a Kind

This article was written for the Bellingham Herald and titled "Grandpa offered words one can live by."

Grandparents Day is Sunday. Coincidentally, it was a year ago this week that our extended family buried a 97-year-old grandfather.

I was nearly dissuaded from this topic when reading the beautiful column by Paul Roley on Sept. 2. Roley wrote about the passing of his virtuous father-in-law. He concluded by wondering why we don't have the sense to realize the old values can do so much to lead to a fulfilling life.

Unlike Roley's father-in-law, my Grandpa Polinder was nowhere near sainthood. Most grandpas and grandmas aren't, but it is still good for us to honor them and to discern the lessons they must teach us. Grandparents can give us some identity, some history, some bearings.

Grandpa Polinder was pre-television. He was a character. They just don't make people like him anymore. I worry that the homogenization which results from a televised culture has robbed us of such characters.

Grandpa had about 25 proverbs that he lived by and shared with his many friends and relatives. T. S. Eliot would have called them "the permanent things." Grandpa called them "fundamental laws."

I have not a clue if this folk wisdom was original. I frankly doubt it. Yet I never hear anyone else using these quotes.

What was it that Grandpa would say? To teach us patience he would say, "What's your hurry? Your mother waited nine months for you."

If he sensed greediness in someone, he described him as "a hog of privilege."

If someone was gossiping, he suggested that he should "believe only a quarter of what you hear, and only half of what you see."

Grandpa figured he had the equivalent of a third-grade education. After that, "experience was his teacher." He read newspapers faithfully, but claimed the back pages were more valuable than the front page if you wanted the real story. His reading gave him something of a global mentality.

He would say, "When I was a boy, during the Spanish-American War, they taught me to hate the Spanish. Some years later during World War I, I had to learn to hate the Germans. A few years later I had to hate them again, and the Japanese too. Since then, I've been taught to hate the Koreans, the Russians, the Cubans, the Vietnamese. Ron," he would add, "I'm sick of hating people."

Grandpa was a farmer, as was his father who moved to Lynden in 1901. As a 12-year-old, Grandpa would drive a team of horses on the corduroy road to Bellingham with a load of sugar beets. The all-day trip would end with the horses finding their way home in the dark. Child Protective Services could have had a hay day with that one.

But he was also a horseman who had the habit of never throwing anything away. Thus the six-horse hitch of Clydesdales has been in the family for decades, but also that junk that laid around would one day provide him a new career.

Retiring in his 60s, he started restoring and collecting old buggies, wagons, and carriages. Over the next 25 years, he stablered a museum on his farm which attracted visitors from every state in the union. He boasted, "I never advertised, never commercialized." Upon his second retirement, then pushing 90, he donated his collection of 40 buggies to the Lynden Pioneer Museum.

He taught us how to grow old. He did more in his retirement than most do in a lifetime of work.

Robert Altman, the film director, rented some buggies for the filming of *McCabe and Mrs. Miller* in southern British Columbia. Grandpa figured the wily Altman took him to the cleaners. He said, "I was so green that if I went out to the pastures the cows would eat me."

Grandpa seemed always concerned about my girth. He called me Jumbo and figured I should be doing an honest day's work, which of course was physical work. He would take his three-fingered hand and poke my ribs as if he was checking the flesh of a Clydesdale he was about to buy. Then he would remind me that "Health is wealth," and "The nation's number-one crime is over-eating." He would tug at his pants and glint, "Thirty-four-inch waist when I got married, 34 today."

Grandpa had a profound sense of transcendence, or as he put it, "the Almighty." He knew his limitations. He would say, "You can't break iron with hands." He knew that much of life was a gift. His way of expressing that was, "You can't buy it, you can't steal it, you can't deal it under the table." Of his own last 25 years he often mused, "I'm living on borrowed time."

There are more quotes worth requoting, by they will likely come out in future columns, almost unbeknownst. That's the kind of influence grandpas have.

On Sunday, take some time to cherish your grandparents. If they are living, visit them. If they are not in your community, call them. Listen to them. Honor them. Love them. It will go well with you. That's a promise.

"Speak For Yourself" column, Bellingham Herald, Circa 1987

Chris Polinder

August 12, 2004

Dear Scott and Dorothy, Angela and Courtney, Uncle Fred and Aunt Glenda, significant others and members of the extended family,

We have waited for a couple of weeks to respond to the dreadful news about Chris. From personal experience, we have found that it was often the call or letter or card that arrived a week or month after a great loss that comforted and encouraged us just when we most needed it. We pray that this letter may in some small way bless you today.

We were driving through the desert of Utah on our return to New Mexico when Phyllis reached us with the awful word. We pulled off the road, stunned. And we remain staggered and bewildered—how could this happen to this terrific kid? We rode for hours and hours, barely saying a word to each other.

To be sure, we have had our losses—our firstborn, my mom and dad's difficult deaths, Colleen's dad a year ago. By God's grace, we never responded in anger. But this one has tested us more than ever before. Sovereign God, how could you allow the devil to do this? This young man would have done great things for you—surely you knew that!!!!!!

We have cried and prayed and tried to understand this with our puny minds.

On Friday morning, we shared the story with our colleagues, who immediately were led to pray for you, and us. But the day was long, with a month of work staring us in the face, wondering how you all could bear up under this devastation. We were glum, almost sullen.

Late in the day, we decided to take the 6-hour trip to El Paso to visit Scott and Shawna—in some ways unable to get back into our work. We picked up our month of mail and in it was a CD from a friend who visited us in June. We decided to listen to it—and then again, and again, and again! For the first time, some solace, some consolation, some hope. Where our words had failed, the poets/songwriters from the past spoke yet again.

"Come thou fount of every blessing, tune my heart to sing thy grace" (Robert Robinson)

"I need thee, oh I need thee…O bless me now my Savior" (Annie Hawks)

"Just as I am, though tossed about with many a conflict, many a doubt...O Lamb of God, I come, I come." (Charlotte Elliott)

And a beautiful song sung in Spanish (which we do not understand), but it somehow touched us!

We enclose the CD with the thought that a day may come in a week, or a month, or a year when it might minister to you as it did to us. You don't need anyone shoving things at you, so when the time is right, maybe it will bless you. If you already have it, pass it on to someone else who may need a blessing.

We expect to be back home over Labor Day weekend for nephew Jeff's wedding. May we stop by with the biggest hugs we can muster? Please know that we are praying for you earnestly and daily. We love you very much!

Warmly,
Ron and Colleen
2004

Donna Spaan: Discovered

When one engages in deep and memorable conversation, there is always the concern about accuracy. How well did I listen and how good is my memory? Of course, the same could be said for the other party. It will demand a mutual reading. So I open with a word of caution that this is my best effort to relay the substance of an altogether wonderful dialogue with Donna Spaan, a second cousin, my Dad's first cousin.

I had wanted to meet with Donna, one on one, for several years. I knew in my soul that we had much in common, given our blood heritage and the experience of heading off to Calvin College from Lynden, WA. Donna had come to Lynden to participate in the 100th Anniversary of Lynden Christian School, where she had attended through grade 12, and then came back to teach for 1½ years in the mid-50's. We met on a Monday morning for coffee, following a splendid weekend in which she connected with dozens of former classmates, students, and relatives. Her heart was full of gratitude and joy.

What was to be a couple of hours at the coffee shop turned into nearly five hours. We connected in such a deep, beautiful, spiritual way—I will always be grateful for a rich conversation that helped me understand this enormously talented and interesting woman. Further, for the insight she gave to understanding myself, my extended family and my religious tradition. And I was impressed with how fair-minded she was, how she wanted to give others the benefit of the doubt, how quick she was to qualify her memory.

Donna was the only child of Cornie and Marie Spaan. She was born in 1933, I think, and was 77 years young at the time of our visit. Uncle Cornie and Aunt Marie were cut out of different cloth than many Lynden couples. They were more inclined to think outside the box, to consider ideas not always accepted by the Dutch Reformed tradition of which they were a part. Donna reported that they subscribed to *Christian Century*, a periodical of mainline Protestantism. The Spaans, the Breens, the Van Waverns, the Jonkers would get together every other Sunday night and discuss agreed on articles and issues.

In the early 50's, when *Christianity Today* started, they also subscribed to it, providing some wholesome evangelical balance. Of course, the CRC has always been in between those two ends of the Protestant spectrum, and so it was for Donna and her family, attracted to aspects of both. But for a girl and young woman, with an active mind and open ears, she was exposed to ideas that few of her peers ever heard. As a precocious 12-year-old, she recalls, she raised her hand in catechism class, and suggested the Hebrew word for "day" in Genesis could be interpreted as a 24 hour day, or a long period of time. The pastor, which must have been Rev. VanDyken, was not at all happy with this display of free-thinking, and wagged his finger at her stating, "Young lady, there are people much smarter than you that have studied these matters, and until you get your thinking straightened out, you are not welcome here." She was summarily booted from the class, and promptly rode her bike home to what must have been a set of beleaguered parents. Surely this was not the first display of audacity that poured out all too easily.

My journey to Calvin College exposed me to ideas and Christian perspectives that were quite new to me. I expected Donna to say the same, but she did not—rather, she noted that so many of the progressive ideas of the 40's and 50's was part of their everyday conversation at home. Knowing Aunt Marie as I came to know her in my Calvin days, I can now see that this thoughtful, expansive woman would have raised Donna in like manner, though there should be no doubt regarding the orthodoxy and profound Christian thinking and character of this family.

Over the next decade, Donna and I would routinely talk on the phone, and if I was in Grand Rapids, we would always go out for a ribeye steak at the Outback Restaurant, and there our conversation would expand and deepen further, always to my benefit.

Donna's varied background included several years of teaching English at Grand Rapids Christian, often with the most talented students, many of whom I met later at Calvin. She told of having filmmaker Paul Schrader as a student and expelling him from class, given his insolence. He spent the rest of the semester in the "office," managing a mere B as a final grade.

Then of all things, she decided she wanted to get a PhD in Theatre from the University of Michigan. This would not be so outrageous if she had a rich background in Theatre, which she did not. Given our caution about movies and theatre in the Dutch Reformed tradition, she had not a single course. But she talked her way into the U of M graduate school.

That in turn gave her opportunity to teach as a graduate assistant to the brightest of students—a 4.0 was expected to be admitted. In hindsight, she would say she saw the seeds of discontent rising up in the 60's and becoming part of the narrative, elitist thinking that prevails today. Donna herself entered into the theater world both in the States and in England. She would acknowledge, "I almost lost my faith."

But Donna returned to the States to take a job working for the Christian colleges (Reformed and Christian Reformed) in Chicago, giving students a big city Chicago experience—on the job no less than 30 years. Upon retirement, she became very active in the Chicago art scene, serving on the New Art Examiner board and recommending theatre awards based on her role as theatre critic.

As our relationship flourished, it became clear that she knew my tribe far better than I did. My Grandma Polinder was a Spaan, likewise a breed of their own. The Polinders experienced pain and tragedy in the immediate family that was never talked about—and best not be even discussed here. But our family of origin had dysfunctions that Donna observed firsthand. To my father's credit, he chose not to expose his family to those issues, which I judge to be honorable on his part.

Donna and I share family secrets. In fact, she claims that I am really not a Polinder, but a Spaan like her, given our boisterous, expressive habits. Her stories are incessantly laughable. To this day, she claims the Kok Road was scheduled to be the Spaan Road until a slippery Kok relative made a clandestine trip to the Courthouse. And she loves to remind me that her Grandma Spaan, the matriarch and an amateur theologian, insisted that a Polinder would never live on the home Spaan place—there's some juicy remnants for you!

But now more seriously, Donna is centrist politically, even libertarian, that leads to stimulating dialogue on virtually every phone call. She believes that the reality of left-leaning elites (on both the East and West Coast) dominating culture at the expense of the middle rural America could mean the end of our country as we know it. On the university campus, she frets about "woke" culture. At Calvin and other Christian colleges, she is concerned about the move away from the liberal arts in favor of the social sciences and STEM.

Such are the conversations that I have with Sister Donna—yes Sister. And I am pleased to be claimed as the Brother she never had.

Haak Family Reunions and a Warm Letter

How cute is that?

Colleen, always the tallest; scrawny Ron off right

Haak family

Haak cousins with Grandma

It was my privilege to be welcomed into the Haak family. Soon after Colleen and I started dating, I would be invited to Sunday dinners and other extended family events. Grandma Haak was an excellent cook, and her meat-cutting husband always did the honors of preparing the meat-plate before the meal (a skill that I should have learned). After meals, there was often a card game or "jarts" outside for the guys. Sister Gloria and brother Vic, and their spouses were usually part of the gang.

Colleen had the blessing of growing up in a safe and secure home, parents that were loyal to church and school. Colleen and I always appreciated the support from her parents who never once begged us to move home. They supported our calling and surely prayed for us regularly.

I did manage to get in some hot water one night when the infamous Cousin Willis came to town, usually carry a slide show of where he had recently traveled. One of those trips was to Russia, a topic I covered in my World Studies classes. When Willis asked if we would be interested in seeing his slides, I quickly piped up with a "yes." Of course, the Haak family had sat through dozens of these slide shows and were not in the mood for another. Worse, the crowded living room meant I had place on the floor, out of sight of Willis and most others, enabling me to quietly fall asleep during the show. That was not hidden from all, and after Willis left, I took considerable teasing, for decades to come, particularly from Uncle Gerrit Haak. I had it coming!

Colleen's extended family had a series of family reunions that we were able to join. They were much anticipated, and the turnout of relatives was usually good. The location varied, though most often in the Midwest including the Black Hills and other places in the Dakotas. Hull, North Dakota was the original home for of the children of John and Marie Haak, four sisters and three brothers, one of whom was Colleen's dad, Albertus (Bubby). (Her mother Harriet came from South Dakota— Pollock and Aberdeen.)

The reunions were loaded with good food—every meal was a feast, though always begun with proper devotions. The laughter and good cheer were abundant, and the card games, especially Rook, were continual.

Occasionally, those card games got a bit tedious, causing Colleen and me to do some exploring. One day we went to the Lawrence Welk Museum, Welk being a native of the neighboring town of Strasburg. The Museum, in no way elaborate, was nevertheless very interesting, including videos of the history of the Russian Germans. I had heard that Russian German classification through the years at Haak gatherings, mostly in relation to their Roman Catholic tradition. The prospect of intermarriage with Dutch Calvinists did not sit well with either group, though some of the marriages worked out well in the extended Haak family.

Off approximately nine miles from Hull was the Strasburg Catholic Church, with a very tall spire pointing to the sky. I suggested to Colleen we drive to Strasburg given my interest in that church. It was an older but attractive structure; I ventured out to see if the door was open. And it was, prompting us to take a walk through it, admiring the stain glass windows and the general architecture.

As we were about to leave, I notice a literature rack, and one particular pamphlet: "Prayers for Rural Families." Listed were the challenging issues that farm families face, and then lovely prayers following each. These examples:

- Prayers for rural families
- Prayer for farm families in crisis
- Prayer for when a farm is passed on to the next generation
- Prayer for when a child drives a tractor for the first time
- Prayer for the family moving off the farm

We took a pamphlet home with us. It comes in handy to make a point that bothers me to this day. We who claim "Our World Belongs to God," indeed Kuyper's "every square inch" have never seemed to muster the creativity or commitment to pray for our farms and farmers like the rural Catholics did, at least not in the Reformed churches of my rural community. Appears those Russian German Catholics got it right!

This Letter from Colleen, October 3, 2005

Dear Haak Family,

Nearly a month has passed since we received a most appreciated and valued surprise – that of a significant gift from the Haak Family Reunion! What a blessing. I cried. Such a mixture of memories and thoughts……. Probably the main one – wishing I had been there, especially after reading the list from Lorraine of everyone who had been in attendance.

From what I've heard from several, it must have been a grand few days. One of the highlights seems to have been the worship service – and we feel so blessed that you chose to remember and give to the ministry of Rehoboth Christian School. Some of you are more aware of our work here than others, but our thanks go to each of you who contributed. We have designated it to be used for scholarships for children whose parents cannot afford to meet their financial obligations. This is a huge challenge for us every year, but with God's blessing and gifts like yours, we stand amazed at the way our needs are met.

I will enclose our October Prayer Guide which you can use as a tool in praying for Rehoboth, if you so choose. Also, I would encourage any of you who have access to the internet, to visit our www. rcsnm.org website and follow the exciting things we are up to.

On a personal note, Ron and I are headed to Chicago and Grand Rapids this coming weekend – RCS business-related for Ron and family visiting for me. Our eldest daughter Stacia and family live in GR. Second daughter Shawna and family are in Washington, DC; and son Rusty and wife are now living in Thailand. We look forward to every opportunity to see our kids and our four grandchildren.

Since I don't have an address for everyone, my plan is to send this note to those whose addresses I have. If you received additional envelopes, please either mail or pass on the extra(s).

Thank you all again so much for giving to the work here. God is good!

Warmly,

Colleen (and Ron) Polinder

Colleen, Gloria and Vic -- 1956

Two beautiful women, Colleen and her mom

Our Children: Stacia, Shawna, Rustin

Tom and Stacia—Uncle Fred driving his team of Clydes

Scott and Shawa—Surely
the Presence of the Lord…

Taryn Hoeksema's H.S. Graduation

Rusty, Katie and Henry—down by the river to pray

When our kids graduated from high school and moved into the next chapter of life, I wrote each of them a rather long "letter," four to five pages, about life and gifts and challenges. These decades later, I reread them, only to discover how the issues raised are still the essence of what our children live with.

These observations:

1. We celebrated the musical gifts that each have enjoyed. High School presents more opportunities to develop those gifts, but these kids still have those instincts. Of course, Mom's piano-playing contributed much. And as a family we often would sing together.

2. Each was commended for their ability to reach out to the new student, the stranger, or the marginalized. They did not only care about the "cool." They know how to talk to kids and adults, some very different from themselves.

3. Each of them was not afraid of ideas. Though they did not all show that on their report cards, they did in our conversations around the dinner table. Our discussions were often robust, age-appropriate, but serious and thoughtful.

4. There is confession, especially from me, about habits and patterns that were not always healthy—too much about work, impatience, demands. I was often distracted as a father and should have been more attentive to their issues. On the other hand, mom was beyond reproach.

5. Through it all, "the love, the love, the love was not the cheapest kind" as a lyric goes in a song by Garrison Keillor. We were not afraid of hugs and tears and "I love you." And it went both ways!

6. Underlying it all was a spiritual foundation that we tried to establish, a commitment to the Christian faith that we discussed and encouraged. Further, the church was understood to be where we learn and grow and often live out our faith.

So what happened to our children in the decades that followed:

Stacia

Stacia attended Calvin University majoring in Social Work. She flourished at Calvin in every way; socially, academically, spiritually. Upon graduation, she decided to work in Romania, which recently had undergone a major revolution. Bethany Christian Services had opened an office where Staci was actually the lone professional staff member, in spite of her youthfulness. Romania did not have Social Workers, so she started a program. Additionally, she teamed with a Jewish Peace Corp worker and started the first Big Brother, Big Sister program in the country. The year was full of adventure, living in the city where the revolution started. Meanwhile, before email and texting, her parents longed for FAXes for a sense of her work and well-being.

At Christmas of that year, her Calvin boyfriend traveled to Romania to present her a diamond, which she subsequently wore around Europe for a couple of weeks. Planning for a wedding from great distance was a challenge, but Colleen was up for it and with only one very expensive phone call, the plans were made and the perfect purple selected. The wedding would be at Bethel, where Colleen and I got married, and the reception would be at our house. In the evening, a dance would take place in our haymow.

These decisions in part were based on our prospective son-in-law, Tom Hoeksema, a Grand Rapids native. While we did not expect a dowry, we sure expected some serious work around our little farm. Staci and I had already power-washed the barn in prep for painting, but other tasks remained— thistles to be trimmed, fence posts to be painted, and a dusty haymow to be swept out for the dance. I doubt Tom questioned his proposal to Stacia, but surely he questioned her old man's sense of duty owed by a city kid.

All went well—Colleen and I often claimed it to be one of the best days of our lives.

The newlyweds headed to Tampa, Florida, where Tom was accepted at U of South Florida to pursue an advanced degree to become a school psychologist. Stacia in turn was hired by a local hospital as a social worker. After two years, they switched roles with Tom taking an assignment in a local school district, and Staci completing her Master's.

In '99 they moved to Grand Rapids where Tom was offered a position with the Christian Learning Center, which lasted until declining enrollment led him into the Grand Rapids Public Schools, still as a school psychologist.

Stac in turn was hired by Hospice of Holland where she worked for several years. She did start some adjunct teaching at Calvin in the evening. That actually grew by the year until it became full-time and she recently was offered a permanent full-time position in the Social Work department.

Of course, life is far more than work, and happily, kids and grandkids have come our way—Taryn and Seth biologically, and Shae and Tayva, adopted from inner city Grand Rapids. They are deeply engaged with Madison Square CRC, a multi-cultural church just a block from home in the inner city.

Taryn's Baptism

Saturday, Sept. 8, 2001—I needed some clips to hang a set of curtain rods in our apartment, a 69-cent item. I figured that someone on campus was sure to have them. With Pete Goudzwaard's key, I checked the shop, then saw Jeff and Tammelyn outside – but came up empty. I figured I better run to town and stopped at the closing out of TG&Y – no luck. The nice lady there suggested Walgreen's—same story. Gallup Lumber is probably the next closest—would you believe that

Gallup Lumber does not carry anything to hang a curtain? By now smoke is coming out of my ears. I am tempted to take a 16-penny nail and pound those rods to the wall in such fashion that they will never be moved.

I decided to drive through town, thinking that may have less traffic on my way to K-Mart. Wrong; I hit every red light from south to north. I passed AC Houston Lumber and gave that a try—another 10 minutes lost. And finally, I arrived at K-Mart where Colleen and I had started the day. I bought enough of those clips for the whole campus and headed for home, having lost nearly two hours. I stewed, not a little, about the obscurity of Gallup, though on my way home I tried to collect my Christian sensibilities. Upon arrival at home, Colleen was clearly shaken, wondering if I had been raptured.

That was Saturday, but Tuesday, 9/11, was coming . . . . Then we all got the sickening news about the attack on our country. The emotions and reflections of times like these can only be captured by poets, which happened Tuesday night singing, "Abide With Me" and "A Mighty Fortress is Our God" at a hastily called prayer meeting. Suddenly I was thankful for the obscurity of Gallup, NM—nobody on earth much knows about us.

That was Tuesday, but Sunday is coming . . . . We are supposed to head out today, Friday, for the mid-west for donor visits and Barnabas meetings. We will yet see if we make it out, given the peril in the skies, and at the end of the next week there will be an event in Grand Rapids, MI that too will seem obscure. A baby will be baptized, Taryn Cole Hoeksema, by her great-grandfather Pekelder, who will recite again the promises: "I will establish my covenant as an everlasting covenant between me and you and your descendants after you" (Genesis 17:7). And "now if we are children, then we are heirs – heirs of God and co-heirs with Christ" (Romans 8:17). And "surely I am with you always, to the very end of the age" (Matthew 28:20b).

The baptism is now a mark on a calendar, but marks on calendars fade and are soon forgotten. The mark on Taryn Cole is indelible, as in everlasting. And there was a cloud of witnesses to see the water do its mystery. At Madison Square CRC, Pastor Sam, a refugee from Liberia, invited the extended family to stand with Tom and Stacia. All those Pekelder's and Hoeksema's were there, a big bunch of them. Only a few from Staci's side, Papa and Nana, Scott and Shawna, Grandma Lois and Cousin Sarah, but the Polinder's and Haak's would have been equally represented if this event had happened in Lynden. The symbol is the vital reality that God has extended those promises now unto our "third and fourth generation," yea, even a thousand generations He promises. We have even lost count of how many generations of these families have testified, "Lord, you have been our dwelling place" (Psalm 90:1).

Why was that flock so numerous? Because so many, though not all, have accepted God's promises, they have lived by the mark on their foreheads. Their home and churches and schools have repeated the "old, old story," and the stories of faith that continue to flow from the faithfulness of this flock.

As Mother Staci, Auntie Shawna and Grandpas Tom and Ron sang promises and prayers, Elder Burger, a believer with African roots, took Taryn with big black hands and strong arms for a walk around the church. Now the whole congregation, the village, could see up close who they had just promised to help raise. With a rousing "Amen," they accepted their responsibility.

Parents Tom and Stacia, a large extended family, a body of believers, likely a Christian School will all play a part in the nurturing of Taryn Cole. It is a glorious reality, a blessing that all too few children will experience in the fractured social and family life of our troubled times. But even beyond this is the eternal covenant, a covenant of grace, which provides deep comfort even while a nation suffers.

It is our prayer that Taryn will always know that her comfort, in life and in death, is that she belongs to a faithful Lord and Savior, Jesus Christ. And we will await yet another day – when she will claim, embrace and profess the promises that were marked on her forehead September 2001.

Papa Polinder

Shawna

Shawna had no interest in pursuing college; rather, took a job with a Nordstrom branch in Bellingham. That is, until Staci came home at Christmas with news that there was an open room in their GR house—and Shawna, "Why don't you come and live with me for a semester. You could get a job as a waitress and…" Well, that is exactly what happened.

However, about three weeks into that experience, and having reconnected with some old Lynden Christian classmates at Calvin, and noting the cute guys on campus, she called home asking, "Dad, I want to go to Calvin." A father cannot easily say, "Sweatheart, I don't think you have the proper preparation—Calvin is a rigorous school." Instead, I promised I would call some Calvin friends and check it out. I soon learned she would have to take Geometry and the ACT. We found the perfect retired teacher willing to take Shawna on, and to her everlasting credit, she caught on and did solid work. Shawna was admitted and discovered she could tackle the demands of Calvin College.

During her sophomore year she signed up for the "Semester in New Mexico." A part of that group was a quiet Freshman named Scott VanderLeest. Shawna started to notice what a quality kid he was, and a romance commenced. Today Scott is our unlikely son-in-law.

During Shawna's junior year, I suggested that as an Art major, she would do well to go the Career Center to explore job options in the world of Art. In the process, they discovered Shawna's affection for children and her experience babysitting our DeHaan neighbors. A week later she got a call from the "career" people indicating there was a prominent Grand Rapids family looking for a nanny—"would she be interested in an interview." Four interviews later, she was hired by Dick and Betsy DeVos to nanny their four children.

The challenges and adventures over the next three years are too extensive to include here, but to say it was life-changing given the travel and responsibility. To this day she has warm relationships with the DeVos family, including the sending of notes of encouragement to Betsy as Secretary of Education.

After the second year of nannying, Shawna and Scott were married. Shawna was insistent in having the three DeHaan and four DeVos kids all in her wedding. She had the right assignment for each. Of course, this would mean the DeVos family would need to come all the way from Michigan, which they happily did, flying their 727 into the Bellingham airport. They were wonderful guests, participating in all the events, including the wedding reception at the DeHaan house.

Again when it was all said and done, Colleen and Shawna created a stunning event, and we decided it was one of the best days of our lives.

Scott was accepted at the Michigan State pre-med program; that meant a move to Lansing. Shawna started her own Day-Care in her basement. She also gave birth to Lathan, their first born. Given Scott's family and ours, both of modest income, Scott signed up for the Army medical program hoping to be trained in surgery. They were assigned to El Paso, TX, their last choice. Further, Scott was disappointed in his superiors and at some point, decided that it is not possible to be a good husband, a good father and a good surgeon, thus putting in for a transfer to do anesthesiology. He was reassigned to Walter Reed in Washington, DC. Shawna in turn, who cried all the way into El Paso, cried all the way out—she made lifelong friends in just one year. And she gave birth to Rushton Rier.

The DC experience was very different: big city, heavy traffic, and Walter Reed during the Iraq War. What Scott experienced with injured soldiers is unspeakable. Shawna did meet regularly with a group of young Mormon moms that became an interesting cross-theology experience. And gave birth to Lerieka in Bethesda Hospital.

The next move was back to Texas, this time the assignment was Ft. Hood. This would be the birthplace of Kortian and brought them closer for us to visit. They lived in Temple, enabling the boys to go to Temple Christian School, and came to love their church and school.

The Iraq war was still going on, and Scott would be deployed to an Army base in central Iraq. Imagine this young family, now with four children, Shawna pregnant with #5, and Daddy headed off to a war. The whole gang moved into our basement, but the day of Scott's departure was one of the saddest of our lives. Scott was able to return home after 11 months and was discharged, having served his country; safely, Thanks be to God.

They returned to Temple to give birth to Renellia, to sell their house, and prepare for life in Lynden. Scott was offered a position with Peace Health in Bellingham, joining a group of 40+ anesthesiologists. Their life is full with a busy family, the kids enrolled at Lynden Christian. Church life, a term on the School Board for Shawna, active kids, all with a lot of love within the walls of a newer home on Wiser Ridge.

Rusty

With a sigh of relief, Rusty graduated from Lynden Christian. School had not been his favorite place, with its thick books and long papers. But he had more ability than he demonstrated which most often was expressed verbally. Already in elementary school, he was diagnosed with ADD, and it plagued him through his schooling.

He was interested in YWAM, having had a couple of mission trip experiences. So it was that he signed up for the base in Los Angeles, Colleen and I wondering if he would last. Indeed, he did quite well, enjoying his Mennonite roommate, both growing weary of endless airy praise songs. One time they came back to their room and sang together "Great is Thy Faithfulness."

YWAM has a four-month discipleship training program and then a two-month outreach. The outreach was scheduled for southern Mexico, though the leader decided each member of his team needed to be "slain in the Spirit" before departure. Rusty was rather sure he didn't need to be slain in the Spirit, and finally after ongoing pressure, he called Dad. I urged him to go to the leader of the base and have him call me. Instead, the team leader Dave called—nervous, uninformed and green. A conversation with a veteran Christian was intimidating, and Rusty was given the green light.

It was a symbol of what was some ongoing frustration with the YWAM way. The next year, he went to Switzerland, where our cousin Debbie and Arnold were spending a year doing hospitality. He was designated driver, making trips to the airport in Geneva to pick up guests—of course he learned a lot in another country. That led to other YWAM experiences, mostly in S.E. Asia, especially in Thailand. At one point, a romance developed with Lynette Miller, from Middlebury, IN. The romance continued and led to marriage in 2003.

Baby Olive Hope was born in '09 in northern Thailand at 2.5 lbs. The proper equipment was not available for a premature baby. The next five months were altogether traumatic. A brain bleed almost surely meant that she would be profoundly disabled. Being in a foreign country at such a time presents almost insurmountable problems. Olive hung on but was often afflicted with infections that threatened to take her.

The details of what happened in those five months is almost a book in itself. As you can imagine, it had a profound effect on both Rusty and Lynette, and the extended families. What became a phenomenon still hard to comprehend was the response of the Christian community to the Olive Hope story. Hundreds, if not thousands, of dear people around the world responded with prayer and financial support.

Finally, on the last day of the year, this afflicted family, with medical support, transported Olive to Indiana. Having already undergone two surgeries, when yet another infection developed on January 22, Rusty and Lynette looked at each other and knew it was time to let her go.

Rusty and Lynette moved from their YWAM affiliation to an indigenous ministry in Chiang Rai. They had by now learned the Thai language and formed precious relationships with the Akha people, with whom they worked most directly. Lynette was also studying midwifery on the side. In 2009, they were again pregnant, and Henry Miles was born on Dec 24 in Bangkok. During Colleen's sickness, we heard his first cry via Skype—"Joyful, joyful we adore thee."

Rusty and Lynette's work in Thailand was coming to an end by 2014 which led to their move back to the States. Lynette got a job as a midwife, and Rusty worked for a Homeless/Alcoholism center in South Bend. At the same time, their marriage was unraveling. With great sadness, they divorced in 2017, leaving both the Miller and Polinder families bereft, concerned for our grandson Henry. How Olive's life and death influenced these developments remains a mystery.

Rusty and Henry moved back to Lynden and some months later Lynette moved to Bellingham to take a position with Peach Health. Rusty in turn took a job with Kidstown International, and enrolled Henry at Lynden Christian. He also moved into my parents' house along the river on

Polinder Road. And he met a new friend, Katie Yoder, a first-grade teacher at Fisher school. They were married on August 1, 2020. We welcome Katie, the newest member of our family, now Henry's step-mom and Rusty's partner. The wedding took place down by the river, beautifully arranged, and spiritually grounded.

Olive Hope

Olive H. Polinder, Sept. 25, 2009 - Jan. 22, 2010

SOUTH BEND - Olive Hope Polinder, 4 months old, passed away in Memorial Hospital, South Bend, on January 22, 2010. Survivors include her adoring parents, Rustin and Lynette Polinder; her grandpas and grandmas, Norm and Carol Miller, Ron and Colleen Polinder; her great-grandparents, Henry and Polly Yoder, Harriet Haak and Lois Polinder. Visitation will be held from 1:30 - 5 PM today in Siloam Fellowship, 61616 C.R. 35, Goshen. A funeral service will be held at 6:30 PM this evening in the church. Friends and family may gather in the Miller-Stewart Funeral Home on Monday morning at 10:30 AM to go in procession to an 11 AM graveside service at Miller Cemetery, Goshen.

Precious Olive Hope—so hard!

Travel

Given Rusty's years in Thailand, Nana and I each made two trips to S.E. Asia. What a grand experience, and to have Rusty as our tour guide made it extra special. His experience with the Ahka people, one of several of what they called Hill Tribes, enabled us to witness his work up close. Becoming part of an indigenous ministry, quite unlike so many of the Western controlled ministries, Rusty and Lynette appreciated working under Luka and Ghan. He had become quite fluent in the Thai language, thus making it easier to become friends. We were able to travel up the mountains to the remote villages where their people lived and where the coffee was grown that they hoped to sell via a cooperative with their friend Pat.

We also took a short trip to Cambodia, which in the mid 70's was turning Communist under their leader Pol Pot, who killed millions, maybe three million. They were also warring with Viet Nam, now united under one Communist regime. Our Viet Nam war contributed to this which is also worthy of further study--our history there had been part of the problem. You would do well to read about Pol Pot and confirm yet again man's inhumanity to man. What we saw there was horrific. We were taken to the "killing fields" (there is also a movie by that name), to skulls and bones scattered in the crude pastures where cows and their manure was spread amongst the bones. There were speakers attached to light poles that played music while they were executing people, so they didn't have to hear the crying of the slaughter.

Back in Phnom Penh, we toured the prison M-21, which once was the biggest and best high school in the city. Now it must be the crudest museum known to mankind—there was blood still smattered on the wall. They showed the torture tools they used on the prisoners. I believe less than 20 ever got out alive, though one was an artist who returned and painted on the wall scenes that he could recall, including the prisoners laying side by side on the floor, chained together. They kept careful records with pictures of each prisoner, the pictures now pasted to the walls and ceilings. Over 12,000 people were executed in the prison. It was one of the most sobering experiences of my lifetime.

In 2017, the renowned documentarian Ken Burns did an eight-part series on the Viet Nam war. History now shows so clearly how mistaken we were to engage that war. And I must acknowledge, even repent, of my own wrong-headed, naïve, hawkish conservatism. It is good for thousands, even millions, of us to admit that we were horribly wrong—and our Ivy League leaders too.

Politics should evoke humility, and Viet Nam is a painful example. Yet, it was also obvious that the communist Cambodia was not nearly as prosperous and efficient as the neighboring, capitalist Thailand.

Grandparenting

The preface makes it clear that this book is intended for my grandchildren, and even great grandchildren. At this writing, I have ten grandchildren and nine step-grandchildren. Mine include Taryn Cole, Seth Thomas, Shaelia Faith and Tavariay Hope of Tom and Stacia; Lathan Prescott, Rushton Rier, Lerieka Marae, Kortian Leitcher, Renellia Linor of Scott and Shawna; and Henry Miles of Rusty, Lynette and Katie.

This is a difficult piece to write because I have never considered myself a very good grandparent. I have had some good role models. Ken Faber could go out with his grandkids for donuts and carry-on conversation for a long time. Pastor Koeman likewise could play with his grandkids, do projects, work in the yard, all the while making spiritual applications. Don Kok along with Shelly would spend many weekends with their kids and grandkids and celebrate their time together.

In turn, for someone who talks to adults aplenty, I grow mute all too quickly. My bantering skills are likewise deficient. I hope that as the kids grow older the conversations and discussions will flow more naturally. In the meantime, I will resort to writing, which seems to come with less difficulty. A few topics come to mind.

The first is music. The genetics are there—you have music in your bones. At least one of each of your parents, maybe more, were good singers. Our kids did less well with instruments, though I am pleased to see some of you playing an instrument. I hope and pray that you will come to love music. It will bless you your whole life, as it did Nana and me.

The Bible has many references to music as a form of praising God. I like that verse Colossians 3:16 with the encouragement to "sing Psalms, and Hymns and Spiritual Songs." Note the diversity—not all one kind. Elsewhere we are encouraged to sing a "new song"—so not just old songs. But there should be some old songs that the church has sung for centuries, rich lyrics and sweet melodies.

Nana and I were never that keen on popular music. We didn't grow up in homes where it was much listened to. And if you study the lyrics, most are unbiblical, even hostile to the Christian faith. Of course, we knew a few, and have some old records to prove it. And our kids were quite fond of country music. We did not object, but we hoped they would see through the shallowness of most of it. If you sing and play good music, it will sink into your soul, and the Holy Spirit will bring back verses, phrases and tunes at important times in your life.

The second would be ideas. It has been said that some people talked about things, others about people, and still others about ideas. Of course, to be human is to talk about all three, but too many people are too shallow to talk about ideas. The Polinder's have not been afraid of ideas. Around the dinner table and at family gatherings, ideas were often the focus of discussion. Ideas have legs—they take you someplace. Good ideas are what we are called to pursue, and bad ideas lead to trouble.

The Bible provides us with the most important ideas. I pray that you will always look to the Scriptures for Truth—therein lies the Truth that stands the test of time. Jesus said, "I am the Truth, the Way, the Life..." John 14:6. The Bible is the greatest story ever told—always test ideas against the Bible. That is why I have been such a believer in a Christian College/University education—you will learn to think like a Christian.

But as noted elsewhere in this memoir, it is not all about ideas, the mind, the intellect. I will quote it again, Proverbs 4:23, "Everything you do flows from [the heart]."

References to ideas would bring up a third category: politics. Our branch of Polinders has been conservative. Up until recently, I would say "Republican," but the Trump presidency has soured us. But I believe conservative principles are still the most compelling, though only to the extent they are supported by Biblical principles. A very good listing of conservative thinking can be seen online entitled "Ten Conservative Principles" by Russell Kirk. I only have room to list five:

- Human nature is constant, and there is an enduring moral order made for humankind,
- Conservatives are guided by the principle of prudence, custom and continuity
- Conservatives believe in the need to restrain human power and passion.
- Government kept local and as close as possible to the people is the best government
- Conservatives uphold voluntary community associations and oppose involuntary collectivism

I do wish conservatives would work more aggressively to address issues related to "the poor, the orphan and the alien," and minorities. They have better answers than the liberals. Likewise, conservatives should be all about "conserving" the Creation, and again they have more sensible answers than the left-wing.

Finally, God created us to laugh. It is such a vital, wonderful part of life. To have a good laugh can be the best part of a day. My parents knew how to laugh, and when we got together at our Grandma's houses, there was laughter. Uncle Fred, Uncle Cornie, Aunt Joanne, Aunt Dort—there were hilarious times. I wish that for you, my grandkids!

Of course, there is something deeper than just laughter—I suppose laughter is rooted in joy. I hope and pray you may live in joy. Again, the Scriptures are not void of references to joy. Nor our music: "Joy to the World, the Lord Has Come" (a sturdy work by Isaac Watts).

Your Papa, in our first year at Ft. Wingate (because our pastor came down with the flu one Saturday) was called on to preach. I had just turned 22, and for some reason, I preached on joy. You will notice that the sermon is not included in this book—but I know it is still in my files. Maybe your parents will dig it out after I am gone and have a good **laugh**—that would be some rich irony!

This addendum regarding Judy's grandchildren, who I have come to know to a much lesser extent: They are my step-grandchildren and deserve mention. Just maybe your paths will cross, or there will be reason to look them up, or this book will fall in their hands. Good kids all, much loved by their dear Grandma Judy: There is James Willis (J.W.) and Wyatt Watkins of Jim and Ame Trull; Jayle Marie and Jena Celeste of Jay and Tara Trull, Lindsay Rae and Clay Isaac of Ryan and Julie Schilperoot, and Isaac William, Addison Rose, and Kassidy Jude of Jeremy and Lori Trull. And of this writing, four great-grandchildren.

We have been blessed—our quiver is full!

CHAPTER 10

FRIENDS

Harlan Kredit – 1999

A brief word about the origins of the Whatcom Land Trust. In the early 80's as Director of Concerned Christian Citizens, I received a phone call from a young man named Craig Lee with the Trust for Public Land. I think Roger VanDyken may have been his first contact, and he in turn sent him on to me. A few phone conversations eventually led to a forum sponsored jointly by CCC and the TPL. This concept had potential and power, and we were blest to have a wonderful collection of leaders in the community attend that first meeting. I will not forget the line of then county councilman Bob Muencher, "This may not seem like much now, but this is an important tool for us to have for the future." That indeed was a prophetic word.

I have always admired the interesting and diverse collection of people that have served on the board. I was pleased that my father Henry Polinder was part of that first effort, and more recently my good friend Dick Beardsley. As good as this day is, it would be better yet if they were here. But in their absence and honor, may we carry on with the high calling of earthkeeping. May God bless this organization and establish the work of your hands. One important way to do just that is to celebrate some of the victories that we see around us, and that leads me to introduce Harlan Kredit.

The Whatcom Land Trust is founded on an underlying honor and delight in the natural heritage of our county, what in my tradition is called God's good creation. One does not need to be a naturalist to behold the beauty and balance, the uniformity and diversity of that creation.

Today, we want to extol that variety, a particular variety, in fact one of a kind. Like there is no county quite like Whatcom, or even close, there is no human quite like Harlan Kredit, or even close. He's as rare as Adam, who took seriously the cultural mandate to cultivate and care for the earth, as uncommon as King David, from whom he learned that "The earth is the LORD's, and everything in it" (Psalm 24:1a), and unique as John Calvin, from whom he apprehended that we are to "feed on the fruits of creation" in such a way that we "neither dissipate it by luxury, nor permit it to be marred or ruined by neglect." And these lessons were engraved in his heart by a lifetime of singing at school and at church: "Summer and winter, springtime and harvest, sun, moon and stars in their courses above join with all nature in manifold witness to thy great faithfulness, mercy and love" (Thomas O. Chisholm).

When God created Harlan Kredit, he said, "Let there be light" that guides his path, his upbringing, his mind, his worldview." But this foundation was established only on the first day of the creation of Harlan—God needed several more days to complete this strange act.

On the second day, God said, "I better move his family out of South Dakota closer to where the land separates from the waters, by the Puget Sound and a river called Nooksack and a creek called Fishtrap, and he will learn to love it and understand how it works."

On the third day, God said, "I want Harlan to discover all kinds of things about vegetation, plants and trees—that lush Whatcom County will keep him occupied. And further, I want him to know about creatures and critters, the fish of the sea, the birds of the air, all those living things. And he better learn about the sun, moon and stars that I have ordained—that will remind him how small he is."

On the fourth day, God decided, "I'm going to make him a teacher. I'm going to make him talk fast and walk fast so that his students have to chase after him. When they catch up with him, they will be excited as he is excited about the design and mysteries of my handiwork."

On the fifth day, God thought, "This is turning into quite a piece of work, but I'm not finished yet. Let's splash some color on this creature—let there be nothing boring about this creation. Let's teach him about player pianos, and model T Fords, and let's give him a dose of liberal politics. And while I'm at it, I'm going to make him an Athletic Director."

Is that enough color, enough diversity in one creature? God said, "This was fun! No one will be able to figure this guy out."

On the sixth day, God again got very serious. He said, "It is not good for Harlan to be alone—I will create for him Linda, a helpmeet, someone to keep him honest and out of trouble, someone to take care of his details, to make him look good. I will make her a patient woman! And I will give them three children, Tim and Kim and Karen, and they will honor their father and their mother."

Finally, on the 7th day, God rested, and he said, "This is quite good; got a little carried away on the nose, the Adam's apple—I don't know what went wrong with that hair." But God rested, though since he created Harlan, all those around him have not been able to rest—he won't let us!

May I introduce to you, ladies and gentlemen, one of God's good stewards, a graduate of Lynden Christian, Calvin College, and William and Mary, Harlan Kredit! Harlan has been teaching now for 38 years in Christian schools, has led people around Yellowstone Park as a ranger for 27 years, and had the vision and commitment to restore the salmon to Fishtrap Creek. It is for this that we honor him today, and he will share briefly his efforts in that regard.

Faber, my Friend

Kenny Dale Faber has been one of my best friends now for decades. We grew up together in Lynden, though he was a couple of years older than me, so a deeper friendship did not develop until post-college.

But he was a popular fella in high school, for two reasons. He was a hotshot basketball player, making varsity already as a sophomore. The key to his game was a unique two-handed jump shot which he drained with high percentage. And he had a quick wit which made him well-liked even with older school mates.

Yet there was sadness in those years. Ken's youngest brother Sam (Nana's and my classmate) had cystic fibrosis and thus was a sickly boy. Ken's mother had four children in six years and seemed overtaken by depression. One Sunday morning, she walked down to the river, across from our gravel bar, and took her life in the river. Can you imagine the pain that afflicted that husband and family? I think sports (he was an excellent baseball player as well) became a distraction for Ken.

Thus, after high school, he went on to Dordt College and played (2 years?) basketball, and then to the military where he played around the Pacific Theatre, a nice assignment compared to Viet Nam, playing with All-American Terry Dischlinger. Dischlinger recognized his talent, and his ability to feed him, the star.

He met his first wife, Nancy, while stationed in Hawaii. After a short romance, they married and moved to Grand Rapids where he enrolled at Calvin College. Ken was never a particularly disciplined student, but with Nancy's nudge, he graduated.

In the spring of 1970, we got a letter from Ken asking about teaching jobs in New Mexico. Knowing there are always openings, we urged him to apply to the Gallup school district. Indeed, he was hired to teach 6th grade in Navajo, NM. We were eager to form a friendship with this Lynden guy, and his pregnant wife. Nana was also with child, both due in the Fall.

We became fast friends, often hosting them on weekends. But on October 16, after a horribly long labor, our firstborn son, Shawn Mitchell, was stillborn. Such will test a friendship. The Fabers were there for us, walking with us through this painful journey.

One month later, their Katie (now Veening) was born; Katie remains the marker and reminder of that collective experience. She has been a special family friend--even as a babe, we welcomed and embraced her.

The Fabers were lonely up in Navajo and sought employment by us in Ft. Wingate. Happily, Ken was hired to teach P.E. and coach at Wingate middle school. Thus we became neighbors and fellow church members, and our friendship deepened.

One of the most memorable experiences was playing on Wingate teacher teams in the Gallup City League. Naturally, given Ken's basketball talents, he was an important part of our team. My role was far lesser given my mediocre ability. But I learned how to feed our big man and coach, Warren Clark, underneath. Thus I got my share of playing time.

We did develop a problem though with our attitude toward one particular referee, Juan Delgado. Faber and I whined too much, causing Delgado to grow weary. Finally, he just started to call "traveling" when Ken got the ball. A couple of those calls cleared up our nonsense rather quickly.

Worse was the six-man flag football league we were part of for a couple years. We had a very good team—a quarterback that had played in the former AFL and could throw a long ways. I was the center, which meant playing on the line without pads, resulting in unsurpassed brutality. The scores were big given wide-open football with talented players.

But the second year, we played a team from the Northside of Gallup, on a field on the Hispanic Northside. The tension was high—they too had some talented athletes. Our longtime friend, John Hartog had joined, he a very fast former soccer player in our Calvin days. Already in the first half, he got in a collision that resulted in a broken cheekbone.

Not too long after, Faber took a cheap shot after catching a pass. In his disgust, he threw the football at the defender's head. Both were kicked out of the game. The opposing player was their best, so we needled Faber that his best contribution was taking that guy out with him.

Now into the second half, I centered the ball and pulled to the right, only to be hit in the back at full speed and splattered into the dusty field. Instinctively, I swore. Well, both of us got the boot also.

Finally, the refs called the game, and given the violence, they actually shut down the league. As for Hartog, Faber, and Polinder, three "Christian" guys, we were embarrassed by our behavior. And thus ended our football careers.

But Ken and I always shared our love for sports, and we watched dozens of TV games together, especially UCLA basketball. We got an LA channel, and he would sneak over to our house and together marvel at the genius of Coach Wooden. To this day, Faber is my favorite to watch games with.

More seriously, after moving to Rehoboth in '72, the Fabers felt somewhat stranded in Wingate. Thus, when an opening occurred, Ken applied and was hired at RCS. That led to even increased activity between our families.

Having lost our firstborn, Ken came to sit with me while Nana was in giving birth to Stacia. Again, it was a miserably long labor, and I was a nervous wreck. But I was calmed by my friend Faber. At last, after 30+ hours, they decided to do Caesarean. After an all-night vigil, we finally saw Dr. Stam emerge from the operating room with a little "peanut" held in his big hand. What relief, what joy, what gratitude!

Thereafter, Ken and I pledged that we would attend to each other as our children were being birthed—we were comrades.

A splendid by-product of our familial relationship was the friendship that developed amongst our kids. The Faber's four girls matched up age-wise with our three. They played together incessantly and are friends to this day. I will never forget many years later, when all the Fabers were in town, we called the girls over to our backyard, at like 9:00 p.m. The story telling and love shared those next hours was of the richest variety. Praise God!

But Ken and I had some differences as well, given my role as his supervisor. It best be represented by the story of a NM snowstorm. It was nasty and lasted three days. This was in the late 70's when RCS was about half day-students and half boarding students.

The teachers were of a mind that since only half the students were there, they would not need to have class. The dorm parents, on the other hand, were quite sure that all those kids should be in the classrooms—how were they going to entertain those kids?

Principal Ron has a divided staff and thus a serious problem. The first morning we tried some outdoor activities in the snow under teacher supervision. It was a flop, as I recall. Day two, I am saying to the teachers, there is activity you can be doing with your kids—there are always lessons you do not get to, or how about meeting with your kids one-on-one?

Faber was hotttt, not sympathetic to the dorm staff. He charged into my office and worked me over. I wasn't about to sit there and take it, and soon we were face to face—picture a baseball manager nose to nose with an umpire. Faber even grabbed his stocking cap and threw it to the ground.

Finally, I decided to appoint a committee of two, Mr. Faber and Miss Ensink, a veteran dorm mother who was not easily pushed around. It worked like a charm, the outcome I expected. The indomitable Ensink won that battle, the good-natured Faber surrendering. Day three we had school.

Our dustup was soon forgotten, Ken and I did a lot together as colleagues and friends. He was JV coach at Rehoboth and contributed strategically to a State championship and two 2nd place finishes.

Our move home in '82 was followed by their move in '87. Once again our families were closer together. But Ken and Nancy struggled with finding their niche, and struggled with each other. Ken settled in as a house and commercial painter.

Yet there was a particularly poignant movement between the four of us. Painfully, Amy's little daughter Abby drowned in the family swimming pool. Of course, as we did as family friends, it was our turn to bring comfort. I will never forget the embrace outside Gillies Funeral Home. They collapsed in our arms, with grief I have seldom experienced. They also asked us to sing with their kids two Navajo songs at the funeral. It would be our last time together as Ken and Nancy, and Ron and Colleen. Their marriage dissolved in 2008.

In our second move back to Lynden, this one in 2009, Ken and I were quick to pick up our friendship, mostly watching the occasional Mariners together, usually with a disappointing outcome to the game.

But in 2010, Ken got a Valentine's card from a woman he had met in California. He showed Colleen and me the card with a sure sense of delight. He questioned whether he had ever received a Valentine's card.

They had already been talking to each other (a lot) on the phone, and he was preparing to pay her a visit. Colleen and I issued the strongest of warnings: "Don't rush into anything!!!" Our council was immediately ignored—within a week we got a call announcing he was engaged to a Susan. Colleen and I implored, "What was the last thing we said to you?" The Faber response? "Here, talk to Susan," who quickly noted, "We aren't getting any younger."

Case closed—they were married on Palm Sunday. So much for a longer romance. But more importantly, the new Mr. and Mrs. Faber were right, and we were wrong. Ken and Susan are flourishing.

And so it is, now a decade later—a friendship reliable and rich.

Don Kok: Remarks

I am honored to be asked to offer some remarks about my friend Don Kok. We have known each other for over 20 years and worked closely and cheerfully as colleagues during my years as HS principal. Interestingly, we developed a habit of verbally needling each other, and enjoying it. Recently Don noted to Shelley that we didn't really mean it, when we said all those unkind things. I responded, "Don't be so presumptuous!"

But tonight calls for kindness. And truly it was my privilege to be an educational teammate of Don for several years. Surely others will dwell on his professional contributions to Lynden Christian, so I am going to move in a more personal direction. What is it that enabled him to serve us so well? What lies underneath that mop of hair? He has long forsaken his comb, but not his heart. His prayer no doubt has been, "Spirit of God, dwell thou within my heart" (George Croly).

Let us not forget that Don got his start on a dairy farm in Wisconsin. Thereby, he learned hard work, humility and some horsing around. And he developed a smell for bologna. He also had a good eye for the girls and already in high school, made his move on Shelley. We now know that he got the best end of that deal. Yet Don and Shelley together have been in so many ways exemplary. Shelley has been a rock!

And then to Calvin College where he caught a bigger vision for Christian education, though one seeded at Waupan Christian back home. And then to a Randolph classroom were you soon find out if you are an educator. The years in the more urban setting in Philadelphia helped Don and Shelley see a bigger world, and then to Bellevue Christian where he served so admirably in that upscale community. And finally to Lynden, where he found a home not unlike his community in WI. To use one of Don's favorite words, the journey has been *positive,* yes always seeing the positive.

But again, more than an educator. I have admired his role as the father of Mia, Nathanial, and Hendrik. How many of us go for runs with our kids? Sickening! But Don was out there, encouraging and modeling. And now he babysits—he considers taking his granddaughter to a ball game a hot date. Poor Shelley! Then there was/is his church life—always in the thick of it, serving on the Council in various places and even now, as an elder at Sonlight in these busy years as a superintendent. Don and I have been in the same Men's group since the 90's where one cannot help but discern the depth of his spiritual commitment.

In the Calvinist day school movement, we have consistently called on the partnership of Home, Church and School. Don did not just talk it, he and Shelley have lived it, and we ought not take that lightly. That Word became flesh and dwelt among us. And we are surely a better school and community because of it!

Thanks be to God, and thank you, Don and Shelley!

Ron Polinder

Koeman's: A Farewell

Dear Ken and Kay,

How does one describe and capture a long relationship—nearly 40 years of friendship and all these good years pastoring our church family. Let us use the word abundance—it has been an abundant relationship.

1. You have blessed our family and hundreds more, both of you. So many Sonlight children, now adults, walking in the truth. In no small part this flows from a church experience that presented them the Gospel in all of its fullness. All five of the Polinders would still say that Sonlight is our favorite church!

2. The affection for Sonlight is directly related to the faithful preaching of the Word – always fresh, always challenging, always something new to think about. And delivered with a calm passion that invited us to participate in the Kingdom.

3. The credibility of good preaching rests first in the truth of the message, but also its incarnation in the messenger. We have appreciated your diligence in studying the Word, reading other authors and living it out in your daily walk – a balance of scholarship and piety.

4. Then too, God has given you a unique gift of so often delivering the right word at the right time. Our earliest memory of this was the word with which you came to Fort Wingate, NM when we lost our firstborn in October 1970 (Hebrews 12:6). Further, the wonderful words of life you presented at Stacia and Shawna's weddings and Rusty's reception. But these were only samples of dozens of occasions when you set the tone just right . . .

5. The hospitality that flowed from your home and Kay's kitchen has blessed hundreds, perhaps even thousands. We experienced it as a family, but more importantly you have modeled Christian hospitality for your congregations. Maybe not all have caught on, or understood your investment in our collective lives. We have wondered if you even

entertained angels unaware! We miss sharing with you those Sunday nooi0kns when we had a table full of folks who needed some warmth and friendship.

6. This more personal note—you always affirmed both of us – those 16 years of working in partnership with me in the Sonlight office, and the encouragement and support for Ron in his work. So it was with dozens of Sonlighters. You seemed to recognize our gifts, even helped us identify them and then came along side of us as we tried to exercise them for the Kingdom. We thank you for your unwavering confidence in us.

7. All of which adds up to not just a relationship, but a friendship with your people. And for the Polinders, it was not just the four of us, but your kids and our kids too. It's a terrific gift, isn't it? It doesn't happen very often. Our move to New Mexico has produced real blessings, but also some real liabilities. There is a chronic sorrow in our souls over the loss of Sonlight and our special comrades in the Kingdom, Ken and Kay Koeman.

We love you, and we will miss you, Ken and Kay!

Sonlight Church

Ken Koeman: Memorial Service—The Right Word

It was 1968 when Colleen and I moved to New Mexico. Pastor Koeman's sister, Mary, reported her brother was moving to Albuquerque, and we should look him up. We knocked on their door one October Saturday, and of course we were welcomed in, thus starting a 50-year friendship with Ken and Kay Koeman.

Though we lived 125 miles west, it did not stop us from frequent visits. There we discovered a very capable young preacher attracting many newcomers to their church. Some years later, they moved to a church in Portland and then by the late 70's as Sonlight Church was starting, we, along with others, suggested to Sonlight they check out that Koeman fella.

So it was that Ken and Kay Koeman, with Kent and Kate, moved to Lynden and Sonlight Church. Pastor Ken preached his first sermon on January 1, 1980, entitled "The Main Thing is to Keep the Main Thing the Main Thing." Those words prevailed throughout his ministry at Sonlight. To this day—they were the right words.

When Colleen and I moved home in '82, we joined Sonlight and our friendship flourished. I can't tell you how many times after welcoming a new family, or a baptism, a wedding, a funeral, Colleen and I would marvel, and whisper to each other, that was the right word. It was our refrain! "The right word"—the theme which describes my dear friend.

Ken Koeman

Thus the title: **The Right Word**

Proverbs 15:23 says: "how good is a timely word!" Cannot everyone present here today remember hearing just those kinds of "right words" maybe in a sermon, in his office, the garden, or on the street. Think about how often from Pastor Ken those "right words" would just roll out.

These examples:

Above all, Ken Koeman was a pastor. It was "family visitation" at our house, an old tradition in the CRC, and he was assigned to that Polinder family. Normally, kind of an intimidating event, our kids seemed relaxed, knowing our friend Koeman was coming. He started with the kids, soliciting questions. The precocious 8th grader Stacia promptly asked him about "predestination." He offered skillful explanation and engaged them further in beautiful conversation, never getting to dad and mom. I believe to this day it helped them to love their church—because he shared the right words.

Koeman was not confined to the church to do his pastoring. Every summer Monday in the backyard the neighborhood kids would show up. He became the Pied Piper! "What was that?" I asked David Vos. "It was his time, his attention, his patience—teaching about Creation," sprinkled with the right words.

There is a men's groups in town, the Weaklings, started 38 years ago by Pastor Ken and others. 26-year member Kevin Pawlowski said it well, "Like a good pastor, Ken would let us wander for a bit into the 'theological wilderness' before he would wisely, gently… rein us back in"—with the right word.

For that Massachusetts family, daughter-in-law Jodi lost her father, to which her father-in law warmly said the right word, "Don't forget, you have another father." And eldest grandson, Jameson, the Calvin cross country runner, Grandpa following the race on live stream, would respond with encouragement, cheers and surely a little pride. For his grandkids, this good grandpa always had— the right word.

Lynda Burke was walking the trail just two weeks ago, the sunshine in her face. And there was Pastor Ken walking in the shadows. Lynda greeted him warmly with "We are going to miss you at Rock the Block!" and he merely said, "Carry on, Lynda, Carry on!" It was the right word, yea the right word for all of us.

Pastor Koeman was so in love with Kay, he often shared how blest he was to have Kay as his helpmate, her hospitality, her eye for the stranger—they were a team for 52 years. A day before passing, when there were no words left, he would rub his mask, and threw her a kiss. His non-word was the right word.

Our congregation, our family, the neighborhood, the brotherhood, children and grandchildren, colleagues, and his beloved Kay have all heard it, many times over—the right word. And so have you!

Like Samuel of old: May the Lord not allow his words to "fall to the ground" (1 Samuel 3:19b).

Paul Van Zanten: Memorial

I am honored to share some words about a man worthy of honor, our friend Paul Van Zanten. I first heard that name attached to Bethel Church, my wife Colleen's favorite Sunday School teacher. Never understate the impact of a great teacher of the catechism or Sunday school.

Upon moving home in 1982, we checked out Sonlight Church. I can't promise that he was the first to greet us, but no one came close to welcoming the stranger like Paul. A charter member, he came to be seen as the elder statesman of this church, a position he held until last week Thursday morning.

But even more important than his title was the esteem, which was carried within this congregation for our perennial elder. A lover of Christ, and His bride the church, even Sonlight church.

The first letter to the Corinthians says we are called to be "saints," a word the Scripture does not use sparingly. It is our calling as Christians, said St. Paul. We have known another saint, the venerable St. Paul of Lynden.

Saints are not so heavenly-minded to be of no earthly good. Our St. Paul understood the call to do justice and love mercy— to seek the welfare of the city. Thus, when Whatcom County was undergoing political reform, the Van Zantens were in the thick of it. Paul had flowers and smudgepots to attend, but Shirley would carry a torch into the field of politics, first on County Council, and eventually becoming our County Executive. And so Paul became known as Mr. Shirley Van Zanten, a title carried with pride and dignity.

Others will speak to more gifts and contributions, but some poetry seems in order for this moment:

There is a poem by Robertson McQuilken, entitled "Let me get home before dark." We use the phrase hoping we get home from, maybe, Seattle, before dark.

But for Paul we find a deeper meaning. We thank God that he allowed Paul to get to his <u>eternal</u> home before dark, that his life was full almost to the end, even a trip to Denmark this past summer for his grandson's wedding. He avoided what this verse describes as:

> *"The darkness of a spirit"*
> *grown mean and small,*

Rather, his end reflected this reality in the poem:

No, Lord. Let the flowers grow lush and sweet,
A joy for all who see;
Spirit-sign of God at work,
stronger, fuller, brighter at the end.
Lord, let me get home before dark.

And so it was with our St. Paul who Jesus called home softly and tenderly.

I close with a hackneyed Larry Ran poem that, with some editing, reminds us of the Paul, who "never knew a stranger"—a one-liner some say originated with Will Rogers.

How Paul loved people, how he loved you!

For Paul, there were no strangers, just people he did not know;
But give him a couple minutes, and the words would start to flow
Paul loved to find out their names, and the place where they were raised;
The schools they attended, and stories of Army days!

Soon they would be conversing, about all their common bonds;
Paul would share his passions, including talk of God!
They would talk about the old days, but also years yet to give.
Of church and school… and the gospel--- and heaven, where now he lives, he Lives,
he LIVES.

Ron Polinder
A Friend

CHAPTER 11

CHURCH

Dare I Say It?

Dare I say it? I am Christian Reformed. I was born into it and expect to die out of it. Some will think it odd that I would much care about this earthly institution, let alone write about it. But one should not describe it as mere earthly. There is something quite heavenly about it. Maybe "providential" helps us.

Colleen thinks it means too much to me. She needles me about my admiration for my tradition. There are others that will be even less charitable, those who have not had such a blessed experience in the CRC, and/or those who never had the patience or the perception to understand it.

But I am holding fast to my tradition. And there I go again, using the "T" word. Rather than defamation, the word needs some definition. Many products of the '60's, and their children, have never gotten beyond defamation of this wonderful reality. But Teyve in "Fiddler" said it well: "Our tradition helps us know who we are and where we came from—without it, we are like a fiddler on the roof." A more sophisticated definition from Jaroslav Jan Pelikan is: "Tradition is the living faith of the dead; traditionalism is the dead faith of the living." I will rest there—in the living faith of our forefathers and mothers.

I have come to this point because I have seen a living faith pouring out of my tradition. I saw it first in my parents, Hank and Mina. Not always so expressive in words, but very expressive in deeds, they lived it out, imperfectly to be sure, in their home and church, school and community, on the farm and with their friends.

They were products of the CRC, as were my siblings, Sherm, Eleanor, Marge, and Karen, and each of their mates. I'm grateful for each one of them, and see in them the marks of their church.

The CRC produced Colleen. She is the greatest gift to me, save the Lord Jesus. Her family raised her in this tradition, and she too has come to "living faith." As have our three children, each the product of the CRC; Staci and Shawna both with wholesome husbands that too were raised in the bosom of the tradition. Son Rusty, roaming in the wider evangelical world, continues to come back to the Reformed tradition from time to time for his bearings.

Collectively, we are products of Lynden Christian School, which was born out of the CRC. Those early Dutch immigrants saw to it that a Christian school was established as early as 1910, before the land was cleared. And most of our family are products of Christian higher education, Calvin College, whose affiliation with the CRC shaped the college, even as the college shaped the church.

At the heart of these institutions were wonderful teachers, Audrey Stremler, Bill Hendricks and Bob Korthuis at LC, and Vander Weele, DeBoer and Miller at Calvin. And rich friendships represented by George and Rick, and couples likes Gary and Carol and Gary and Pat.

I have always been active in the life of a CRC church, as a youth sitting at the feet of pastors like Van Houten, who exemplified the grace of the gospel, and Ackerman who taught the truth of the gospel. And then as a married couple to have minister/mentors who became soulmates liked Rolf and Nella Veenstra and Ken and Kay Koeman, all products of the tradition.

My heart was fashioned by the songs of the church; "This Is My Father's World," "Fill Thou My Life," and "Take My Life."

My mind has been shaped by the tradition's scholar & authors: Wolterstorff, Plantinga, Schaap, to name a few. While reading Neal Plantinga's "Engaging God's World," I resolved to write this essay. How can we not respect a tradition who produced such a gifted thinker/theologian?

It has been a joy to see others embrace the tradition, who in turn have blest me with their insights: Jim Skillen, who really introduced me to Abraham Kuyper; Frank Stiedl, who became my partner at LC; Cheryl Bostrom, a true sister in the Lord; and Kevin Pawlowski, a true brother in the Lord. Donna VG, Cal F, Jim DK, Don K, and true-blue friends. How rich are these relationships!!

For us, the church gave us roots, but also wings. It kicked us out of our comfort zone and propelled us into areas unknown, to the obscurity of Ft. Wingate, NM and the Navajo Reservation with a remarkably bold vision to have a transforming presence wherever God would place us. And in the process, we came to know CRC folks of a different color, who in turned enrich our lives enormously: the Edward T. Begay family, Board Chair Ed Carlisle, converts Art and Emma, colleague Lorretta, artist Elmer, and *shi' kis* Stanley.

Interestingly, it did the same for our kids, exploring worlds unknown. Staci went to Romania, Shawna to the rich and famous DeVos family, Rusty to more nations than all of us combined. Each of them was determined to make a difference in the lives of those dissimilar than themselves, their decision fostered by the sometimes clouded vision of their church.

Each of them has been blessed by friends who are products of the CRC tradition: Staci by Beth, Shawna by Wendi, Rusty by Mitch. And their friends have become our friends, making it possible to have young friends as well, like Eric and Becky, Rocky and Ruth Ann, Dirk and Stacey.

All these names are both models and representatives of another layer of God's children who too have a living faith that has sanctified our lives. Truly our lives have fallen in pleasant places, amongst people whose is faith alive.

The CRC is far from perfect. Its weaknesses may also be reflected in my life. Prayer and evangelism have not been hallmarks. And the stranger within our gates has not been welcomed as the Bible calls us to do.

And there is one other flaw, maybe <u>fatal</u>: It is overly self-critical and contentious, to the point of eating us up from the inside. And we may be in danger of, *dare I say it*, peeing this gift away.

Ron Polinder
February 2002

Thanks To the Third Power

As I celebrated with you this Sunday evening past, my mind flooded with memories and thanksgiving for growing up in Third Church. With Arv Blankers, I claim Third Church as "my church," even though I am no longer a member. The arithmetic Arv prompts me to conjure up a math symbol to describe what God has been up to in history. That is, the "power" in Third Church is that of the Holy Spirit, who has been multiplying goodness and faithfulness unto the 3rd and 4th generation of them that love Him. I am eternally thankful for the ways in which Third Church has formed and "reformed" me. To share a few:

1. My earliest memory, age four, was down in the basement. I think my dad had to take me out of the service. I wonder if he took me back in after doing the discipline, as was often the custom in those days? Third Church was where hundreds of us learned how to behave in church. It is a wonderful gift.
2. I remember my Grandpa Otter walking in with the consistory, sitting in the elder's row. Later in life, I was told of his judgment and wisdom, often delivered with a touch of humor.

Well-placed humor does much to diffuse the heat of a church meeting. We could use a few more Grandpa Otters.

3. I remember Rev. Ackerman "working over" the liberals, that is those who denied the deity of Christ, His virgin birth, His bodily resurrection. He said they had robbed the gospel of its power, that good theology was important. He was right. Rev. Ackerman wanted me to go to Calvin College. I resisted. Still don't know what got into me (was it "Third Power?"), but I went. He was right—again!

4. I remember playing softball for Third Church. We started as high school kids and got beat a lot. But we stuck together. We were managed by the generous Pete Douma, who played even me, and led by the incomparable Dean Douma, who pitched and batted the team to an eventual championship. This was a fine group of guys: Jack Veltkamp, Bob Vander Hoek, Rod DeJong, Dale Hendricks, Bruce Bode, Ken Kok, Willie Libolt, Gerald Van Loo, Jack Byeman, Bud Brouwer. We were friends—and still are.

5. I remember the support of Third Church in our New Mexico years, emotionally when we lost our first-born, financially when we worked for Home Missions, prayerfully when Rusty was so sick. And then to come home in the summer, to sit again in the familiar pews "amid the thronging worshippers" (as the 1912 Psalster versified Psalm 22), and to feel the firm handshake of Jake DeWaard and many others. I learned something about community.

6. And then there was the sudden and tragic death of our mother, 1982. Love and sorrow stood up together in the response of the church. To our extended family, it seemed like our emptiness was matched by a love that knew no ending.

7. Which brings us to this past May, when again the church filled, this time to help us say farewell to a father. There was no place I would rather have been than in my home church, Third Church, where our parents had taken us kids faithfully. Now they were both gone, but the church, with Christ as its head, remains "our dwelling place" (Psalm 90:1). One wonders where my family might be without this church?

8. God bless Third Church! You have been faithful. The gospel, in its fullness, has been preached. You have kept covenant. The kingdom is present! May the love that I, and many others, have experienced continue to dwell in you richly (John 13:34,35).

Ron Polinder
November 1998

Third Christian Reformed Church

Sonlight: A Case Study in Executional Weakness

Our family has been enormously blessed by Sonlight church. I start this way to make that a matter of the record. The subsequent critique is made in the context of gratitude for wonderful brothers and sisters, for staff members who contributed much, for a faithfulness to the gospel.

Yet Sonlight has suffered from the same weakness of many churches and non-profits. In short, there can be a dreadful lack of accountability and execution of the mission and vision of the organization and the decisions made toward that end. The result is that countless meetings are held in vain, leading to disillusionment. And organizations flounder.

The Sonlight narrative is littered with examples, but a couple short stories will make the point.

1. At its founding, Sonlight produced a document called "Sonlight Aims and Goals." It was revised a couple of times through the years, but somewhere in the 2000's the document was lost. In 2012, when asked to chair a new Long-Range Planning Committee, I had to find a copy of it in my personal files and pass a copy on to the church for its files.

A very fine committee was appointed to serve the long-range process which met many Saturday mornings to craft an updated document, based on the original. Titled "The Identity and Values of Sonlight CRC," the document went through a Town Hall process and was approved overwhelmingly by the congregation. Further, the document insists on two-thirds congregational approval if changes are to be proposed.

The problem was that it hardly saw the light of day after the congregational approval, in part because the new pastor, while originally agreeable, wanted something shorter. Thus, countless hours of work went for naught, though the new chair of the Council has pledged to devote time to it each of the next 12 months.

2. One the key provisions in the document calls for a deliberate effort to become more "missional." With the participation of the Missions Committee, the Long Range Committees and Christian Reformed Home Missions, two documents were submitted to the Council to adopt a strategy to lead the congregation in this direction. Again, no execution, no accountability. Those carefully crafted documents too have gathered dust, and Sonlight is not one inch closer to becoming a missional church.

This pattern is repeated over and o9ver again in organizations, prompting the publication of an excellent book entitled *Execution: The Discipline of Getting Things Done* (Bossidy & Charan). I bought the book in the early 2000's, and subsequently bought copies for our Administrative Staff at Rehoboth, where we were struggling with the same issues. It made an impact, though since then, Rehoboth has fallen into some of the same habits with its foundational documents.

As a member of the Board of Trustees at Calvin from '89 to '97, we adopted an expanded mission statement, 62 pages in length no less. To Calvin's everlasting credit, not one new program or major change happens on that campus without a tie-in to the Expanded Mission Statement. This is the pattern for which I am calling—use it, or lose it.

Recently, I had a conversation with my daughter Stacia about these same issues. She has come to the same conclusions and frankly said she is weary of the same old story. She hardly has the energy to serve on another committee or board unless there is assurance of a change in behavior.

Those who read this may well take to heart this phenomenon, and remember: execution, execution, execution!

CHAPTER 12

RETURN TO REHOBOTH: (2000 – 2009)

Gates Foundation, 2000: Introduction

Having made the decision to return Rehoboth, one quickly begins to think about needs and possible contributions. The spring of 2000 included a major announcement by the Gates Foundation to expand their work to include education reform. To lead the effort, they named Tom VanderArk as the Executive Director. I had come to know Tom given an online workshop we had we both participated in, and I learned he was a relative of Dan VanderArk, the CEO of Christian Schools International. Further, the annual summer convention of CSI was scheduled to be held in Seattle, and Tom was chosen as one of the speakers.

I made contact with Dan wondering if we could schedule a lunch with Tom to see if Gates would have interest in providing support for private schools, particularly those serving minority students. Dan warmed up to the idea and reached out to Tom for a lunch at the Red Lion. Tom himself a graduate of Denver Christian, was naturally interested. Warm conversation ensued, and while he did not make any promises, we could tell he was interested.

Fast forward to September and I get a phone call from Tom VA's secretary indicating Tom was going to be in New Mexico that week, wondering if he could visit our school. Needless to say, the calendar was cleared, some dignitaries invited, and the flavor of Rehoboth was passed on. His first response was his comment about Christian schools, reminding him of his school experience—the halls were empty, the teachers were teaching and the students engaged. There is a culture of accountability.

That afternoon we drove to the Zuni pueblo, wanting to tour the Zuni Mission School. The 45-minute drive enabled some stimulating conversation including the question, "Tom, how did you get this job?" He answered with is usual charm, "They asked me if I had any recommendations for the new position at the Gates Foundation—I thought for a bit and couldn't think of anyone better than myself."

Upon arrival in Zuni, we first met Pastor Mike Meekhof. After some introductory chit chat, Mike asked, "Are you any relation to Rev. Harry VanderArk? Tom responded, "That was my grandpa." Mike, "I was at his bedside when he died—he had given me all his theology books—we had become close..." Tom reached up and took a book off Mike's shelf. He opened it and there inside the cover was his grandfather's signature. He was speechless. In the obscurity of Zuni, NM, the providence of God made an appearance. The prospect of us getting a Gates grant suddenly improved, indeed, we received $1.4 million between our two schools—put to good use in private schools known for their quality and results.

What did he discover?

- He liked our size. The Gates Foundation is taking very seriously the growing body of research that shows that small schools are generally more effective.
- He liked our longevity and focus. He rightly concluded that to have survived as private schools this long (99 years 94 years) in this environment proved that we were serious, committed and successful.
- He liked our effectiveness. He sensed that our graduates were leaving our schools, succeeding at the next level, and moving into leadership positions with college and other post-high degrees.
- He saw discipline, rigor, and respect. He saw dedicated, competent teachers, and involved, supportive parents willing to invest in their kids and pay tuition, even though many are low income.

The Gates Foundation is interested in funding success, leadership, vision. They are not going to pour money into lousy schools. They want to create models of excellence, and hope that it can be passed on and replicated. In fact, they have talked to us about Phase II of a grant that would challenge us to share our best practices with our neighbors.

Now comes the challenge of being good stewards of $1,405,000, the kind of money that schools like ours are not used to seeing. As good private schools, we know how to pinch a penny and use every dime we have been given. That is the only way we survive!

Denny and Ruth Van Andel: Farewell

I count it a privilege to be able to reflect with you for a few moments about my friend Denny Van Andel. Some of you know, but not all, that Denny and Colleen and I were classmates at Lynden Christian School in our hometown of Lynden, WA. In fact, Denny and I were classmates from first grade through college, and we even did some summer graduate work together. Notice I said first grade, which explains why he is so much smarter than I am—Denny went to Kindergarten—I didn't. "Everything you need to know you learn in kindergarten!" I have been trying to catch up ever since.

Denny was likely the best all-around athlete in our class, which may surprise some of you—an excellent trackster even on the college level, a solid basketball player and fine baseball player. He knew the game well—as youngsters we collected and traded baseball cards, and I could never get the best of him. Denny was a good student and a good kid, better than the rest of us. His moral character was shaped at Lynden Christian School, at Bethel Church, and in a solid Christian home. His father, long the mayor of our hometown, provided the example for the Van Andel family with extensive service in the school, in church, in the community. His cheerful mother provided stability at home.

Through all of these years, I have counted Denny as a loyal friend. Denny is true, earnest, sacrificial.

Beyond our friendship, I have always respected him as an educator. Early in our careers, I could sense in him unrest with the status quo. He always wondered if there was a better way to do it. Beyond his solid preparation at Calvin College, he got his master's degree from Indiana University, now nearly 30 years ago, in Outdoor Education. It was a rigorous and innovative program, which helped him to think outside the box, outside the classroom. I have often thought that the day-to-day weight and demands of the Superintendency prevented Denny from showing his true colors and instincts. Given time and room, Denny could have tackled some very interesting projects on this campus.

You may wonder how Denny and Ruth came here in the first place. They were teaching in Korea in the early 70's when they inquired with Colleen and me about teaching in New Mexico. We were teaching in Wingate at the time and offered to try to find the right channels into the Gallup McKinley County Schools. I am sure we talked to our friends John and Ruth Hartog and sent them the right forms and waited. Well, it was the middle of May and they had to decide about where and how to ship their belongings from Korea. There was no email in those days, only the telephone with expensive long-distance rates. Somehow, we decided a phone call was in order—3 minutes would be $12.00. Well, have you ever known me to limit myself to three minutes, and our eldest Stacia was born besides—Colleen was still in the hospital. We got the bill: 13 minutes, $54.00, which in 1972 was a lot of money.

But I got to thinking, what a terrific investment that was. Denny and Ruth sent their goods to Gallup, and now for 30 years those "goods" have multiplied enormously—good teaching, good modeling, good friendship, good leadership, good living. Those goods have been sprinkled like salt around this community, first at Red Rock School and then at Rehoboth Christian School, both Denny and Ruth, at Bethany church and now in county pre-schools that Ruth serves, in Kiwanis, on the tennis court, in the coffee shop.

We had the good sense to hire Denny away from Red Rock, and that was now 25 years ago. Who can number the goods and services that Denny has performed as teacher, elementary principal, and Superintendent? Of course, only God is allowed and able to number our days and deeds, and to establish the work of our hands.

One of the ways God has blessed Denny is giving him Ruth. She has been a steady, encouraging, thoughtful partner. Behind nearly every good man is a good woman, and Ruth has been enormously supportive to Denny's work, all the while being mom, and distinguishing herself as an excellent educator in her own right. And together, they have raised two great kids Brent and Kelly who now are headed for their own lives of Christian service.

Perhaps I know Denny best as a Christian. Through the years, we have shared much and deeply. These last two years, we have been in a men's group together. His comments are slow in coming, but always worth waiting for, because "still waters run deep." Only through a glass darkly of course, but I feel better than many of us, he knows God—his Word, his will, his voice, his calling. Denny was called to serve—here. And has done so out of obedience and gratitude.

He has served young people far beyond any of them will ever realize. He has served his church, faithful in attendance, serving in leadership, quietly doing ministry. He has been committed to service to the Native American community, mixing it up, getting off this campus to spend time with the people he has come to serve and grown to love.

A number of years ago, former Rehoboth principal Bernie Koops, was described by a colleague as having only one weakness—"He was too good!" I would like to edit and pass on that supreme compliment by saying to Denny. "You may have been too good for us!"

Well Denny, they have already named a restaurant after you. I think one of these buildings should be next, but knowing your humble spirit, you would object! But I doubt Denny will object to this request: "Will you pray for us, and will you continue to participate with us?"

Toward that end, finally, we are looking for school board members—I cannot think of anyone more qualified! Do you agree? Please help me usher Denny into this new assignment that he has not yet accepted!

Ron Polinder
May 2002

Mohammed Aysheh

I think the year was 2001, when my friend, Edward T. Begay, then Speaker of the Navajo Nation Council, suggested that I needed to meet one of Rehoboth's neighbors, Mohammed Aysheh. In fact, thought the three of us should go out for lunch together.

Mohammed was owner of the LaQuinta Hotel, bordering our Rehoboth property, plus he had two substantial Native jewelry and craft stores just down the road. I did not take Ed's proposition all that seriously, until a day or two later he said he had made the date.

Oh my, I had never met a Muslim before. What would the protocol be? How need I behave? What would we talk about? That was settled in the first three minutes of our encounter—this was the most friendly, charming fella I had met in some time. What transpired in the next 90+ minutes was pure delight. Imagine the Arab American, Native American and Dutch American gabbing over Chinese food. It started a friendship that has been sustained to this day.

Mohammed's story is similar to the stories of some other immigrants—rags to riches. His education consisted of two or three grades. Dropping out of school, his family expected him to try to scrouge for a few cents a week. To this day, he remains illiterate. He left Jordan at age 15 and headed for Brazil, living a riotous life. At 21, he came to America with $35, to sell Turkish rugs door to door.

Hearing there may be a market in New Mexico, he moved from Denver to Gallup, again selling door to door. But somehow he became involved with a prominent Indian Arts businessman, Gilbert Ortega. That relationship flourished, enabling Mo to learn the business and eventually to buy in.

I noted earlier that he could not read or write, but I have rarely seen anyone as skilled with numbers. His memory of transactions and his eye for a profitable venture has been remarkable. He is now owner of hotels and real estate, making him a multimillionaire. Often he says, "America, the best country in the world." u

However, he has been much less successful on the personal side of life. There have been several failed marriages and a dozen kids, most of whom he has no relationship with. He claims he spoiled them, and now they have stolen from him.

Mo did have at least one failed business when he went in partnership with me. Learning of Rusty's Thailand connection, he saw profits from Thai's produced bronze statues, which he wanted in his stores. If I would help him make the connections and take care of the details, we would split the profit 50/50. Unfortunately, this was around the recession of 2008, and those statues would not sell. Finally, feeling sorry for me, Mo bought me out such that I broke even.

Through it all, we have remained friends. He loved Nana and now Judy. In our last encounter, he said, "We are not just friends, you are "family." Thus we stay at no charge in his LaQuinta in Gallup. And he has been generous in other ways.

You will wonder, how about our faith issues? Maybe it is best described by his inquiry into having his youngest daughter attend Rehoboth. My standard response to non-Christians: "We will expect them to take Bibles classes and attend chapel—and the whole Rehoboth experience may lead her to becoming a Christian." Immediately, his response, "No, that cannot be."

When Mohammed and I complete a phone call, it always ends with, "I love you, Ron." In turn, "I love you too, Mohammed."

Gail VanderPloeg DeYoung

Gail VanderPloeg was yet another of those outstanding student teachers that came to us from Calvin College. Our school and community have been enormously blest by the gang of several dozen young folks who populated our campus and classrooms. There was none more talented and dedicated than Gail Vander Ploeg, not yet Gail DeYoung.

I can recall exactly where on campus I said it to my colleague Stan Pikaart: "That Gail is so talented we should hire her whether or not we have a position available." And that is exactly what we did—we manufactured a place for Gail. I don't recall what all we had her teach, but I know one was Home Ec, which occupied a room just west of the Science lab.

If I had my way about it, we would still be teaching Home Ec at Rehoboth—what could be more important than teaching our kids about family life, parenting, and nutrition? Gail did outstanding work—we still have a quilt with which her Home Ec class gifted us when we first departed in 1982.

Hiring Gail was more complicated than I have just described. She had a problem—she was in love with some "ne'er-do-well" from Southern California, who in chauvinistic manner thought he was more worthy of a job than his bride-to-be. This Mike fella was actually given a job before Gail, which he still believes was because he was the more important—delusional soul that he is.

Gail proceeded to distinguish herself in a variety of ways—haven't we all lost count, including what a good softball player she was. But professionally, she will most be remembered for the big heart with which she went about her counseling and teaching at the Middle School. And it was that same heart that poured itself out year after year, season after season into our music program, poised at the piano with skill and grace.

And the list goes on—her work at church as a musician and elder, her devotion as a wife and mother of three, and now grandma, her loyalty to an extended family in Pella and beyond, and her hospitality to the Rehoboth family including current and former students. There were the painful good-byes to precious young people who too soon went to be with the Lord.

May I close by celebrating a gift that dozens of us have experienced, that is, her friendship. Who of us would not quickly say that Gail was and is one of our best friends? Surely that was our family's blessing, as now nearly six years ago we released Colleen to her heavenly home. And it was Gail (and Mike) who came to Lynden to play piano to welcome Judy, into a new circle of friendship.

God has given you many gifts, Gail DeYoung, and you have used them so we would all testify (with the words of song writer Debbie Kerner), "Beautiful, beautiful, Jesus made beautiful things of your life."

Ron Polinder
May 2018

Mike DeYoung: Retirement Remarks

Mike DeYoung and I have been harassing each other for over 40 years. He usually gets the best of me. His quick wit leaves me in the New Mexico dust. Above, I added to his humility; now is time to show some respect.

Mike's first assignment at Rehoboth was teaching 7-9 earth science and math where he quickly distinguished himself as a good teacher. He also proved to be organized and efficient, and within a couple of years, as I took over superintendent duties, I was quick to appoint Mike as my assistant— he was my detail guy.

We were young; too young, I suppose. I was 31, Mike was 24. When it came time for some detective work, we were aggressive. With his clipboard in hand, we soon developed an image. Discipline cases were plentiful. Mike later became the 7-12 principal from '86 to '99, a long stretch.i

Mike did some Earth Science instruction at the Gallup branch as well and for the Calvin program for a few decades including Teacher of the Year in '96. What we have here is a faithful teacher and administrator for a long time. Throw in some coaching and astronomy work, and we have a picture of a solid servant.

Mike has never been void of a sense of humor. Old-timers will remember a disrespectful, though stellar imitation of Johnny Carson's Carnac the Magnificent, "An Apple, A Pear, and a Lemon" (Blow open an envelope) "What would be New York City, Dolly Parton, and the Rehoboth Christian School Board?"

Then of course, Mike was always, always concerned for when there was possibility of snow and the potential danger. He place his hand over his heart, and sanctimoniously pronounce that school should be called off "for the children."

But Mike, no matter what your own kids say about you, I am going stick up for you.

At last Mike was able to move in '99 from the frying pan of administration into the fire of IT. Surely, the Rehoboth staff would be patient and grateful for all of Mike's warm and tender ways as he serviced one building after the other. Do any you recall a crabby, cranky, surly, sour, Network Administrator? Go ahead and raise your hands—No sense in being bashful—after tonight, you don't have to deal with the guy.

I'm sorry, here we go again. Let's consider how many times he comes out at night to open the observatory, how many miles he drove carrying the equipment for the choir, how often has he run the sound system at school or at church? We owe you a lot, Mike. You have been our friend.

One of my most favorite times was when we hauled our chairs up a hill above Wingate and read "Blood and Thunder" and imagined the bloodshed down in the valley. It symbolized a relationship with a history, a culture, a friendship. Mike, thank you for our friendship—I will cherish it the rest of my days.

Ron Polinder
May 2018

More New Mexico Friends

Goodness sakes—what am I getting myself into? So many people have been so good to us! Who am I going to offend by not including them? Nevertheless, I must name some folks, and the blessing they were in our lives:

Ernie and Martha Hurst—now deceased, Martha was Colleen's supervisor in the Wingate Middle School and Ernie was mine in the High School. They taught us so much about Native kids, went to church together, visited at night and played cards—they were our surrogate parents.

John and Ruth Hartog—moved to NM in '69 and have not left. We spent endless hours with them—family friends. John, the teacher, became a fine principal, and honored referee in NM. Ruth, the Bethany church secretary, was enduringly loyal. I could write several more paragraphs about our precious friendship.

Gary and Pat Nederveld—our teammates as dorm parents. We depended on their experience and good judgment in our rookie year. And our friendship has endured for decades even though their politics are messed up and their sports teams are losers.... (Our needling each other does not diminish the mutual love and respect.)

John and Jo Van't Land—Another long friendship with our twice sojourn in NM. John was truly an outstanding Math teacher, preparing unnumbered prospective engineers, doctors, and nurses for the rigors of college. And a marvelous photographer. Thoughtful Jo, well-read, compassionate, prayerful—good folks.

Rich and Elaine Stam—Rich our pediatrician, there for the birth of our kids. And so steadfast regarding Rusty's early childhood ailment. Elaine also, special friend to Colleen and to our whole family. Many hours of stimulating, fun visits, our families together. Missed them when they moved to Albuquerque.

Phil and Elsie Belone—Elsie was Colleen's favorite student at Wingate. Upon return to Rehoboth, we were thrilled to see Elsie on the Rehoboth School Board. The next year, she came to teach at Rehoboth. We worshiped with Phil and Elsie often at Tohlakai. Elsie honored us by participating in both of Colleen's memorial services.

Bob and Mary Ippel—All heart, both of them. Superman Bob can teach at any level, started the highly regarded choir, and is now the Rehoboth superintendent. "Super" brings up other words that also apply to Mary's leadership as a dedicated nurse—the Ippels are superb, even superior—and they will likely invite you for supper.

Stanley and Sharon Jim—Stanley has been the lead pastor on the Rez for well over 20 years. Seminary trained, his preaching is first-rate and insights into ministry and culture exceptional. I am proud to call him my friend—so many good conversations. In turn, Sharon served well as Elementary Secretary--light-hearted and cheerful.

Jim and Short Holwerda—"salt of the earth" best describes Jim. Quiet, thoughtful, diligent, supportive—such a good man. On the other hand, there is Short: noisy, naughty, but still nice! And she knows how to teach! She recently turned 65, prompting me to plead, "Please don't start acting your age."

Cal and Jeannie Feddes—Montana Cal, the most earnest elder I know—he should be full-time. As a science teacher, he was so diligent, I encouraged him to look for other work, which he did. Now he can more enjoy the effervescent, fun-loving Jeannie, who for us, and many more, was the ever mindful, always cheerful nurse.

Stu and Flo Barton—too late we came to know and love the Bartons, now both deceased. Rehoboth grads, who as their grandkids enrolled, became active grandparents. Flo was our best cheerleader and referee critic, from the bleachers. Stu, before our departure said, "We're going to miss you, you think like an Indian."

The Jones family—from Mexican Springs, met them at Tohatchi CRC. Mother Elizabeth had 11 kids—she was the matriarch at church and most everywhere else. We met most of her adult children at church—solid people, and good leaders. Lots of grandkids at Rehoboth. When she passed, I insisted her "obit" make *The Banner*.

The Carlisle family—Ed and Dorothy, both loyal Rehoboth grads from the 50's. Ed was for many years the excellent Chair of the RCS Board. Their three kids graduated, Donovan now working at Rehoboth in campus maintenance. Overqualified, but loves the school. Wife Audrey--my mischievous, loyal *shi*-buddy.

The Zylstras—Jason and Ken, no relation to each other, both making enormous contributions to RCS. Jason for years the CFO, a strong leader who started the role at age 24, maybe. I can't imagine being superintendent without Jason. Ken became our Director of Development, also grew into the job, and has performed so well. Both good family men!

Ed T. Begay and family—Ed a revered Navajo leader as Speaker of the Council and Vice President. Long-time Bethany church leader. Father of Shar, our baby-sitter decades ago, now a mother and forever friend. Sandra, brilliant engineer at Sandia Lab. Honorable Rehoboth grads all. Honored to be at their table for Easter dinner.

Ray Pinto—A Letter

January 21, 2019
My friend Ray,

I am writing this on Martin Luther King Day, which is symbolic of a theme I want to highlight in this letter. Dr. King represented so much of what was good and just, and what we needed to learn and become, especially cross-culturally. He was killed in April of 1968, four months before we moved to Ft. Wingate, now over 50 years ago. It was in August of that year that I first met a future colleague and friend named Ray Pinto.

Ray, you were the first Native American that I came to know and form a friendship with. In God's good providence, our lives became intertwined at school, at church, in the community. This young, naïve, 21-year-old, began to learn about your story and culture. I will always be grateful for your kindness and patience—you must have rolled your eyes at times given my immaturity and easy answers.

But together, we invested heavily in the lives of our students at school and in the youth group at church. We formed relationships with them, we fed them, we went on outings together. I remember picking pinons toward Ramah and each spring a venture to Wheatfields. And how could be forget our entry in the hide race at the Wingate rodeo, me on Sonny Tafoya's horse and you behind, hanging on for your life. We came in third—not bad for having practiced but once.

We also tackled substantive matters. You may remember our mutual unease about the quality and climate at Rehoboth Mission school. One day I wrote up these collective concerns into a three-page letter to Home Missions. You, Ed T. Begay, and I signed it, and received back a very positive response, which may have helped start some major changes in program and staffing. A few years later, you served on the RCS Board, and even as chair as I recall.

Ray Pinto and me at Wingate Rodeo—Students teased me for no cowboy boots or hat

With Stanley Jim: leading pastor, beautiful singer

And then I became principal, first at the elementary and then K-12, having all four of your capable kids in those years. Mona, the eldest, who participated in "saving" Miss Helland one day (Mona needs to tell you that sweet story), the talented Renee we passed a grade given her brilliant mind, Lisa, Staci's classmate and friend, and the tailender Jeremy, now a Ph.D. As you know, Mona and I have an ongoing relationship—we are big pals.

Somewhere along the way, we drifted apart. You and Marge parted ways, and you moved in a more "traditional" direction. Surely this created some apprehension between us, yet on the rare times our paths crossed it was always warm and friendly. Surely that represented the deeper respect and love that we still shared. And I should add that it would be true of how you viewed Colleen as well—she too was your friend.

When Mona told me of your birthday, I knew I wanted to reflect again on our friendship, and thank you for it. I wish we could still find about three hours to sit under a pinon tree, with some cold fry bread to chew on if we got hungry. I would wish we could talk about faith and culture, Christianity and Navajo tradition, Rehoboth and Wingate, and likely a whole lot more. Certainly we would brag about our kids and give thanks for them. We would also talk about our suffering, of which you and I have had plenty. I do remember some painful aspects of your family of origin, and you will remember some of my suffering, from losing our firstborn to losing Colleen. I suspect we would weep together.

But we would also laugh and give thanks for much of life. Psalm 90:15 says "Make us glad for as many days as you have afflicted us, for as many years as we have seen trouble." As I number my days, I would testify that I am still way to the good.

And now I hope and pray that you will have a rich time with your family. I hope you can count your blessings, and "taste and see that the Lord is good" (Psalm 34:8a). I hope to be in NM the first week of March—it may be too cold for a pinon tree, but we should be able to find some soft seat somewhere, softer than the saddle and hide we rode at the rodeo.

Happy Birthday—

Love you *shik'is*,
Ron Polinder

Keith Kuipers Funeral

I am so pleased to be with you today, among so many old friends and colleagues. My name is Ron Polinder, and I had the privilege of knowing Keith Kuipers as a supervisor (he hired Colleen and me), a colleague, a neighbor—and a fellow pilgrim at this place called Rehoboth. It is an honor for me to stand here and share with you some thoughts about this good man.

The family has asked me to include some reference to II Timothy 4:7,8. Most of you will find it familiar: *I have fought the good fight, I have finished the race, I have kept the faith. Now there is in store for me the crown of righteousness, which the Lord, the righteous Judge, will award to me on that day—and not only me, but also to all who have longed for his appearing.*

That verse is so packed, and I am not the one to deliver the sermon today, so let me just try to note quickly three things that relate to our brother Keith.

1. When we hear that word "race", one automatically thinks of competition, and thus we think of Coach Kuipers. I "fought" the good fight"—most of you probably don't know this, because we think of Keith as kind of a mellow fellow, but Keith liked to win; he was more competitive than it appeared—he wanted to win those games. So too, when he played tennis, or went fishing—he "willed" to win or catch the big one. Keith Kuipers had some "fight" in him, and it contributed to his amazing record as a coach,

    But he always competed with honor, with respect, with dignity—always keeping his faith as central to what he was representing. Never, in my recollection, did he embarrass his school, his community, his Lord.

2. Now the verse says Keith is wearing a crown of righteousness. There is a tendency to think that such a crown was his due, given his humble manner, his faithful service to Rehoboth Christian School, his warm affirmation for so many students and parents, fellow church members and neighbors (in the broad sense). We think of all the meetings he went to, all the tough conversations he had with kids and parents, all the classes he taught, all the Latin he conjugated. And let's not forget his years of service, in the military, in Kalamazoo, his state championships in two states, his years as administrator, and teacher and volunteer and bus driver—wow, what a guy.

    He must have earned that crown—surely—all that good work? Keith would say to you and me, "no, no, no—it is the righteousness of Christ that has been bestowed on me. I didn't earn anything—it was a gift. I am just another sinner, saved by grace. If I did anything good, it was out of gratitude for what Christ did for me." That is Keith Kuipers.

3. And then the verse ends with a word that Keith would pass on—it is not only to me, Keith, but also to you who wait his appearing, his coming. So you too can live in the hope of the new creation. But Keith would ask, "Have you surrendered to the Lord, confessed your sins, turned your over your life to the One and Only who can cover your guilt and shame with his righteousness?"

In closing, I have yet this memory of Mr. Kuipers, I wonder if others do? It's a line that often was spoken in his prayers—I always liked to hear it, from II Peter—He would pray from II Peter 3:18, *May we grow in the grace and knowledge of our Lord Jesus Christ.* That's good line, a good word—I need to include that in my prayers. But here's the deal—Keith just didn't pray it, he *lived* it.

I will always remember Keith as a man growing in grace, his instincts were always gracious, his response to students and to parents and to the rest of us sinners was always toward grace. And that is why he was so loved, because grace oozed out of him. If he erred, he erred on the side of grace.

And too, that we be growing in knowledge—let us not forget that he devoted his life to Christian education, so that children and young people would grow in their knowledge of the Lord Jesus Christ. That is what Keith Kuipers lived for: basketball, and English, and Latin, and history and science and math, all of life and learning, point us to our Lord and Savior. Keith Kuipers—a man of grace, who gave his very life to this school, that many of you would come to know this Lord and Savior, Jesus Christ.

In preparing these remarks, I believe the Holy Spirit reminded of a song that I know some of you know. I invite you to sing along, or at the very least, pray along. It's a song that will forever remind me of our brother Keith Kuipers.

My friends may you grow in grace, and in the knowledge of our Lord and Savior.
My friends may you grow in grace, and in the knowledge of Jesus Christ
To God be the glory, now and forever, now and forever, Amen
To God be the glory, now and forever, now and forever, Amen
(written by Sean Diamond and Timothy James Meaney)

Karen Schell; School Board Chair and Friend

Dear Karen,

This is a day none of us have wanted to come—the day you would be leaving the Rehoboth Christian School Board. Your service to the Rehoboth school family has been exemplary. Let me count the ways—well some of the ways:

- Time and miles—how many meetings have you attended and how many trips have you made to campus to fulfill some need or obligation? And you have done it cheerfully.

- You allowed the Board to make you the Chair, even though you were unsure and frightened. But you grew into the position beautifully and have created a wholesome atmosphere and level of accountability.
- You love this place—it is truly your school. You want it to serve God and to serve His people. You have respected its history, and you have worked for and prayed for its future.
- Your leadership has been marked by principle. You have some spine—you have stood up for what you believe, and you want Rehoboth always to be true to its Christian foundations—without compromise!
- You have been a great ambassador for the school, both in the local community, but also around the country, whether on choir tour or with our national advisors. You represented us with class and character.
- You have been a good mom through it all—never sticking up for your kids, but always wanting them and the staff to live up to high standards. We have appreciated your good sense and balance.
- You have been a friend, to both Colleen and me. Thank you for that, even the passion to clean this place up. Karen and Colleen, that was a team—they could get things done!

So, there will be a huge hole left as you depart. But we will trust the Lord to fill it with servants of different experiences and gifts. And we will not let you off the hook—even as there is a lot of Karen left at Rehoboth, there is also a lot of Rehoboth left in Karen. So we will see you around, and fully intend to put you to work!

Karen, we thank you! And we love you!

Ron Polinder
June, 2008

Lorretta Smith

When Colleen and I arrived back on campus in August of 2000, we came upon a major mess in the office, particularly related to admissions. In short, we did not know who would or would not be coming to school a couple of weeks hence. Outgoing Van Andel was in the hospital with intestinal issues, and the Admissions Director was on National Guard duty.

Mother/daughter, Lorretta and Nikki, our hard-working partners in the office

But slugging it out was Denny Van Andel's secretary Lorretta, filling in on admissions issues and trying to organize the paperwork. We quickly discovered this woman was not afraid of work, knew the families and loved the school—Colleen and I were quickly attracted to Lorretta Smith, and we became a team.

Lorretta Smith was born in the Tohlakai area of the Rez, to a family that was not functioning well. Her grandparents and father were primarily involved in her childhood. Additionally, there were four boys and sister, Rena. She graduated from Tohatchi HS and participated quite faithfully in the Bethlehem Chapel, a little CRC in her community.

There is more than a little mystery surrounding her post-high years, but they included working at the Gallup Police station as a janitor. Transportation was a problem and thus she would sneak into a backroom at her workplace to sleep. At last, one of the officers found/caught her, a Sgt. Hawthorne, who eventually became romantically involved with Lorretta. They got married and became the parents of Nikki. They also moved to Las Vegas for a few years. Tragically, on a trip back home, Nikki's father died of a heart attack six days after she was born. Lorretta had no choice but to move back to the Rez.

Lorretta knew she wanted Nikki to attend Rehoboth, which also led to her election to the Rehoboth School Board. Superintendent Gord Kamps recognized some of Lorretta's gifts and offered her part-time work, which of course led to a full-time position and a 26-year tenure working at Rehoboth

The teamwork that developed between Colleen, Lorretta and I lasted for the years we were together. Lorretta and I relied on each other in so many ways—admissions, tuition charges, candidates for the School Board. More importantly, Colleen and Lorretta bonded in such a wholesome way. This is best described by a term we learned from some Australian visitors, also Christian School administrators. They described the partnerships they formed between their aboriginal staff and the expatriate staff, what they called "two-way." This enabled the best of their respective cultures to be represented in decision-making. And such was the relationship between Lorretta and Colleen—they needed and complemented each other.

We worked hard, but we also had fun in the office—Colleen would make her famous "health bread" and various cookies and bars. Or Nikki would run to town for some French Fries smothered in green chili. Our office was the old high school dorm, very plain, by still functional. It is where Colleen and I lived and worked when we were dorm parents. We turned the old girl's lounge in a very attractive Board room.

We made Lorretta part of our Administrative Staff—she was the only Native, and we needed her voice. Lorretta's voice was not subtle—she had opinions and was not afraid to express them. At times she could test our patience with her outspoken, even critical views. Yet, she was a strategic presence. To her credit, not having a college education, she worked hard to understand the essence of Christian education and Reformed theology.

Her blunt style served another useful purpose—she was not afraid to challenge colleagues regarding cultural sensitivity. She ruffled some feathers, but most employees came to appreciate her honesty. Rookie Jeff Engbers came as our new A.D. and coach. Lorretta loved to hang out in our new Sports and Fitness center, where she was always the ticket-taker. It gave her a place to observe and advise Jeff with her forthright style. I shall not forget Jeff's tears of friendship when he had to say good-bye to Lorretta.

Likewise, our departure in 2009 was tearful and painful. Colleen and I were both so grateful for this woman in our lives—what she taught us, how she lived out her Christian life, how she mothered Nikki. And she tried to keep her brothers together, playing a mother-like role. Often she shared portions of her meager check to help out relatives. Her faith was simple, but not hidden.

And then the worst would come to be—Colleen's brain cancer. I can only imagine how Lorretta must have suffered at a distance. But I often claim it led to what our family calls the gift of Lorretta's finest hour. After the funeral (July of 2012), there was a wonderful gathering in our backyard. I asked Lorretta to make some opening remarks. What flowed out of her soul was pure, rich, and authentic.

She described how "this plain Navajo woman became a friend of this elegant tall, white woman, who taught me how to study the Bible, to raise my daughter, to set a table and make chocolate-chippers. I grew up around mostly men—I needed help. This was not what usually happens in my community, but Colleen had this friendly, warm way that was appreciated by the parents—and I especially had this blessing in my life."

Lorretta also was dealing with health issues, but we were never quite sure of the diagnosis or the prognosis. But 2017 would reveal that "cancer was back" and she all too soon was confined to her bed. This was especially hard for Nikki, who had given birth to Mykal four months previous. Sadly, as we planned for a substantial thank you event, Lorretta was slipping away and could not attend. She died just a few days later.

But saying our goodbyes was bittersweet. Bitter for her family and friends, but sweet in how it happened—gathered in her apartment singing both in Navajo and English, raising her up to heaven.

I had the privilege of leading the memorial service based on Lorretta's favorite passage: Psalm 27:1, *The Lord is my light and my salvation, Whom then shall I fear? The Lord is the strength of my life, Of Whom shall I be afraid?* This is the assurance that our friend Lorretta lived with and died with—Thank you Jesus.

The DeVos Family

Presentation to the honorable Rich DeVos, who along with
Mrs. DeVos, were Rehoboth's major benefactors

Rich and Helen DeVos, one of the founding families of Amway, faithfully contributed to the RCS annual fund for years. But as we approached major campus renewal and the building of a new middle school, we knew that we would need some million-dollar gifts.

Daughter Shawna, having worked for Dick and Betsy, knew her way around some of the key players of the DeVos Foundation. She knew that Dad better dress up in his finest suit and tie to see Ginny VanderHart, the director. It was an enjoyable visit, and the start of a friendship with Ginny, and eventually the DeVos family. Thus we prepared a million-dollar proposal for a six-million-dollar building. When we received positive word of our first million-dollar gift, the celebration and gratitude was widespread.

When the building was completed, and the first 8th grade class was going to graduate, we invited Mr. and Mrs. DeVos to come for graduation, and for Mr. DeVos, a noted speaker worldwide, to speak at both the 8th grade and HS. ceremonies. He was outstanding! Our parents were so authentic in their expression of thanks—no pretense; jeans and cowboy boots, or traditional dress would work just fine for that Thursday night.

With HS graduation on Saturday afternoon, Friday was spent going to Zuni, 40 miles south. That proved to be fortuitous for Zuni, but that is another story. That evening we gathered our School Board for dinner with Mr. and Mrs. DeVos at the historic El Rancho. As was my custom, we asked Board members to tell their stories, which in Indian country most often happens through tears. It was a beautiful, powerful couple of hours.

Until the final board member, Harry Begay. He spoke of his troubled childhood, his education, the pleasure that his children attended Rehoboth. And then he launched into a case for a place at Rehoboth "where the whole school community could gather." I am on the other end of the table in a cold sweat wondering what Harry may say next—this visit was supposed to be a time to thank them, not to ask for money! Harry did not get the "memo."

Harry continued, "What we really need is a new gym." At which point, Mr. DeVos said, "Are you making a pitch?" Without missing a beat, Harry said, "I sure am!" And lifted his water glass saying, "Let's drink to that!" Mr. DeVos led the room in uproarious laughter. It was the most unscripted ask in the history of philanthropy.

What followed over the next two days was Mr. DeVos's peppering me with questions about what all we had in mind. Truth be told, we had yet to come up with a design beyond some big picture dreaming. The last thing Mr. DeVos said to me on his way to a car after church on Sunday, "Now you get me that proposal!"

A few days later I called Ginny, who was along on the trip. Previously, Ginny had warned me that we would be fortunate to get another million dollars from the DeVos's.

"Ginny, How did that go by us," I inquired.

"Oh Ron, They had a marvelous time."

"Do you think we could ask for more than a million dollars?" I asked.

Ginny responded, "I wouldn't dare say what you should ask for."

"How about five million?" I posited.

"I think you should ask for five million," Ginny replied.

That summer we hastily prepared a proposal with conceptual drawings, asking for 4.8 million of what would be a $11 million project, including a turf field and track. In October, I got a call from Mr. DeVos indicating they would give us five million "to start with."

Thank you, Harry Begay, for following the lead of the Spirit and for the courage to say and ask what we may have been too timid to do ourselves. The providence of God is a glorious reality.

But I'm not finished. The DeVos's came out to participate in the dedication of the Sports and Fitness Center. Mr. DeVos took me aside and indicated that if some of the other gifts did not come through, they would pay the balance. Given our impending departure, it was a great comfort to know that the building would be paid off.

This beautiful reality—our athletic facilities are equal to the finest in the region. Our turf field, a beautiful green, stands out as people drive past on I-40. Our gym with three floors enables the athletes who come from great distance to get home on time to do homework, and for guests to have seats for the "big game." Too, for the large funeral, or our own graduation can now be done on campus—what a gift!

Jim DeKorne; True Friend

Jim DeKorne became one of my best friends through my New Mexico years. He had the sharpest of minds such that every time I encountered him, he would say something provocative and unusually insightful. He always made me think.

It started during his student teaching year, 1974, when he came to Rehoboth to teach math and science. He was the guy who took a shine to Gretta, who had come the previous year only to break her leg—so seriously that she could not complete her semester. Thankfully, she returned, and it wasn't long before Jim and Gretta were flirting—like seriously.

They did part ways—Gretta for a year in Wisconsin and Jim for a year in Guam. But the next year, they were back with Jim taking on a full-time position at the HS. He soon became a solid, respected teacher. As noted elsewhere, as I took up the role as Superintendent, we called on Jim to be the part time business manager, a task he took to quite naturally. He did superb work, maybe a bit prone to procrastination, but always done well—trustworthy.

As the years move forward, we moved to WA, and Jim took on the substantial task of starting Desert Christian High School in Tucson. And after that assignment, he became to the Superintendant of a Christian School in Colorado Springs. During these years, we rarely saw each other, but occasionally had meaningful conversation. I could tell he had a creative way about him.

Jim took on a couple of other interesting roles, but it was his work with Christian Schools International that brought us together such that our friendship would be cemented. He became Director of Support Sevices at CSI which made him available as a consultant at RCS. We utilized his considerable skills in long-range planning and evaluation. More importantly, he became a trusted advisor to Colleen and me, during a time when the challenges at Rehoboth were considerable.

Jim and I had a particular experience that will go down in CSI history. We decided to have the annual CSI convention at Rehoboth, in 2006. We were a team, and we crafted a program and a speaker's lineup that was first class. We were told numerous times that it was the best CSI convention ever—the participants had their feet on the ground, in the sand, lined up for Navajo Tacos. The hiking and the beauty of the Southwest was overwhelming, far better than a high rise in one of our big cities. Lest we claim too much credit, let it be said the Lord saw fit bring the right team together.

Jim eventually took a job with the National Heritage Academies, a charter school movement in Western Michigan. This cast him into another role, a good one that placed him in the presence some fine educators, and quality schools (though not all).

Behind my good friend Jim is an equally good woman named Gretta. They have established a fine family of four spread around the world doing the Lord's work, not unlike their parents. All of which started with a nasty broken leg, with bone protruding. How would God bring redemption to such suffering? Given a little time and the enchantment of New Mexico, Jim and Gretta found each other by God's good providence. And together they have been faithful servants.

Rolf Veenstra Memorial Poem (Circa 1986)

(Delivered at the naming of the Rehoboth library, to which he gave oversight in his retirement)

Rolf Veenstra: the Peculiar Padre

Padre, you say?
Yes, Padre – father.
My father, my priest, my padre,
So Catholic, you say!
Well, catholic, as in comprehensive;
broad in sympathies and tastes and interests–
A Calvinist who could wear a clerical collar.
He was a prophet, a priest,
a king, and a clown.

I
A prophet, you say?
Yes, a prophet, one gifted with more than
ordinary spiritual and moral insight.
Prophets are strange, odd, curious –
Peculiar people whose deeds and creeds are
eccentric–off of center.

Rolf was peculiar
- he wrote letters on used paper and mailed them in used envelopes
- he crawled along the freeway on an old bicycle with a funny red flag
- he preached his farewell sermon without telling his congregation
- he never took that gift trip to Nigeria

His poignant preaching was practiced,

his principles played out.
Rolf would say "Our world-and-life view must
become our world-and-life do" –

He word became flesh, and dwelt among us –
frugally, modestly, humbly, stewardly,
peculiarly, prophetically.

II
A priest, you say?
Yes, a priest, one who represented us before God,
who mediates, who intercedes
Priests say it better than we can, and more often.
They talk good to God

Rolf prayed
- who else kneeled during his congregational prayer,
- who else prayed for each household as he walked around campus,
- who else prayed for our Rusty like Rolf, as he anointed his body with oil,
- who else prayed more for you, who else?

Rolf would quote Tennyson, "Prayer has wrought more
than the world has ever dreamed of."
He words lobbied the heavens, his life was a sacrifice
of pleading and prayer.
Rolf was our priest.

III
A king, you say?
Yes, a king, with a royal inheritance, who sitteth
with Christ in the heavenly realms
And he sat there long before December 29, 1990.

He was not a king of human carriage,
of pomp and circumstance, on center-stage,

Rolf was an obscure king riding on a donkey
whose only and best claim to fame was being the

child of a king.
In Christ he conquered principalities and power,
in Christ he was exalted,
In Christ he was triumphant.

Rolf made proclamations.
- by greeting us as "saints"
- by the numerous notes he slipped under our door,
honoring us like we were royalty
- by urging us "not so much to get into heaven,
but to get heaven into us."
- by likening our sin to a chicken with its head
chopped off.

He said from Ephesians: "Keep looking down; we're in
charge here, on top of the situation, and above our
circumstances."

Rolf lived like a king.

IV
A clown you say?
Yes, a clown – a clown with a crown, mind you,
but instinctively a clown, comedian, jester, a jokester,
a wily wag whose witticisms won him the title
wordsmith,
and apt author of alliteration.
Rolf was a punster:
- when given the comb as a gift for his bare pate,
he responded, "I assure you I shall never part with it."
- when he caught you working in the evening he would
remind you "Six days shalt thou labor, not six nights."
- when analyzing school attendance patterns he observed
"Education begins by being present."
- when on his deathbed he would welcome the "upper taker"

Can you picture the twinkle in the eye of that glorified boy, can you imagine
his with renewed mind, cracking some good ones?

I see that peculiar padre, that clown with his crown,
as he sitteth in heavens and laughs.

May 1991 RP

Our beloved Rev. Veenstra—
sketch by Elmer Yazzie

Nella—none like her

Farewell again, from our 2nd home

Gallup Independent: Nella Veenstra, A Huge Hole in Gallup

In a few days, Gallup, New Mexico will be diminished. Only a handful of folks will notice, for this is one of those times when the economies of this world do not quite add up. This is a story of weakness rather than strength, of loss rather than gain, of humility rather than pride.

On September 10, a woman by the name of Nella will be moving away from our community to a retirement center in the Midwest. The Rehoboth community and a number of Gallup citizens will weep as she departs. This precious 82-year-old woman has been a rock for us for over three decades.

How is it that a modest preacher's wife, a woman of minimal financial means, someone who has not held a "professional" position for 50 years could accumulate such affection? What is it about her life that has touched hundreds, maybe thousands, and made us all better along the way?

Nella Veenstra moved here in 1969 with her husband Rev. Rolf Veenstra and their three elementary-aged sons. She believed her highest calling in life was to be a wife and mother and considered herself a "liberated woman" who did not have to work outside the home. She devoted herself to loving Rolf, her boys, and two step-daughters. In the process, she seemed to have so much love left over for the rest of us.

The essence of her life was her Christian faith. She took to heart what her husband preached every Sunday, that when we become Christians, we are "new creatures," that Christ lives in us, and that we can live a glorious life of faith, hope and love. Every day for Nella was and is an invitation for Jesus to reign—like it says in Philippians 1:21, "to live is Christ."

Such faith will surely inspire a life of prayer, and so it has with Nella. She prays way more than most of us, and she has seen the results. So have many of us who have had the privilege to know her, and to pray with her. We have wanted Nella to be praying for us—there is something special about that.

She believed the Tennyson line, "More things are wrought by prayer than this world dreams of." So before Rolf passed away, and after, they/she would pray for each household on the Rehoboth campus as they walked past. My wife and I wonder where our kids would be today without Nella's prayers.

Nella's spirituality was also earthy—she cared about this world in all of its complexity. She loved a good poem, an exciting ballgame, a new dress—these were all gifts from God for the people of God. Sweet potato casserole at Cracker Barrel was a special treat from God. Once, while eating fresh raspberries in Washington State, she became convinced of what led to Eve's fall.

There is little about this woman that dried up with age, certainly not her sense of humor. Having been married to the ultimate jokester, she has laughed so steadily that after eight decades she can still give you a hoot with her voice and a twinkle with her eye. She has little patience for a dour or sour faith.

Nor has her mind gone stale. Recently we hosted, at Rehoboth, the annual convention of Christian Schools International. There was Nella, at every keynote speech and most workshops, taking it all in. This summer she cheerfully sat through three consecutive sermons on a Wednesday evening at First Baptist in Gallup.

Which illustrates another key to Nella's Christian walk—while she loved and respected her Dutch Calvinist heritage, she knew that other church traditions had insights and patterns that were God-ordained and inspired. She was catholic—small "c" – and loved her friendships with Christians and non-Christians of all stripes.

And her walk was literal—to this day, now a slower pace, she walks. Exercise was a matter of taking care of the body that God has given her. Before Rolf's passing in 1991, they would ceaselessly ride their bikes to town—some of you old-timers will remember those old bicycles, each with a tall red flag. It was a bit of a comedy.

All this done in the obscurity of Gallup, New Mexico—more particularly, Rehoboth. Content to live in an older mobile home for now nearly 30 years, it was not the kind the world would esteem. But out of it flowed warm hospitality, in it lived a model of contentment, from it will move a "hero of faith." And our community will be smaller, much smaller.

Ron Polinder
Executive Director, Rehoboth Christian School

Rehoboth Pain

The greater Gallup community including a portion of the Reservation has been afflicted with horribly painful events. The Gallup Independent and the Navajo Times almost daily contained a litany of sadness, crime, and death. It is a society racked with abuse and dysfunction.

Naturally, some of that spilled over to the Rehoboth community. While we never counted it up, the number of single parent homes was surely higher the any other Christian school. The counselors would report sad tales of abuse, especially alcohol abuse. The broken families were legion, and death was too often the result.

In that context, Rehoboth too suffered through some painful death, some crime-related, but certainly not all. I will try to list those, though I am no longer sure of exact dates. I do know that in 2002, Board member Alan Landavazo was taking his two boys and a third to a soccer event in Albuquerque. It had snowed that morning, late Fall, as is often the case near the Continental Divide. Several cars were off the road and the Landavazo gang stopped to be of help. Given the chilly weather, Josh ran back to the car to get his coat, only to encounter a sliding car headed straight for him. He was killed, while having stopped to help others. It was a travesty, felt deeply by his fellow high school students, and the broader community.

I believe it was the next Fall that a young man who completed 8th grade at Rehoboth but transferred to Tohatchi for high school. One day we got the shocking news that he had died, from an apparent suicide. That could not be confirmed—more likely, given he was something of a prankster, he could have been trying to choke himself for some sort of "high" for doing such. Regardless, it shook our community again to its roots, and many of us, including his former classmates, headed to yet another funeral.

But there is more—so much more. In the Spring of the 2006 school year some of our students and their teacher headed to Santa Fe for a United Nations event/contest on a Sunday morning. There were two cars, one of them driven by a student. About thirty miles from Albuquerque, the young man driving the car fell asleep at the wheel. The car rolled a couple of times as I recall, with horrible results. All the students were transported to the hospital with various injuries. As three of us were driving to the hospital in Albuqurque, we got a call that our German exchange student, Maria Holcher, had passed away. Two others had very serious injuries, one a broken neck and the other serious lacerations on his upper leg and buttocks. One can only imagine the scene at the hospital!

But then we had to inform Maria's family in Germany—I believe the exchange student organization took the lead on that. Her mother rather quickly flew out to Rehoboth, a sweet, but grieving woman, to share in the tragedy of that horrific event. Maria had won the hearts of her schoolmates and was a thoughtful and seeking Christian. Her mother escorted her body back to Germany.

Maria was a gung-ho member of the Rehoboth choir. Her mother actually offered several thousand dollars to the choir to fly to Europe after school was out. That proved to be powerful event for our students and a marvelous witness to Maria's community. But the pain ran deep.

Two were hospitalized for several weeks, but slowly recovered, though one, an outstanding soccer player, would not play again.

Given our use of a student driver, there were liability concerns. To be sure, a few weeks later, we were served notice that a lawsuit would be forthcoming. Our insurance company was Church Mutual, who responded with care and professionalism. Rather than going to court, all sides agreed to mediation. One August day, we all gathered in a tall building in Albuquerque. Our mediator was a former Attorney General for New Mexico, a very bright, talented, skilled man.

The whole group met together to start the process, I asked if I could pray. I don't recall exactly what I prayed, but I know I asked that we come away still being friends.

We then divided into about six rooms, and the mediator would go from room to room. My friend and our CFO Jason Zylstra and a representative from Church Mutual were in a room together. I will forever be grateful for the gentleman from Church Mutual, and later wrote the company a letter of gratitude. The final settlement was very large—5 million plus as I recall. And the School Board made doggone sure our policy about student drivers was radically changed—I felt some heat!

There was precious Megan Ortiz who had a childhood illness the name of which I have forgotten. She missed much school with breathing issues. She was slight, but charming and winsome. She was wonderfully confident in her faith. Nana and I knew her family well from Tohlakai church, especially Grandma Hubbard and Auntie Kat Meese, who cut my hair for years. We had great assurance and a hope-filled funeral for this sweet girl.

Of greater sadness was the story of Brooke Spencer, an outstanding athlete, both Basketball and Softball. As too often happened, she thought she could make the big time by transferring to Gallup H.S. There was also a boyfriend involved, one who was likewise athletic. I pleaded with Brooke as strongly as I ever did with any student. I said, and wrote, while talking to her: "This is not good for you academically, socially, spiritually and romantically." I asked her to keep that paper in her wallet. But off she went and starred at Gallup High for two years. The night after graduation, at someone's party, she tried to break up with the boyfriend noted above, who was under the influence of alcohol. Unbelievably he took out a knife and stabbed her—she did not survive. Like so many others, she is buried in the Rehoboth cemetery—the young man sentenced to 30 years in prison. Both families had long-standing roots at Rehoboth and met each other again on opposite side of the aisle in the courtroom. Such sadness!

A girl not known personally to me, but she had attended Rehoboth a couple of years before our return. I did know her father, and she had a younger sibling in our school. One day we read in the paper that a girl had been found in a ditch a few miles outside of Rehoboth clearly the victim of foul play. Soon we learned it was our former student. The full story never was uncovered, but yet another painful event.

Then there was the sweet 7th grade boy who the week before school was out, went to his grandparents for the weekend. There was a horse accident, the details I do not recall, save he was kicked in the head. He was flown to Phoenix with a severe brain injury, on life support. He died a week later, on 8th grade graduation day. Can you imagine the gloom that surrounded those students and their families.

The last day of that school year would be followed by events that occurred on the first official day of staff meetings that August. We had gathered for our Staff Retreat at Sacred Heart Retreat Center, south of Gallup. Full of anticipation for a new school year, Pastor Ken Koeman was brought in to lead us, and James Schaap would read us a couple of his stories.

Midway through the first session, the phone rang for Chuck Johnson, our middle school Science teacher. He quickly left along with a couple of others. At the break, we were given the news that his son, Chris, went down with his helicopter in Iraq. He and his entire crew perished. Of course, we were stunned—we took a half hour to process it, during which time Pastor Koeman revised his entire message to meet the need of the hour. After a quick lunch, Jim Schaap selected a story that likewise spoke to our deep distress. Emotionally drained, we departed early, to go home and face the pain and distress of yet another family.

Of course, Nana and I promptly went to visit Chuck and Mary. They had received the official visit from other officers. There we were with a weeping mother and a stoic father. What do you say? I have no idea what we said.

I don't recall the time frame, but I will never forget when Chris's body arrived back in Gallup. We were told the time, and our entire student body lined the street on campus, waving small American flags. The hearse was followed by veterans of every stripe, including many of motorcycles. It was at once sobering and honorable. Chris was laid to rest in the Rehoboth cemetery up above the other graves, surrounded by red rocks, with an American flag flying, I hope to this day.

When I started this story, I surely did not expect it to be this long. But maybe that is fitting, because it was a long, painful journey. Still, this most honest and perceptive verse from Job 1:21: "The Lord gave and the Lord has taken away; may the name of the Lord be praised."

CHAPTER 13

ASSORTED STORIES & OPINION: REHOBOTH 2ND TIME

Ron Donkersloot—Colleen and I were relieved when it came to our attention that Ron and MaryLou Donkersloot from British Columbia were somewhat interested in returning to New Mexico to take up the Superintendency at Rehoboth. The Donkersloots got their professional start at Crownpoint Christian School. But there was one obstacle in that he had just completed a sabbatical and owed Vancouver Christian School another year of service.

That in turn prompted the idea for us to take a leave of absence from Lynden Christian and fill in for a year at Rehoboth. Sure enough, that was approved by the powers that be, and plans were made accordingly.

In preparation for our year, I already had made a trip to Grand Rapids to meet with our consultant who would school me on the agenda for the coming year. It was quite a revelation, making two remarkable statements: First, "you are going to have to do Rehoboth up right, or put the place out of its misery." That means, secondly, "You are going to have to learn how to ask donors for a million dollars." Such statements will put you on your heels.

Upon our arrival back on the Rehoboth campus, it soon became clear that consultant Sal was altogether correct in his analysis. The campus was tired, some of the buildings in tough shape, the infrastructure long overdue for renewal. As the Fall progressed, Sal was proposing that we should consider the college model, that is a President (or Executive Director) and a Provost (or Academic Headmaster). Given the fundraising demands, with a new Middle School on the drawing board, this concept gained traction with the Admin Staff and the School Board.

To Ron Donkersloot's credit, he too saw the wisdom in this arrangement, if we would be willing to stay on beyond our one-year arrangement. Colleen and I wrestled—were we prepared to give some additional years to the Rehoboth cause? At last, we decided to do so, and then made the difficult call to Mr. Kamps asking to be released from our agreement, to which he assented. Colleen and I sat in my office and wept—but just then our friend Steve Timmermans rounded the corner outside. I raised the window, asking him to come in. He was just the calming voice we needed.

Ron became the "inside guy" overseeing education, and I was "outside," traveling widely to build relationships with potential donors. Thus, we called our Parent News column "The Ins and Outs," as noted a couple columns hence. Ron was an incurably cheerful guy who built wholesome relationships with the Native community and the staff.

Eventually, he chose to make the difficult decision to return to a role as an Elementary Principal at the neighboring Indian Hills of the Gallup School District. Ron and MaryLou made significant contributions to the Kingdom, from Crownpoint Christian School to Rehoboth School to RMC Hospital to Bethany Church—to be sure, substantial gifts.

Tim and Mona Stuart—this story starts in the lobby of Sonlight church when a young couple walked in by mistake. They were looking for Sunrise Baptist and ended up Sonlight CRC. Met by the irrepressible Paul Van Zanten, he greeted them and shoved them into Newcomers class close to where they were standing. Colleen and I taught that class for years, and thus met Tim and Mona.

It was the start of a rich friendship that was enhanced by Tim's being of partial Native blood. When we decided to return to NM in 2000, the Stuarts likewise became intrigued by the possibility of working at Rehoboth. The high school principalship opened in '02, and we promptly hired Tim who was well-trained, talented, and charming.

The Stuarts were with us for four years, and their influence was substantial. Tim was our first Native administrator and soon related nicely with our diverse student body. Rehoboth for too many years saw too much separation between Native and Anglo students. During the Stuart years, that began to breakdown, and at last the kids were sitting together in the Dining Hall, which persists to this day. Somehow, the Lord used Tim toward that end.

In turn, Mona was a superb writer and soon found a role in our Development and Public Relations Department. I recall in particular as we sought to find new ways to tell the Rehoboth story, we would do well tell stories of Rehoboth families now into their third generation of attendance. Such was the seed for the Schaap book (see below).

Tim and Mona's instincts were toward international education, and after four years they departed for Indonesia, Singapore, and Ethiopia. The Rehoboth community honored their work. Happily, our friendship has been sustained, always thankful for their contribution to Rehoboth Christian School.

Jim Schaap—at some point around 2008, I received a letter from the distinguished Dordt College professor and writer James Schaap, that he was looking for a new adventure, having mined aplenty the Dutch Calvinist tradition. He wondered if there may be a teaching position or something at Rehoboth where he could be useful.

I wasn't sure this college prof could easily adapt to high schoolers. But surely we could use his writing skills. In fact, the project that Mona Stuart and I had discussed quickly came to mind. When presented to Schaap, he warmed up to the idea. Rather quickly we decided to identify a dozen "old-time" Rehoboth families, interview them and tell their stories of growth and struggle and faith.

Jim and I needed to team up, given Native reluctance to open up their hearts to a White guy from the Midwest. Having been around for a couple decades, the families took my word for it that Schaap was trustworthy. I sat in on some of the interviews, or for a portion, or not at all. We selected nine Native families and three Anglo families.

As Jim completed stories, I did some very modest editing and presented them to the families for their approval, all of whom gave their blessing with little correction. The DeVos Foundation agreed to underwrite the project and by September of '08 it was off to the publisher.

By November it was ready for distribution, which prompted us to gather the twelve families in the "newish" middle school. Jim Schaap came for the event. As we gave each family five free books, Jim shared one unforgettable quality or lesson about each family. It was precious and poignant. The families lingered late into the evening, taking pictures and signing each other's books. The spirit was of the Spirit.

As we departed, Jim observed, "I am not sure I will ever experience on this side of glory what heaven will be like, the good feelings, the laughter, the cross-cultural friendship." Such summarized one of the finest hours of the century-old Rehoboth story.

The Ride to Window Rock—Window Rock is the capital of the Navajo Nation. It is the home of President's office, the Courts, and the powerful Tribal Council. The Navajo government is much less uptight about the separation of church and state than the U.S government. To their credit, the Navajo people understand that spirituality relates to all of life. Thus, never was it said about our efforts for support to be a violation of the separation of church and state.

However, that did not mean politics and sheer favoritism did not enter into the process. The Nation had taken over the old Navajo Methodist mission in Farmington and turned it into a place where the traditional religion was favored. So our first effort was a modest request for $125,000, which after several trips to committees was granted by the full Council.

The next year, we increased our request to $150,000. Again, plenty of trips to Window Rock, but that year our first graders came sing to the Council. Their teacher, Elsie Belone, was also the Navajo language teacher, so those kids could sing several songs in Navajo. As are all the classes at Rehoboth, there is a mixture of races, but all the kids learn some Navajo. As they lined up to sing, I noticed some of the kids in the front row were white students. I thought, "Elsie, put those kids in the back row." But it was too late. That little choir was outstanding, receiving a standing ovation. During the brief recess, several delegates came to thank them. Others were chatting, and I heard it said, "Did you see those white kids singing Navajo, they knew their songs like the Native kids!" Lesson? Elsie got it right.

The third attempt was for a half-million for building our Sports and Fitness center. Again, lots of trips, lobbying, lunches, all taking time and costing money. Should we continue the pursuit—it did not seem to be gaining traction. One delegate accused, "You are just here to take advantage of our Navajo people." That stung! And we were not granted our request.

But here is the lesson I learned—on all those trips to Window Rock, I would get a pit in my stomach. Often, I was the only white guy present, and further, I did not know all the protocols. How to shake hands—firmly or softly? Should I greet in Navajo or English? Light-hearted, or serious? When do you stand, or sit? I was a nervous wreck—how do I act when I am the minority?

The *big* lesson—how do we suppose Navajo people feel when they are the minority coming into an Anglo-dominated setting? When they come on Rehoboth campus (though that has changed a lot)? When they fly to Grand Rapids for committee meetings or Synod? When they come into our house, sit around our table, observe the luxuries we live with as compared to theirs?

To be sure, there are many Native people who are perfectly comfortable in such cross-cultural settings—they have been around and learned the protocols.

But many have not, are less cross-culturally comfortable. And they too have a pit in their stomach.

Opinion & More

Gallup Independent: Let's Play Ball

Let's play ball! Such is the well-used phrase of coaches and umpires calling athletic teams to action. Simple enough, it would seem. But is it? In our culture today, do we even remember what it means to "play?"

A partial answer to the question comes from Gordon Dahl, "We worship our work, we work at our play and we play at our worship." Ouch!—we "work at our play?" On what basis can we make such a statement?

Allow me to try to make the case but follow with an example of wholesome play.

The professional athletes, of course, hardly play at all. It is a job for which they are often paid millions of dollars. Good athletes "work" during the entire off-season to get better at their "play" during the season.

How about the Olympic model? These folks often work for years (not "play" for years) to qualify for the Olympics. For most, there is nothing "amateur" about it—it is an obsession.

Big-time college athletics these days is loaded with exploitation, and the notion of "playfulness" being a part of Division I sports is a joke.

And the purity of high school athletics is an endangered reality. The pressure on fragile teenagers by communities, coaches and parents quickly can take the play out of the activity. To play 20 basketball games during the off season no longer cuts it—40, 50, or 60 is the standard for many high school teams these days.

All of this gloom and doom was contrasted for some of us last week Thursday, when the Rehoboth softball girls played Menaul for the regional championship at Ford Canyon. Two evenly matched teams played nose to nose into extra innings. Smiles plentiful, sportsmanship obvious, competition real.

The same spirit prevailed in the stands amongst parents and supporters from both schools. Everyone was having a dandy time cheering for kids, acknowledging good plays on both teams, and feeling sorry for those who made the occasional error.

This was all enhanced by a pleasant gentleman behind the microphone, Mr. Chavez, whose editorial comments and ongoing conversation with the crowd brought smiles to everyone's faces. There was a playfulness about the entire event—it felt so good.

Rehoboth won the game in the bottom of the 8th inning by what seemed like divine intervention. The joy and jumping of the victors was delightful, the sadness of the other team genuine. Such is play and competition—part of it is the risk of losing.

I ask this question—how often do we see examples of such play? Do we still remember how? Do we know how to "play" ball? Or is what we see so often distorted, out of balance, lacking in moderation?

God has built play into the fabric of his creation. For us to not play is to forsake a piece of our humanity. Note the kingdom vision of Zechariah 8:4,5: "Once again men and women of ripe old age will sit in the streets of Jerusalem, each of them with cane in hand because of their age. The city streets will be filled with boys and girls playing there."

Those of us who work at our play, or don't play enough, or play too much, thereby neglecting our work, best look at our "playlife."

It is certainly one of the areas of my life that is out of whack. Recently, I took a day off to go on a trail ride with my friend, Mike Mataya. We joined Hugh Williams and about 50 other horse people for a glorious day in the creation. Reminding myself that "this is the day the Lord has made, let us rejoice and be glad in it" (from Psalm 118:24 ESV), I was also feeling guilty about not being at work.

I comfort myself, and you, with the biblical notion that usually we need to first be thinking right about something before we can begin acting right. I am hopeful that if we begin to think right about play, we will begin to redeem the role of play in our schools, our communities, and our personal lives.

Ron Polinder
Executive Director. Rehoboth Christian School

Gallup Independent: The Outrageous Idea of Sportsmanship, Circa 2008

The need for this article occurred to me sometime during the first half of the Navajo Pine/Rehoboth basketball game a week ago today. It is born out of the heat of battle between two teams, two sets of fans, two communities, though one could easily substitute any two schools in America and come to the same conclusion.

What is about to be shared here is truly outrageous! Most folks, if they get beyond these opening paragraphs, will conclude that I am losing my marbles. These ideas for many will be outlandish, excessive, over the edge.

And they come to this page from a flawed and fallen soul who has not always practiced what he is about to preach. So I am preaching to myself, and allowing others to listen in. It is a sermon I have to bring up nearly every game I go to, and being a veteran school administrator, that means hundreds of ballgames in my career.

The first outrageous idea is that we are "playing" another team. One cultural critic Gordon Dahl has noted that these days we "worship our work, work at our play and play at our worship." When we go to another gym, we go to "play." That would suggest we need to lighten up and not act like our entire self-concept as a school or community is going to depend on whether we win or lose, and how well some teenagers are "playing" the game.

The second outrageous idea is that we should love the other team, welcome them, and thank them for coming. If they had not come, we would not have anyone to play with. We can only have a game if those good folks show up, so let's show our gratitude for all the miles they drove to play with us. The essence of competition is that two parties (or more) have agreed to come together to play and compete. In the process, the other team will enable us to *enjoy* the God-given gifts and talents of all those represented. Imagine loving the other team—that is absurd—or isn't it?

If that were the case, we would not likely tease the other player when they shot an "airball." After missing a free throw, we would likely not yell "let's have another one, just like the other one." Instead, we would compliment the other team, their fans, and thank them for coming to our school. Never would we taunt our neighbors.

A third outrageous idea is that we would even have respect and admiration for the referees. Imagine what kind of game we could have if we did not have referees? It would be chaos—it would not be a game. There could easily be injuries, and maybe even a brawl if those good officials did not keep control. Surely Kevin Jones and Danny Lujan did us all a huge favor last Saturday by calling a good, tight game. Thank you, fellas—and forgive us for not lining up afterward to express our appreciation.

The next idea will seem less outrageous until we examine the behavior of fans even towards their own players. To be sure, there is often much adoration of one's own team. But what happens when they start messing up? Then one hears all kinds of advice from fat old fans who could barely run down the floor. "Pass the ball!" "Don't dribble so much!" "Drive for the bucket!" Insults are hurled, even within earshot of a player's parents. Shameful, outrageous I would say—at least let us be positive toward our own precious kids!

Well, you add all these outrageous ideas up, and it comes out to be *sportsmanship*. Honoring the other team, respecting the officials, cheering for your own kids—that is how we can create an atmosphere that will bless our community.

There is really a very simple and loving solution to some of the bad stuff that happens at games. Be positive, positive, positive!

Cheer for your team, not against the other team. Positive cheers are awesome, negative cheers are awful!

Notice how often the refs get it right! Admire the giftedness of players on the other team! Reach out and shake hands with a fan from the other team!

This for Navajo Pine—what a terrific team you have, and supportive fans! You played well and made us better in the process. We look forward to another good game at our place in a couple of weeks!

We love our basketball around here—let's make sure we love each other in the process!

Gallup Independent: "Defining Religion - Culture – Identity" Circa 2007

More accurately this title should be "*Toward* Defining Religion, Culture and Identity." It is foolish to think that one could clarify these terms in a mere 750 words. But can we move toward clearer definition and better understanding? Having returned to live in New Mexico now five years ago, there is clearly enormous confusion and misuse of these terms. Religion, for many, is synonymous with culture. Identity is complicated and confused by issues of religion and culture. The confusion regarding these concepts crosses cultural lines. Some Native Americans easily equate and interchange culture and religion. Some Anglo-Americans want to deny any relationship between religion and culture. Radical Muslims equate everything American with Christianity.

All of the above messes with one's identity and sense of self. Practically, this comes to expression in the following examples:

- Navajo Christians are often made to feel like they are lesser Navajos because they no longer subscribe to traditional Navajo religion. Their frybread may be superb, their mutton stew outstanding, their use of the Navajo language impeccable, their family and clan relationships in harmony, and yet somehow they are second-class Navajos? Hogwash! Such a projection reflects the inappropriate equation of religion and culture. It is fully possible to be culturally Navajo and spiritually Christian.
- Secular Americans would deny the right for religious Americans to allow their religion to influence how they live in culture. They desire religion to be privatized. So they are offended by religious claims about marriage, sanctity of life, or wholesome sexuality. They make the opposite mistake of the above example and desire for religion to have little or

no voice in the culture. Here too, I say, "Hogwash!" My religious faith has enormous implications for how I live culturally. As a Christian, I am always trying to transform the culture – even this article is an attempt to influence how we live together.

- Radical Muslims identify America as the great Satan. They too mistakenly equate culture and religion. Because America has a significant percentage of serious Christians, they believe that all the cultural manifestations are a result of Christianity. MTV, Jerry Springer, and Howard Stern are the antithesis of Christian faith and morality, but they have failed to make that distinction.

- All of the above confusion contributes to serious identity crises. If the only way one can be a true Navajo is to believe in traditional Navajo religion and speak the Navajo language, then there are going to be thousands of Navajo youth and adults who will spend much of their lives trying to be someone who they are not. They will over-reach trying to "prove" they are the real thing. Christians who happen to be Americans, if they believe the secularists, will be at best muted (or mutated) Christians who actually buy into the notion that their faith has nothing to say as to how they do business, politics, or entertainment. Their identity as Christians has been compromised.

- Then there are those Americans who actually think they are Christians because they believe this nonsense about a "Christian" America. They identify themselves as Christians if they believe in the Constitution, know a couple of the 10 Commandments, and salute the flag. They need to know that America never was or ever will be a Christian nation. Influenced by Christianity? To be sure, but never to be identified as authentically Christian.

All of this to say:

- *Religion* is recognition on the part of humans that there is a transcendent being(s) entitled to obedience, reverence, and worship
- *Culture* is a way of living and a set of values built up by a group of people over a period of time and passed on to the next generation.
- *Identity* is the condition of being oneself, which may or may not have a sameness with one even several groups.

If we were to stay true to these definitions, there would be much less misunderstanding in our community, our nation and our world.

Gallup Independent: Honoring the Artist but Abusing the Art, Circa 2008

One of the marvels of our region is the number of great artists who live and work here. A trip to any store that features Native American art will reveal stunning jewelry, rugs, or pottery. Don't we all stand in awe of a Navajo rug weaver who without sketch or measure can produce a tapestry of perfect symmetry? Imagine the folly of bringing together for a great banquet some of our leading artists, analyzing, honoring, paying tribute to their work, and then on the way out smashing, ripping, degrading the art pieces that we have been praising. Such behavior would be unimaginable.

In fact, what happens is that we place on our walls or display for all to see the glorious work of the hands of a great artist. We save up to buy and then protect and insure these masterpieces. And well we should!

There has been one artist who has been at work for hundreds, thousands, millions of years, but is all too often unrecognized. His name is God. We would do well to get to know him better. Don't we all enjoy being in the presence of a great artist so we can ask questions and try to figure out his technique?

When we want to get to know someone, we usually ask them about their line of work. Have you ever wondered what God does for a living? Amongst other things, he is an artist. He is creating all the time—designing landscapes, painting sunsets, carving canyons. Our great local artists are merely trying to imitate God.

Some of us go to churches where we give considerable time and money to honor the Great Artist. We sing to the Artist and at least pay lip service to the work of his hands. We make melody about "all things bright and beautiful, all creatures great and small" (Cecil Frances Alexander). We sing "praise to the Lord, the almighty, the king of creation" (Joachim Neander, trans C. Winkworth). We shout "Ah, Sovereign LORD, you have made the heavens and the earth by your great power and outstretched arm. Nothing is too hard for you" (Jeremiah 32:17).

I suspect that often God is less than impressed. Why? Because after we leave church, we proceed to ignore the beauty and creativity of the world in which we live. Worse, we degrade, pollute, abuse these great works of art that come from the Creator.

Some of my fellow Christians get more of a thrill from debating how old the earth is than from spending time appreciating and caring for the creation. It is like parents who keep watching the video of the birth of their child, and then neglect to love and nurture their precious gift.

Others are so fixated on one aspect of God's work that they never see the big picture. Their focus is on "fire insurance," all the while forgetting the fullness of what it means to be a follower and fan of the Great Artist. Anglican John Stott has said that "some Christians have a fully developed doctrine of redemption, but an underdeveloped doctrine of Creation."

I have never had the privilege of an "Art Appreciation" course. Surely it would help me see so much more in great works of art. So too, I regret that I was not a better science student. My colleague Cal Feddes has so much more material with which to praise the Great Artist. Cal, a science teacher at Rehoboth, understands the design and technique behind the creation. We Christians ought to become great scientists, and it will give substance to our singing to the "Lord of Harvest."

While I would hope to bring balance to Christians to honor and respect both the Artist and the Art, the Creator and the Creation, I fret even more about those who seem to worship the art, but don't give a rip for the Artist. This is strange behavior!

I cannot imagine buying an expensive work of art, celebrating its beauty, and not trying to get to know something about the One who created it. Oddly, much of our world today is in that boat— worshipping the Creation rather than the Creator. I want to know the one who made "mother earth" and "father sky." The Bible has a wonderful way of putting us in our place. For those inclined to discount or disregard, to defile or abuse either the Art or the Artist, Creation or the Creator, Job 12:7-10 teaches:

> "But ask the animals, and they will teach you,
> or the birds in the sky, and they will tell you;
> or speak to the earth, and it will teach you,
> or let the fish in the sea inform you.
> Which of all these does not know
> that the hand of the LORD has done this?
> In his hand is the life of every creature
> and the breath of all mankind."

Ron Polinder
Executive Director, Rehoboth Christian School

A Miscellany of Writing

God's Providence and Rehoboth's Future – 2004 Rehoboth News

Like many folks associated with Rehoboth, but certainly not all, I grew up in the Christian Reformed Church. Part of that experience, for those less familiar with the ways of that particular denomination, was the regular instruction in the teachings or "catechism" of the church. We were taught from the Heidelberg Catechism certain basic biblical truths that remain, for many of us, the framework of our faith.

While I was less than a willing student, by God's grace, one of the lingering lessons of my church experience as a youth relates to God's providence:

> *"Providence is the almighty and ever present power of God by which he upholds, as with his hand, heaven and earth and all creatures, and so rules them that leaf and blade, rain and drought, fruitful and lean years, food and drink, health and sickness, prosperity and poverty—all things, in fact, come to us not by chance but by his fatherly hand." (Heidelberg Catechism Lord's Day 10, Q & A 27)*

I cannot tell you what enormous comfort and confidence that reality gives us as we go about my task for Rehoboth Christian School—that "all things…come to us…by his fatherly hand." In the face of a $3 million annual budget, and a $6.5 million capital campaign, and trying to do private, quality, Christian education in the 3rd poorest county in the nation—well, if that doesn't test your faith, nothing will.

But the unfolding of God's plans and provisions for Rehoboth are before our eyes routinely. This issue of *Rehoboth News* is laced with stories of the Lord making straight his path. Usually it happens in the form of people, God's people, who through the prompting of the Spirit are moved to participate with us.

- Key parents, alumni, and friends of RCS present themselves at just the right time as we wind our way through the legislative process of the Navajo Nation Council in an attempt to get financial support.
- We need a road and parking lot built, and four talented couples make themselves available from Lynden, Washington, along with a civil engineer from Midland, MI, who makes his 6th trip to Rehoboth to help with such projects.
- As we build our new buildings, we think that sidewalks, curbs and gutters could possibly be done by volunteers. And two church groups from Washington and one from Michigan, all loaded with able people make plans to come.
- Planning a choir tour is an enormous project, especially if you want to include Southwestern arts and crafts to tell the Rehoboth story. Graduate artists Anthony Emerson and Elmer Yazzie offer to take the lead and accompany the choir.

- Cal Van Huekelem from *Colorado Hardscapes* in Denver hears that we are building, may need some decorative cement work and stained concrete. He comes down to check us out and departs eager to play a role in our project.
- The tale of two sisters, former students, starting a business in Shiprock leads to a story and reminds us again that God's word does not return empty, that the partnership of Christian home, church and school yield fruit.

The stories are endless—they go back 100 years, all proclaiming the mighty acts of God at Rehoboth. In the midst of all our challenges at Rehoboth Christian School, *"we can be patient when things go against us, thankful when things go well, and for the future we can have good confidence in our faithful God and Father… (Heidelberg Catechism Q&A 28).*

Ron Polinder
Executive Director

Rehoboth Creed

Rehoboth Elementary Creed, recited by K-6 students

We go to Rehoboth, a Christian school.

We believe in God the Father, God the Son and God the Holy Spirit.

We believe the Bible is God's Holy Word which is completely true. It is a lamp to our feet and a light to our path (Psalm 119:105).

God created me in His own image, and He loves me beyond my imagination (Psalm 139). He calls me by name (John 10:3). He wrote my name on the palms of His hands (Isaiah 49:16)!

At our school we are each different, but we are one in Jesus. We respect each other and honor the gifts that God has given each of us.

At Rehoboth we learn that every inch of our world belongs to God! Every subject is His. I will work hard to learn and grow in knowledge and in wisdom.

I will follow Jesus Christ and listen to His voice. He calls me to use words of kindness, to respect God's creation and all authority, and to encourage and serve the people around me.

"We will be called oaks of righteousness, a planting of the Lord for the display of His splendor" (Isaiah 61:3b).

Ins and Outs (administrator's column in the weekly Parent News)

The Ins and Outs (Spring 2003)

Surely you see something different about the look our *Parent News*. With our 100th anniversary, we thought it wise to study and update our public image. We have counted up about 10 different images or logos that we have used in publications, signs, and articles of clothing. It is time for us to unify our image. Further, we have wanted to denote that this is our centennial year.

Many of you who have gone through this know that the design and adoption of a new logo is more complicated than meets the eye, especially if you want to be somewhat democratic in the process. So we have been working at this for some months. We were particularly blessed by reconnecting with Rehoboth grad, Mike Muller, who now is part owner of a graphic design firm in Grand Rapids, Michigan. Mike was a joy to work with and was very gracious throughout the process.

Several samples were presented to our School Board, and there was virtually unanimous enthusiasm for the image that now graces the front of this newsletter. It still connects us to our previous image, and it prominently places front and center the historic name of Rehoboth. The background outline of what we locally call "Pyramid" and "Church Rock" reflects our geography and the "end of the Red Rocks" translated in Navajo as *Tse Yaaniichii*. Finally, the cross is a focal point in the form of an extended Zia/New Mexico symbol.

We have also adopted a new motto that we think captures the essence of Rehoboth Christian School. During this school year, our Administrative Staff has been discussing the best-selling book *Good to Great*. It stresses the need for companies and organizations to identify what it is that makes them exceptional and distinctive. We have wrestled with that and identified four things that makes Rehoboth an extraordinary school.

1. **Vigorously Academic**—RCS through the decades has been noted for its academic standards, and its ability to produce graduates with the skills and discipline to move on from here to college and/or the workplace and be successful. Rehoboth has never claimed to be an exclusive prep school; rather, a school that has been able to take a variety of students, and with a dedicated staff help students be accountable and productive.

2. **Beautifully Diverse**—RCS has a splendid balance and array of cultures represented in its student body. Students who are in schools where the student population is homogenous miss out on a significant learning opportunity. As our world becomes more global and diverse, young people are blest to be able to be with and learn with kids different than themselves. Rehoboth students thereby become bi-cultural or even multi-cultural.

3. **Thoroughly Christian**—RCS has always taken its middle name seriously. Christian education is more than prayer to open the day and a weekly chapel service. As important as that is, even more critical is that our young people learn that our world belongs to God, that every subject in school is taught from a Christian perspective, that Bible is the source and basis for truth and wisdom. Christian faith isn't just a hobby at Rehoboth, it permeates all of life and learning.

All of the above happens in the context of community—**Rehoboth is a small, safe, caring, learning community!** Our academic life, our diversity, our Christian expression are done in an environment where teachers and students and parents are committed to each other. In an era where many schools have become lethargic, chaotic, secular and even dangerous, the Rehoboth setting is both rare and precious.

As we prepare for our 2nd century, we believe that God has taught us lessons from the past that will shape our future. We give thanks for healthy habits that have persisted, turn away from patterns that were harmful. Boldly we believe that our best days are ahead.

And we hope a refreshed image will facilitate our telling the "ins and outs" of Rehoboth Christian School.

Ron Polinder
Executive Director

The Ins and Outs (Fall 2003)

This school year, our 101st, will go down in the annals of Rehoboth history as the year of the "big building project." To be sure, there have been other building projects, and big ones, but this one more than ever is ours. It has been locally dreamed, designed, and executed. It is a "big deal," and we want you to feel it, experience it, enjoy it.

It is wholesome to hear the old-timers tell stories from the 50's and 60's when they were involved in building projects. One senses in chatting with the veteran Roland Kamps the great pride and involvement in building our current gym—what an undertaking back then, and how it has blest this community for decades.

So too, I write this in an office that was once a dorm room. With the decrease in need for boarding facilities, this building has transferred nicely into administrative offices. But it is fun to have former students come through who helped pour the cement and lay the brick back in 1959. They take pride in it—a pride of ownership!

What will be the memory of our current students and parents about the building of our new Middle School and Code Talker Communication Center? We want there to be some of that pride of ownership! We hope elementary and mid school students will watch with awe and interest this year as their new school is being built. We hope parents will wind their way up to the building site and marvel at this gift that is being "unwrapped" right before our eyes—a gift that will bless our children and grandchildren for decades to come. Grand gifts are something to treasure and cherish and care for.

I suppose it could be seen as just another school building, not unlike those erected by the BIA or a school district. Because there is so little personal investment, there is little personal ownership. How do we prevent that from happening at Rehoboth, that we just take it for granted and ceremoniously tip our hat to a wealthy donor? How to we build a sense of longing and passion and stewardship for this new building?

I am not sure we have a simple or single answer—no doubt there are many creative ways to promote this kind of passion and pride. But I am calling all parents and staff and students to ponder how you as a family or class, church or individual can take part in the project. Let me throw out some ideas:

- Walk up and watch the progress.
- Or drive over on a weekend with your family, and before leaving, offer a prayer.
- For that matter, pray often for the workers, the fund-raisers, the donors.
- Make a prayer request at church for the school and project or suggest an offering.
- If there are opportunities to volunteer in certain parts of the project, sign up.
- Bring cupcakes or donuts or fry bread someday to the work crew on site.
- Consider how you may participate financially with your own hard-earned dollars.

You add to the list! And live one or more of them out—and God will take your gift and spirit and multiply it unto the "3rd and 4th generation."

Ron Polinder

RON POLINDER

Executive Director

The Ins and Outs (2015)

This past Monday evening provided a grand experience for the Rehoboth community. You have seen advertised the "Preparing the Way" community event. A fine turnout of 350-400 community members, parents, staff and students gathered to receive a challenge to participate in the financial support of the new high school.

It was a festive occasion—as people flowed in, the Cantabile vocal group was singing in the Sports and Fitness lobby providing a nice background for people to visit and read the displays prepared by our staff. The buzz was warm and genuine. From there, the folks gradually moved into gym where food awaited them. More visitation happened around the tables. The Winginit group formed of RCS staff members played and sang terrific music.

From there the folks moved into the seating to hear Rehoboth Stomp, more Cantabile, the Preparing the Way video and a challenge from Supt. Carol and Development Director Ken Zylstra. The evening ended with dessert and people writing checks and making financial pledges to build our new school.

A good event can often be judged by how long people hang around afterwards—so it was Monday eve. The folks lingered, visiting with each other, often with people they have not seen for a while.

There was something particularly special about this gathering—it was the mix of the people. Numerous ethnicities, Gallup folks and Rez folks, leaders and followers, long-time supporters and people new to the school—and who knows how many denominations? That is the way it is supposed to be—it is the beauty of Rehoboth Christian School.

I was asked to welcome the crowd with some opening remarks and chose to center my comments on the increasing ownership we are experiencing from the Gallup community. Now with annexation, we want to be seen as an important institution in the greater Gallup community, one of their schools that they can promote and be proud of.

Of course, with ownership comes financial responsibility, and we are seeing that happen not only from our parents, but former parents and grandparents and Gallup business owners. My honored mentor, Ed Carlisle, former RCS Board president would often remind me and our parents that "there ain't no Santa Claus." Rehoboth is here because someone is digging deep—private, Christian education comes with sacrifice, pure and simple.

So we will continue to call on you, our community, to join in the excitement and challenge of supporting this terrific school, and thereby experience the joy of giving.

Many thanks to those who give, and who faithfully continue to give—and to those staff members and sponsors who staged such a grand evening. To God be the Glory.

Ron Polinder, Former RCS Supt.

Graduation Day Beauty

Did you see how gorgeous our girls were—so many dressed Native, stunning jewelry, warm smiles, happy parents! A good graduation— *"Nizhoni"* as the Navajos say. As beautiful as it was, that was only half the story, the most obvious—it was the events afterward that added texture.

Actually it started before the ceremony at the Ballenger brunch. Classy, as one would expect from Virginia; we were gabbing with some seniors over enchiladas, one of whom had tested us severely. How they had grown-up, how comfortable they were in chatting with us older adults, how they talked about their future. It was beautiful.

After graduation, we hustled to the Largo gathering. Funny John and sweet Brenda making everyone feel welcome—practicing hospitality that they learned in their Native churches growing up. A Christian mom and dad, cherishing these moments with their only child, with Christian relatives, unto the third and fourth generation, all around. It was the Church. Christ and his church have made John and Brenda and Jessica so gracious and modest and loyal—the fruit of the Spirit pours out of this family. Beautiful fruit!

To the Jones—we all know that nobody can put on an event like the Jones. Efficient, orderly, warm, with Grandma Elizabeth at the controls—celebrating Jacob, who is a man, and has been a man in the house for a good while. Home, church, school? —see Jacob! The occasion planned months in advance by Auntie Felicia, who charged each of her 10 siblings $20 a month, beginning in October of '08, to pay for the party. Speeches, testimonies, and then Pendleton gifts, none more precious than to Lorretta, whose tears barely enabled her to say, "No one has ever done this for me before." Beautiful! The Jones—a beautiful family.

Now the Terry's—big, warm crowd—Crownpoint and Tohatchi people and points in between, lots of Holyans, rodeo folks—for SunniRose and Ashley's graduations. A previous generation left Rehoboth estranged, but they have come back, reconciled. And at enormous sacrifice—just consider the miles from Crownpoint, to all those games, concerts, board meetings. Aunt Betty helps. Harrison Henry gives ringing endorsement for Christian education. Mom Jo Ann thanks us for letting her kids hang out at our house during meetings—Colleen would make them supper, sometimes leftovers. Such a small thing created such appreciative tears, and a Brent painting. Those tears were beautiful.

Raymond, Colina, Felicia, Chris Yazzie—in some ways an unlikely Rehoboth family, given their traditional and Mormon tendencies. But what a grateful family! Raymond attended Rehoboth for only his sophomore year in the 70's and testifies how that one year made such an impact on him—wishes he had finished . . . this coming from one of the most successful Native artists in the country. We have known portions of this extended family for 40 years—what is God up to in this Yazzie clan? What will be the Kingdom end? A beautiful adventure!

Hustle to Esco and Anna—will they still be partying? They were; celebrating that Daniel, what a great kid to celebrate. Too, we have known beautiful Anna since she was a little girl and God has blessed her with those beautiful boys—talented, musical, leaders, fun! And that smiling stepdad with his legendary *pasole*! If you know Grandma Maudine, you know where much that grace and charm comes from—Southern beauty!

Whew!! Is there any energy left for Kamps, Cherneys, Holwerdas—of course, but let's go put on some jeans. Parked in the driveway was the outrageous VanDrunen Tin Bean, adding to the color and caffeine of this glorious day. Bryan and Linda's place was teaming with people, all now rather stuffed and worn out, in the mood to sit in a soft chair and have some winding down conversation. What a mixture—not a melting pot, but a crazy quilt of tribe and tongue and nation—sharing, reminiscing, celebrating. Beautifully diverse!!

May 23, 2009—a beautiful day in the life of Rehoboth Christian School!

Ron Polinder
Executive Director

Cheerleading

Already in my first stint at Rehoboth as principal, I would occasionally lead the student body in a cheer. *Goooooo Lynx* (the RCS mascot) (three times) and then *Go, Fight, Win!* I only did in close games, when our players and fans needed a boost. In becoming principal at LC, I did the same for the Lyncs.

In moving back to Rehoboth in 2000, a few alums remembered that cheer and urged me to revive it one more time. So I did, somewhat selectively, always at the crucial point in the game. It does take some guts to do it—you must be willing to make a spectacle of yourself. Most Native people, given their instinctive shyness, would likely never do such a thing, but what would you expect from a loud-mouth white guy?

Our last year there, we drove to Farmington to play Navajo Prep to watch our girls play. We were not favored to win, and too often got beat by them. During half-time, they had a long ordeal honoring all kinds of former players, overextending normal half-time break. By the end of the third quarter, we were down seven or eight points, and I knew it was time to lead the cheer if we were going to have a chance.

I went out to start the cheer and their A.D. promptly came out to tell me to get off the floor. I pleaded my case, noting I was the superintendent and led this cheer routinely at our school and other schools. He was not convinced, nor was I. He told me he was going to turn me into the NMAA, to which I said then I was going to turn him in for having such a long half-time show.

All the while, our fans are observing this to their great delight—watching their Superintendent get the boot, but only to see him refuse to leave, and proceed with the cheer, which they joined in with more enthusiasm than ever.

It was a few months later that we would be leaving Rehoboth permanently, and parents would express their concern that we were departing. Ironically, they did not ask about my successor, or indicate that my leadership would be missed, or question who would be doing the fund-raising. No, no, no, they asked, "Who is going to lead our cheer?"

Yet another lesson in humility!

Cheerleading

Native American Education: One (mostly) Successful Story

Ben Gibson's articles these past months (published in CPJ's Capitol Commentary c. 2015) regarding Native American Education have been instructive, and may I say typical. Ben (with whom I share a hometown, Lynden WA) is to be commended for devoting two years of his life immersed in one of the greatest educational challenges of our time. Native education around the country, even continent, remains a grim story. We hear talk about failing inner city schools—merely add "inner city and reservation schools" and you get the picture.

My story offers some hope, but not much because of the injustice in the funding of American education. It happens that there is a private, Christian school in Gallup, New Mexico called Rehoboth Christian School that has started in 1903 by the Christian Reformed Church to serve Navajo and Zuni children. Rehoboth was one of four mission schools, the other three started by the Methodist in Farmington, NM, the Presbyterians in Ganado, AZ, the Roman Catholics in St. Michaels, AZ. These old mission schools did most of the early education for Navajo people, and their graduates were often the early leaders of the Navajo Nation. Unfortunately, because of lack of funding, the Presbyterian and Methodist schools closed in the 70's.

To be sure, these were not perfect schools, and more than a few serious errors of judgment were made through the decades. Particularly, there were years when students were punished for speaking their Native language and there were some painful experiences in the boarding schools. Many of these mistakes were rooted not in a mean spirit as much as the sheer lack of respect for Native culture, language, and religion. The white folks reflected the dominant culture, and they were often determined to acculturate the Natives.

When Rehoboth celebrated its 100th anniversary in 2003, we included a "Day of Reflection" which ended with a time of "Confession and Reconciliation." It was a powerful, sometimes tearful experience. Upon the advice of one of our elder statesmen Edward T. Begay we published summary proceedings with full-page ads in two local newspapers, including the Navajo Times.   L i n k : http://www.rcsnm.org/confession.pdf

In spite of these errors of the past, Rehoboth did a lot right through the decades, including the delivery of quality education for hundreds of Native young people. A Rehoboth education came in the context of accountability, discipline, and a culture of success. Several 8th grade grads were part of the WWII Navajo Code Talker experience. When a high school started in 1948, many graduates went on to earn college degrees as well as successful military careers. Prior to that, in the early 2000's, the Speaker of the Council, the Supreme Court Chief Justice, the Attorney General, and several highly place Navajo Nation Division leaders were all Rehoboth graduates.

Today, Rehoboth has a student body over 500 students. All families pay at least partial tuition, some full tuition, though more than half the student body qualifies for free and reduced lunch. It is likely one of the most diverse Christian schools in the nation, with 2/3 of the student body being Native, and the rest a mixture of Hispanic, Caucasian, Ethiopian, Filipino and more. The percentage of Native teachers is also steadily increasing.

Dating back to the early 70's with the advent of Red Power, Rehoboth parents wanted a stronger voice in the governance of Rehoboth school. Given the authority from Christian Reformed Home Missions, a local School Board with a Native majority took over the day-to-day operations of the school. With that came greater responsibility for the financial affairs of the school. Tuition now covers 38% of annual operating costs, which is remarkable given the average income of our parents. The transition to local control has been highly successful.

Financially, substantial support comes from Christian supporters around the nation, most of CRC roots. While the actual financial support from the denomination has ended, the entire campus has been deeded to the Rehoboth School Board. This carries significant meaning—how many Native people actually own their own school, with no government strings attached?

Rehoboth now graduates between 40 and 50 students each year. Over 90% of our students go on to college or the military, which is remarkable given half of Native students are still not graduating from High School. Over a dozen of our students have earned a Gates Millennium Scholarship and many others a Daniels Scholarship.

What has led to the ongoing success of this school? One, we didn't quit—for 112 years, we have been trying to learn and do it better. Secondly, our parents are involved, e.g., we get 100% participation in K-8 parent/teacher conferences, and 70% at the High School. Third, we have had a relatively stable staff with enormous dedication, some serving for an entire career. Fourth, there is that sense of parental ownership, of taking responsibility for their children's education—the culture surrounding the school is simply markedly different from the neighboring schools.

All of this is in large part a result of having never wavered from our mission of being a Christian school. Rehoboth has never compromised its Christian heritage or Biblical roots. Many students come from families that are 3rd and 4th generation Christians. But in many parts of Indian country as a neo-traditional Native religion emerges, the work of Christian missionaries and mission schools is disparaged. It is not politically correct to support a school based on Christian faith.

So this bitter irony—Rehoboth Christian School, which recently was named one of the 50 best Christian schools in the U.S (http://www.rcsnm.org), which is arguably the best school in the nation serving Native students, which has a waiting list and would triple in size if there was choice in education, which offers quality education in an entire region of failing schools—is systematically ignored by the power brokers because of its middle name. Justice in (Native) education continues to be "a long road to freedom " (Nelson Mandela).

Ron Polinder

CHAPTER 14

COMING HOME (AGAIN): THE END OF A SOJOURN

Published in Gallup Independent (2009)

A sojourner is someone who stays for a while but is not a permanent resident. That describes my wife and me as we approach our last month in New Mexico and write this final article for the *Gallup Independent*. At the end of June, we will be moving back to our "rez" in Washington, where we both grew up. To us, Lynden, Washington is still "home."

We have been tempted, twice, to convert to New Mexico. We first came in 1968 for what we thought would be for a couple of years and then we would retreat to middle America. Two years became 14, split between Ft. Wingate and Rehoboth. We returned in 2000, for one year, and that has become nine years. It would appear we were almost persuaded.

Possibly Native people understand it better than most—the lure back to roots and land and place. While we have grown to love the blue and the brown of NM, we are still oriented to the green and the gray of WA. As we traveled back and forth for a combined 23 years, we learned to love the diversity of creation and culture. We really have two homes.

But we now say farewell to our second home, which at once we love and occasionally loathe. We love the blue sky, though not the nasty spring winds. We love Gallup people but wish this town would clean up. We love New Mexico but wish we could find more excellence.

All of which prompts some more reflection on what we have come to honor and admire, or regret and scorn.

Some easy ones—the great burgers at Glenn's, the breakfast burritos at Aurelia's, the friendliness at Earl's, the patty melt at the Roadrunner, served by Maribell. And how are we going to find good green chili in Washington?

Favorite writer—Elizabeth Hardin-Burrola, who consistently writes with fairness, insight, and sensitivity. And speaking of journalism, have we not been wonderfully blessed by Van Drunen and Haveman publishing the *Gallup Journey?* Too, that little paper of Hartsock, *Town Talk.*

A couple of wholesome adventures—this column in the Weekend Edition which started in '02 and gives voice to the spiritual life underlying this community. Religion and faith are too often neglected in the public square and discourse. And then there is the Red Rock Coalition, gathering the High School principals in the county for friendship and professional enlargement - thanks to a Rehoboth/Gates grant aimed to boost our schools.

My biggest concern for this community? The lack of authentic economic development that will provide honorable, livable-wage jobs. And the lack of quality education, which is far below standard and worse than most folks realize. (Europe and Asia continue to kick our behinds.) By the way, there is a solution: involved, committed, supportive parents and good, hard-working teachers, and most problems are solved. And that doesn't cost a lot more money.

The biggest community farce? The Fire Rock Casino, draining resources from the 97% Native families who walk through the door. Gallup business folks, once in favor of the concept, are feeling the drain. And that is only economics; consider the long-range social blight!

Deep concerns that nobody dares to talk about? Illegitimacy and sexual abuse. And men who beat up their wives, though that one is finally getting some attention. We will not miss the painful headlines in this paper reminding us daily of the violence, abuse, even murder that some families and children have to live with.

Greatest joy—when young people move on, well-prepared for their next level of education, with values and morals that will bless them for a lifetime, and a worldview that is biblically based. Or to quote III John:4: "I have no greater joy than to hear that my children are walking in the truth."

Greatest privilege—to be entrusted with leading Rehoboth Christian School for nine years, by a School Board of 15 people, who never quarreled, but were consistently sensible, thoughtful, and godly. And to work with a staff of enormous talent and dedication—whose hearts are as big as watermelons, and whose Christian faith is solid and seeable.

Working For Calvin

Calvin College Down on the Farm

From time to time, I have the urge to write some things that are on my heart. Last week, I hung out at the Lynden Fair, the finest fair in all of Washington. I went every day for at least part of the time—it's a great place to do Calvin work. And I was inspired to write this piece after seeing again the old family picture not only on display by my brother's cows, but also included in the beautiful 100th anniversary hardcover book of the fair.

Please view the picture below, note the sweatshirt, and then read "Calvin College Down on the Farm" following the picture.

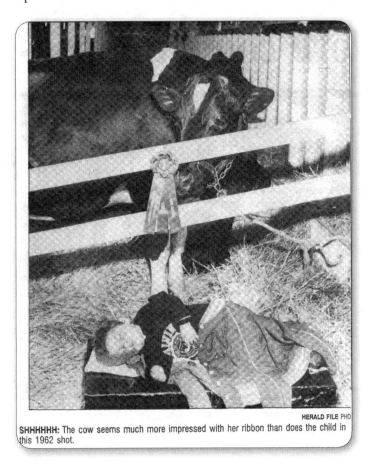

HERALD FILE PHO

SHHHHHH: The cow seems much more impressed with her ribbon than does the child in this 1962 shot.

This picture was taken in 1962 at the Northwest Washington Fair in Lynden, WA, published in the **Bellingham Herald**, and actually sent on the AP wire around the country. That is my little sister

Karen, born the previous year, just a month before our oldest sister, Eleanor, headed off to Calvin College. Eleanor, the first in our family to go to Calvin, came home with a Calvin sweatshirt. For what must have been a cool summer day, Karen wore the sweatshirt bearing the name of the college we came to love. It was show day and our cow, Ronelee Stylemaster Ethel, was grand champion.

But the picture represents much more than our family in some ways. It represents a piece of Calvin College that rarely gets much thought or attention. One wonders how many students came to Calvin having grown up on family farms—my guess is it would be thousands. And most of those folks, I propose, would be grateful for the privilege of their education at Calvin College, and the education they received back home on the farm. Life on the farm and a Calvin education was a good mix.

There is an unfortunate arrogance that crept into our tradition and culture—that is, it didn't take a lot of smarts to be farmer, or if you could not do anything else, you could always farm. I suspect most of us can remember off-handed remarks from a teacher or classmate who looked down their noses at farm folks. Herb Brinks tells of a Reformed pastor from the State Church in the Netherlands who described our lowly Afscheiding forebears as "dumber than the cows they fed."

I never bought it. I was always proud of my agricultural roots. I knew my dad and mom were good farmers—together, our family, each doing our share, made the farm work. When I headed off to Calvin College in 1964, I suppose I was the only freshman to have a picture of his favorite cow on the bulletin board. And my new friends on 2nd floor VanderWerp were intrigued. Pre-med student Don Batts and others loved to converse about cattle, their anatomy, physiology, and genetics. My plan was to do two years at Calvin and then follow my brother Sherm to WSU Ag school—until I met up with freshmen Chemistry. I soon realized I wasn't smart enough to be a farmer.

It is not to Calvin's credit that our sister college in Sioux Center, IA was the first to start an Agriculture program. Given the vast amount of agriculture in the Dutch tradition, we should have applied our theology decades before the 70's when Dordt finally took up the task. Calvin professor Janel Curry has asked, "What theology sits in the tractor seat?" Good question! Calvin College could have shaped a theology of stewardship and had enormous influence in American and Canadian agriculture. If we had pre-Med, pre-Engineering, why could we not have pre-Agriculture.

Happily there are examples of Calvin grads back on the farm. This spring I was able to tour with Calvin Worship Apprentices the farm of Dan and Carolyn DeGroot in Sunnyside, WA, both Calvin grads, and now Calvin parents. By the time we were finished, those young people realized that a farmer today is an agronomist, a nutritionist, an economist, a geneticist, an environmentalist, a veterinarian, an accountant and manager of people and resources. Here in my hometown, classmate

Rod DeJong's three boys, with their Calvin education, have joined full-time in the family dairy farm. Son Mark is now on the Friends of Agriculture Board in our county.

And there are no doubt dozens of others—this spring in Montana I met Dell and Nell Kamerman, dairy farmers in Manhattan, MT, who have nine children, seven of whom attended Calvin College, three of whom are now back on the family farm. Speaking of Montana, Calvin College is fortunate to have a rancher on the Board of Trustees, Dale Venhuizen, former President of the National Hereford Association. Dale and Nancy have four daughters, all Calvin grads, all of whom know their way around that ranch. In the 80's, modest Jersey farmers, Bert and Ruth Tjoelker, from neighboring Sumas, WA, had four kids in four years, all at Lynden Christian, and then all at Calvin College—it must've set a record of some kind. Those farm and ranch kids thrived at Calvin!

Way back in the 60's my dad delightfully reported that President Spoelhof visited the Harm teVelde farm in Southern California. Harm was so impressed with the President that he gave the name "Spoelhof" to one of his prized young bulls.

The current Hekman Library was renamed in the 90's after the Hekman family, which was represented then by entrepreneur and businessman Edsko Hekman. A little-known fact of Calvin history is that Edsko also was part owner of a dairy farm in Colorado, Paclamar Farm. At one time, they owned the two best registered Holsteins in the world. I had the privilege of being on the Board of Trustees at the time and at the reception I talked to the elderly Hekman.

I said, "You had some good cows in your day."

"Yes," he said, "we had two real good ones."

"That would have been 'Milly' and 'Snowboots,'" I retorted.

I shall never forget the warmth of that Hekman smile! Nor the delightful incredulity of President Diekema that we would be talking about cows at such a distinguished occasion in the old Manor House.

Sometimes in our Calvin College world, we can be a little too easily impressed with the big bucks and high test scores. I thought it worth reminding ourselves at the start of a new year that lots of Calvin families are pretty ordinary folks who love their kids and their college and are scratching to make it affordable. They send their kids to Calvin praying that they will more fully come to know God, his Word and world. It happened in our family, four of us, having graduated, including that little girl napping on the tack box and sisters Eleanor and Marge—and now a batch of the next generation. For many of us, it started on a farm—thanks to the likes of Ethel, good crops, hard work, and God's blessing.

Ron Polinder
August 2010

Letter to Manhattan Elders

Board of Elders
First Manhattan CRC
7950 Churchill Rd,
Manhattan, MT 59741

Dear Brothers,

We received word recently that you declined an offer to have our esteemed retired chaplain, Rev. Dale Cooper, preach the Gospel to your congregation. We are disappointed and saddened by your decision. Chaplain Cooper has served Calvin College and the Christian Reformed Church with distinction for 45 years. He has preached in literally hundreds of churches, mostly Christian Reformed. Never has there been a complaint about his preaching, or his character. He has blessed thousands of students, including students from Montana. Frankly, this is an affront to this good servant of the Church and the Kingdom. In the spirit of Ephesians 4:25, we need to remind ourselves "we are all members of one body."

We realize that you are also trying to make a statement to Calvin College. Calvin is your college, and if you could witness all the wonderful things that happen on this campus daily, you would give thanks. At the same time, it is not a perfect place. When something goes awry, we work hard to try to make it right. We would believe the same about your congregation—surely you have been a good and faithful church through the decades. But we suspect you are not perfect either, and when something goes wrong, you diligently try to fix it. Ought we not give each other some grace in this process?

Chaplain Cooper and his wife Marcia will be worshiping with you, Lord willing, at the evening service of April 3. Following the church service there will be a "Calvin Alumni/Friends of Calvin" event in your Fellowship Hall. We want to be sure to invite you to that event so you can meet Chaplain Cooper and see how he represents Calvin College. Further, he will be leading staff devotions and chapel at Manhattan Christian School. After school, he will be doing an in-service for the staff because they hold him in such high regard. We are sure you would be welcomed guests at those events. And if you would like to meet with him personally, he would welcome the opportunity.

We have about 150 Calvin alumni in the Manhattan/Churchill/Bozeman region. We believe they have blessed your community. They have been leaders in your businesses, churches, homes, and school. Imagine your community through the decades without Calvin College—we believe it would be much diminished. Even in recent years, we have had some outstanding Calvin students from your community, one of whom, a granddaughter of your congregation, will graduate in May. Let us give thanks for each other, support each other, pray for each other. Of such is the Kingdom!

To be sure, I am the voice of a single Calvin employee who has the privilege of working for the college and representing it throughout the Northwest, including Montana. But I know that I also speak for hundreds, even thousands of parents and alumni who are enormously grateful for the gift of Calvin College and the blessing it has been to our families and our denomination. I would plead with you to give thanks for Calvin College and weigh all the blessings that flow from its devoted leaders, its talented, Godly professors, its earnest and bright students, and its over 50,000 graduates sprinkled around the globe living out the gospel.

Sincerely,

Ron Polinder
Development/Admissions Representative, Western US/Canada
Calvin College

Jeff Pluymert—My Calvin Friend and Colleague

We hardly see each other, but we can warm up the phone from time to time. It all started in the late 80's when I was elected to the Calvin Board of Trustees. Little did I know that a fund-raiser would soon be breathing down my neck. Actually, Jeff Pluyment, a Social Worker by training, had been hired by the Development Office at Calvin, and was assigned to the Northwest.

Jeff invited me out for lunch, snooping around for information as to who the potential donors maybe in Lynden. He did it in such a way that I took a shine to the fellow—those lunches became annual. And a friendship flourished. Jeff could tell a good story and welcomed mine in return. Turns out, we laughed a lot.

Our move back to New Mexico in 2000 carried with it the expectation that I would be doing some fund-raising, a new assignment for me. I decided the first person to talk to was the best fund-raiser I know, who is Jeff Pluymert. He taught me a lot—he is very good at what he does.

Eight plus years passed. We stayed in touch and he would mentor me, even introducing me to some people who became good Rehoboth donors. On one of those trips to GR, I called Jeff to inform him that Colleen and I had decided it was time for us to leave Rehoboth and take on another assignment in our "waning" years. Jeff asked, "Where are you calling from?" I indicated that I was in Grand Rapids, to which his response was, "Get your behind over here—we need to talk."

Within a couple of hours, Jeff had me convinced I should apply at Calvin to join the development staff given my Rehoboth experience. Further, he set up an interview with the Vice President for Development. Within a few weeks, I was offered a job, allowing us to live in the Northwest and also to do some admissions work. And Jeff would be my colleague.

In September of '09, Jeff came out to accompany me for a week of donor visits. In one week, we made 24 calls—we hustled, and I watched Jeff in action. He was a master at his craft—listening, questioning, joking, informing. Most notable was his love for Calvin—his deep loyalty to what Calvin was about and trying to do.

Through the years, I met Sue and his three children. A splendid family indeed, often attending Christian High and Calvin sporting events. I would follow Calvin from a distance sometimes calling Jeff mid-game. That included DIII National Championships in both men's basketball and women's volleyball—his daughter Jennifer excelling in volleyball. What joy we had and still have rooting for the Calvin teams.

My stint with Calvin lasted four years, interrupted by prostate cancer, the death in infancy Olive Hope, and then Colleen's succumbing to brain cancer. Jeff walked with me, in Middlebury, IN and then in the cemetery in Lynden. I can't think of anyone who I needed more in my hometown than my friend Jeff Pluymert.

By this time, we were true brothers—people remarked about our similarities, though he would be the younger. In one of our recent years, I decided to go diet, which agitated Jeff. He declared, "I can't stand the thought of Ron being skinnier than me." We both had success, but not enough, nor sustained. It has been noted we could survive a few months of famine.

Most seriously, C.S. Lewis said thus in *Mere Christianity*: "You have not chosen one another but I have chosen you for one another. Friendship is not a reward for our discriminating and good taste in finding one another out. It is the instrument by which God reveals to each of us the [virtue] of others."

Surely Shirley

It was the early 90's when serving on the Calvin Board of Trustees that a new member joined, an attorney from New Haven, Connecticut. Having a couple of years of Board experience, I was paired with Shirley Vogelzang Hoogstra as a mentor. It was not a big deal, except that we became fast friends—friends to this day.

Shirley and I found ourselves in agreement on many of the issues surrounding Calvin, not the least of which was a deep loyalty to the institution and profound gratitude for how it shaped our thinking and thus our lives. She was also obviously so capable, well-spoken, light-hearted, and capable of a good laugh. But, all things must end which for me was eight years stint on the Board.

Fast forward, a couple of years and Calvin was looking for a new VP of Student Life. Son-in-law Scott was named as a student representative on the search committee. Occasionally I would ask him about that experience which he enjoyed, but indicated the committee was not all that pleased with the candidates. He actually thought I should apply, which I thought beyond my capacity.

On one of those inquiries, he noted that there was some enthusiasm about a woman from Connecticut, though she was not a professional educator. Not knowing it, Scott said enough for me to know exactly who that was—it had to be Shirley. But he still thought there was enough doubt that I should allow my name to be offered, which he did to the Chairman.

Within an hour my phone rings with the Chairman urging me to apply, in fact, extending the finalists from three to four if I would submit a worthy application. Now I am thinking that they may actually be interested in me, so I scurry to put together a thoughtful application. Two days later, I get a call indicating they have narrowed the field to two, Shirley and me.

I was instructed to not make any contact with Shirley. A week later, we were both in GR for interviews. I decided to attend an early service at Sunshine church the day before my interview. As I was exiting, none other than Shirley was walking in, however, she did not see me. I did an immediate 180 turn, leaving out a back door.

The interviewing process was the most rigorous I had ever experience, essentially 12 hours. I did get the feeling that I was the back-up, knowing that they really needed a woman on the Cabinet.

And, I had a hard time imagining that my gifts surpassed Shirley's. But in a weak moment, one begins to imagine that just maybe they would choose me.

A couple of days later I got the call that Shirley was their first choice. I do remember I was disappointed, that I had talked myself into believing I could do the job. That lasted but a few hours as I considered the weight and complexity of the assignment. Even the size of the budget was intimidating. Surely, Shirley with her marvelous set of gifts had the better qualifications.

Maybe the sweetest part of this whole experience was my phone call to Shirley. She had no idea I was the other candidate, and further said, "Ron, if I had known it was you, I would have withdrawn." We wept together over the phone marveling at the good providence of God. And Shirley went on to serve with great skill and distinction. Thanks be to God!

I believe the year was 1998, and now over 20 years later, some amazing things have transpired:

- Shirley's husband, Dr. Jeff, became the pediatrician for Taryn, Seth, Shae and Tayva.
- Each visit to campus afforded me a wonderful visit with Shirley. Our friendship only deepened—we are like a brother and sister.
- When told about a Dr. Vogelzang in Las Vegas, and realizing he was a 1st cousin, she was quick to write a note urging him to take me on as a patient, which he cheerfully did
- Shirley's leadership was marked by advocating for the rightful role of women faculty, staff and students.
- Shirley became the President of the Coalition for Christian Colleges and Universities, (CCCU) requiring a move to Washington DC, and commuting on weekends. Her leadership has been stellar.
- The CCCU has various workshops around the country for college leaders, including a June gathering at Cedar Springs in Sumas, affording us at least an annual visit.

It was that 2012 visit that was so remarkable. Shirley as very aware of Nana's brain cancer, in fact wrote in Caring Bridge routinely, maybe more than any other. Just three weeks before Nana's passing, Shirley came for her visit. The sweetness of that visit, which included Shirley's feeding her some ice cream, conversing, singing, even laughing, was most precious – as much a blessing for her as it was for Colleen.

And this visit, just days ago from this writing, revealed Shirley has breast cancer, already having undergone treatments. The prognosis is hopeful, but prayer is requested.

Such is the story of my very dear friend, Shirley. Surely, she has been one of my richest blessings.

CHAPTER 15

COLLEEN'S CANCER AND PASSING

Nine grands

Rushton and his Nana

Desolation?

It is not an accident that I chose this portion of my life to be written last. I postponed this project as long as possible. You likely already guessed, this is about Colleen's journey with brain cancer, glioblastoma to be precise. Here is a revisit.

In March of 2011, Colleen and I were attending the State Basketball Tournament in Yakima, WA, which included, as usual, both Lynden Christian boys' and girls' teams. These were always grand times for the school community, as our teams often placed well. It was Saturday morning, and we were looking forward to some good games.

We were actually staying in Judy's apartment--Judy had gone to Spokane for the Sunnyside Christian games. Colleen was relaxed on the couch when suddenly there was commotion. **She went into seizure**. It was horrible, and I didn't even know the exact address. I ran outside to the upstairs apartment, the Ellisons, who then called 911.

So much I don't remember, but at last she was loaded in the ambulance for the 40 minute drive to Yakima, the longest of trips in spite of the 80 miles an hour. We were to meet Jack and Diane Veltkamp for lunch, so I called them to meet us at the hospital. I remember the comfort of seeing our good friends waiting.

All this time, I am wondering if Colleen would even survive this traumatic event. But maybe an hour into emergency, we learned that she was gaining consciousness. Enormous relief, and soon both Diane and I were talking to her. Finally, we were given a room, from which she could undergo various tests.

Judy, home from Spokane, came to visit us Sunday. Conversation happened quite naturally. On Monday afternoon, a young resident came to share some test results showing a small spot on her brain which they diagnosed as a likely stroke. We were given the green light to be discharged the next morning.

We were able to get an appointment rather promptly with a neurologist in Bellingham whose testing seem to confirm that indeed it was most likely a stroke. But with the passing of a couple months, I noticed some other irregularities, particularly her aversion to noise. Also, she seemed to struggle with her balance at times.

By August, her eyesight seemed compromised at times, and then one eye would open wider than the other. At an August 19 wedding, I needed to hold her arm for balance as we found our seats.

The next day, with Stacia and Tom home, we took the entire family on the ferry to Friday Harbor, where the symptoms only worsened. A trip to the E.R was planned for Monday.

It was the MRI on Monday, that caused the ER doctor to ask Scott to join him to review of the scan. A short time later, they returned with the worst of news, "You have a brain tumor." It was August 22, our 44th wedding anniversary. I don't recall the term, glioblastoma, but there was clear indication this was serious. The rest was a blur.

Within a day or two, we were able to see a Bellingham brain surgeon who informed us of a new clinical trial for which Colleen could be eligible. Soon we were on our way to Swedish hospital in Seattle, the first of countless trips to meet the remarkable Dr. Foltz.

Dr. Gregory Foltz was a concert pianist headed for the Julliard School of Music when his plans were interrupted by the death of a friend from brain cancer. His story is told on YouTube, *Brain Surgeon pianist*—and we had to blessing of having him as Colleen's lead doctor. Further, Colleen qualified for the clinical trial, the first in the Pacific Northwest.

Surgery was scheduled almost immediately, with Dr. Foltz reporting positively as to the amount of the tumor they were able to remove. But a problem developed—Colleen did not wake up. Nor the next day, or the next. It was swelling they figured, but on day three, suddenly I heard my name over the hospital loudspeaker to report.

They concluded there was a "brain lock," something that Dr. Foltz had seen only twice when he was a resident. They quickly took her to surgery, and we waited much longer than expected for him to come with the result. At last he arrived, smiling, to report that the first two procedures he tried did not work. Finally, he merely irrigated the brain with a saline solution and saw the brain loosen from the skull. There was little doubt that we almost lost Colleen.

But within a couple hours, she was giving me thumbs up. Thus, onward in preparation for radiation and rehabilitation. Those surgeries seriously weakened her, even cognitively. The journey had just begun. Thanks to my kids, they set up a Caring Bridge account enabling us to keep friends and relatives updated. What happened on Caring Bridge will be told more fully below.

The days at Swedish were full—lots of Rehab, some blessed visitors, and always singing. Elsewhere in the book I have written about the consistent singing, and the rediscovery of a songbook from home *Let Youth Praise Him*. The songs of our youth enriched us tenfold. Nearly every night we ended with Cleland Boyd McAfee's lyrics "There is a place of quiet rest, near to the heart of God."

Our singing spilled over a couple of rooms to an African American family; the mama Curtistine had her leg amputated. Soon we became friends, and discovered they were a Christian family. "We've been singing in our room; would you like us to sing you a song?" Of course, and that one song became five or six or seven, and most every day depending on who was visiting. It was more blessed to give than receive.

As the month of September wore on, I was mindful of my work for Calvin. They were good to me, but I still felt the need to perform. In the coming months, that pressure remained. But I was able to get some work done as others attended to Colleen. We were given September 29 for her release. She was so eager! Yet, through tears she asked, "Am I still the same person? Will I be of value to anyone?"

But the day of her arrival home was terrific—so glad to be in her own house. Stacia came home to help, and Shawna of course. By then we had also designated Kay Koeman as the Captain. She offered as a friend and with her nurse's training, to oversee all the medical issues and caregiving. The house was ready, along with some chicken soup from her mom, Grandma Haak.

The next months were filled with treatments in Bellingham and trips to Seattle. We were overwhelmed with the numerous ways our Lynden community supported us, with well-wishes and prayers rising around the nation and the world. With the help of my sister Eleanor, friends Judy and Diane D.W., all of whom wrote on Caring Bridge so beautifully, for Stacia and Shawna coming and going as best they could, we had lots of support. All the while, Rusty and Lynette are in Bangkok, Lynette pregnant and on bed rest.

As I read Caring Bridge, I realize how much I was still on the road, and thus all the more grateful for Captain Kay. As we approached Thanksgiving and Christmas, Pastor Koeman, prayed "no more let sin and sorrow grow, nor thorns infest the ground…." While treatments seemed to be going well, the test results hopeful, the vaccine from the trial started, we knew and Colleen knew the battle was engaged, and the songs and prayers were what seemed to sustain us.

We were able to sneak Colleen into the back row at Third Church for the Christmas cantata—so good. The day after Christmas, we asked Pastor Koeman and a couple of elders to come to anoint Colleen with oil. At the same time, we had Skype on knowing that Lynette was in labor. As the gathering was breaking up, we heard the cries of a newborn baby in far off Thailand. What cause for rejoicing, well-born Henry Miles Polinder! Imagine the joy in the heart of his Nana!

Grandchildren

What may seem odd, Colleen and I planned a trip to Bob and Eleanor's in SoCal in February. It was a fine time, though I left for some of the days for Calvin work. The highlight seemed to be the Gaither concert, filled with music and humor that warmed our hearts. Long Uncle Bob's favorite group, we were filled to the brim, believing "He Touched Me" was the Spirit's extra portion of blessing.

Could it be that we would need it? But first we needed to observed Valentine's Day on the 14th and Colleen's birthday on the 15th, her 66th. Through our 50 years together, counting courtship, I would buy a goofy Valentine card and a serious birthday card. It was the 14th on which another trip to Swedish was scheduled, for another MRI. Yes, there it was, a growth in the brain that looked suspicious, and yes, we did need that touch of the Spirit.

The indication was that a follow-up MRI would be needed a month hence. And if there was growth, a new procedure called "cyberknife" would be administered. On March 13, Stacia wrote, "We did not get the news we were hoping for today." In addition to growth, there were other spots, and the cyberknife was scheduled. I confess, deep down, an ominous feeling prevailed.

The cyberknife procedures were for five days, meaning a daily 200-mile round trip to Seattle. Colleen was fitted with a special mask for the 40-minute treatment. But there was also anticipation for the arrival of Rusty, Lynette, and Henry Miles. That middle name Miles was chosen intentionally given the journey's our families had taken. But what joy there was to see this "Thai" family, and for Nana to embrace her grandson.

It happened that the first week in April spring vacations were simultaneous. The kids came up with a plan that we all meet in California, Huntington Beach no less. It included a day in Disneyland. Bob, Eleanor and nephew Rick generously arranged all the transportation for our tribe. Colleen rested and soaked in the pool for hours as the grandkids played and attended to their Nana. It was grand, a rich blessing for all.

The next week we had an appointment with our second doctor Dr. Hensen. He informed us that Colleen was not in that part of the trial receiving the Vaccine, but that now they would be giving it to her to see if it had any affect. We were both disappointed, yet pleased that she would be a recipient. They also increased the steroid doses. In reality, these are all signs that the cancer is advancing.

A trip to Calvin was scheduled, so Rusty and Lynette were home to help Captain Kay. Sister Marge came the following week from Dallas and wrote a beautiful post on Caring Bridge generating many responses. Likewise, a piece that Stacia wrote for Caring Bridge some months previous was sent to the *Banner* which came out the week I was at Calvin. Numerous comments were directed at me, but also on Caring Bridge. The title was "How's Your Mom?" in which she offered three answers, the last of which was 'she is dying.' By now, this is the reality we face and it is moving toward us.

Then my youngest sister Karen came for a week, and she entered a poignant post on Caring Bridge, followed by Pastor Ken describing a smallish church service with just our family. All of these generated remarkable responses, to great comfort for Colleen. I enjoyed reading them to her, and her comments that followed. How can I say it strongly enough—Caring Bridge with all the entries of countless folks blessed us richly.

'Mid the desolation

Mom and Stacia

Mom and Shawna

Mom, Rusty and baby

In May, Stacia came home and was here on the 17th, her birthday. We decided to invite some of Colleen's friends, most of whom had not seen her for months. It was a lovely day, and we bundled her up to sit on the back porch. The love that was poured out toward her, but also reciprocated, was astounding. That evening, this time inside, Staci and Shawna's friends came by. It was so beautiful to see these now young women embrace and talk to this dying woman who they too had come to love—a mom not unlike their moms, who would leave two young moms and a young dad motherless. The old spiritual came to mind, "Sometimes I feel like a motherless child."

Because of a certain medicine they were administering, it made sense for that to happen in our local county rather than the 200-mile round trip to Seattle. We were able to connect with a Dr. Crews, new to Bellingham, a charming young oncologist, who seemed to take a shine to Colleen. During our first visit, we even invited her to come out the Lynden. Sure enough, the next visit was a house call, no doubt orchestrated by former student Kim Kredit.

It also became time for us to engage Hospice. Stacia, being a former Hospice social worker, was so helpful in this process. And the timing was fortunate, as the morning of May 23, while resting on the couch, Colleen went into seizure, and not just one, but again and again. We called both Hospice and 911 with dreadful minutes passing before their arrival. We wondered if she would survive, but at last Hospice arrived with the right shot to settle her. She slept for hours.

Within the next couple of days, there was a rebound of sorts. She was more engaging, and this strange little interlude occurred. Nana became obsessed with apple fritters, and she was not to be denied. At times we had to scramble to Safeway to replenish. It was both comical and sad, because this was not her nature. After a few days, it subsided. And a slow but steady decline resumed.

The next month was yet a time when Colleen was conscious and able to see the grandkids and other friends or family that stopped by. But she slept more and more. By mid-June we would best describe it as "lingering." We wondered each day if the Lord would take her. And on June 30, at 7:50 in the evening, she went to be with her Lord. Actually, Grandma Haak was in the room when she quietly passed.

The long journey ended seemingly painlessly, which was our prayer. But the stark reality of a lifeless Colleen lying in her bed was a scene, a reality that reduced us all to tears. My wife, my best friend, faithful companion was gone. Stacia, Shawna, and Rusty (and mates) were now motherless indeed. 10 grandchildren were without their Nana—a sad reality.

The following days were jammed with planning for a fitting memorial service. I wanted to write a eulogy, and Stacia, Shawna and Rusty wanted to make it with voice and images—a video. It was labor intensive to create it, with music and recordings from Grandma, Auntie Gloria, and Uncle Vic—plus the four of us. But they pulled it off, ready for a July 3 service. It can still be seen on YouTube, "Colleen's Eulogy."

We decided for the funeral service that music should have an important part. Pastor Koeman stated at the outset that the service was going to be "Navajo style," that is to say "unhurried." I suspect we sang for 30 minutes, with Jack Koning at the piano and Gaye Davis at the violin. Sonlight Church was full on that busy holiday weekend. Pastor Koeman was at his best, with just the "right word," speaking of the "double portion" of blessing and giftedness that Mom had received.

We invited whoever would like to join us that evening at our place for berries and ice cream. We were blessed to have my friend Jeff Pluymert come from Calvin, and colleagues and friends from New Mexico, Lorretta Smith and daughter Nikki, Elsie Belone and daughter Philana, Carol Bremer Bennett, Ruth Hartog and Jason Zylstra. Each were given opportunity to make remarks.

The service at Rehoboth, in September, was similar, again unhurried, with Gail DeYoung at the piano and Sara Zylstra at the violin. The girls sang, Rusty prayed, Pastor Ken spoke, and we all sang together.

There was a part that was particularly unique, as we asked our Navajo friend, Elsie Belone to take the lead with singing two Navajo songs, "Victory in Jesus" and "Where Could I Go but to the Lord," songs that Native people love to sing in the Navajo language. Following Native style, the invitation was made to come forward and sing. In Native churches, practice is altogether unnecessary. What happened next will forever be with us—the people stood and came forward. It was like a human wave. Auntie Eleanor counted 70 and knew that she could not see everyone—so likely 80. They sang their hearts out, honoring Nana, and the Lord she served.

Jim Schaap described it as "one of the holiest days of his life."

The reception followed in the Fellowship Hall, orchestrated by Ruth and Ruth, Lorretta and Sue and Mohammed. The open mic gave opportunity to our friend and revered Navajo leader, Edward T. Begay, to say it best; "Look around, look at the diversity in this room, from so many different places here together—this is community, this is the church…"

The title of this chapter started out as **Desolation**. But I could not live with it. That was/is part of the story, but not near the full measure. Throughout this rendition, we have quoted and praised the Caring Bridge experience. No desolation there! And then we are reminded repeatedly that there is a heavenly home. No desolation there! Thus, the added question mark, symbolizing the paradox, the contradiction, of family and friends who grieve and the truth of our hope in Christ. Thus, Colleen/Mom/Nana—now "like a child at home" (from Isaac Watts's version of Psalm 23, "My Shepherd Will Supply My Need").

Kay Koeman: From the Bedside

I'm grateful to be at Colleen's bedside much of the time since her journey began last March. I recognize that this is a place of honor and I have felt the high privilege it has been to be in this place of caring for my friend and yours. She is such a compliant and grateful patient that I am not sure who is blessing whom.

Our families have been fast friends for 42 years and we've walked alongside each other through many dark days as well as bright ones. But we've never had a season like this—a journey together largely spent in a hospital—facing a very real enemy in brain cancer. From walking her to the door into the surgery suite, to being at her side in the neurological critical care unit and now to rehab floor, I have been privileged to watch your friend and ours face very difficult days.

From the bedside, I see our friend, my sister in Christ, as a person who came into this experience not unequipped for such a time as this. It's true that being told you have a brain tumor is an indescribable shock, and I've seen plenty of tears. But Colleen, and Ron, did not come into this storm without ballast. All their years of singing the great hymns as children and adults, marinating themselves in Scripture, and bringing so many of life's issues to the Lord in prayer have put them in a place of preparedness for this fiery trial. They are so rich in faith and friends. They have a history of God's faithfulness, and I've watched a patient whose faith is firm, even when anxieties stormed in, as they have so much during this season.

From the bedside I see a couple who 44 years ago at their wedding made vows before God, family and friends to love one another in sickness and in health. I see that pledge being carried out steadily, consistently, tenderly, in loving embraces and affectionate words.

From the bedside, I've watched a family pour out so much love upon a mother, singing to her, praying with her, kissing her, weeping with her, and, as Polinder's do so well, laughing with her.

At the bedside our day always began with reading Sarah Young's *Jesus Calling*, wondering what the Lord might have for us through her for that day. It was often so fitting that Colleen asked me to read it again during the day. Then in the night (by the way, Colleen was quick to correct me for saying *in* the night; no, the veteran teacher and secretary said, our Minnesota way of saying the phrase was not right. The *right* way was *during* the night) if she awoke, or was restless, often she asked that we sing "There Is A Place of Quiet Rest, Near To The Heart of God." We have sung it countless times. And without fail those old words have centered our hearts back into that place of quiet and peace, and afforded Colleen the precious rest she needed in her recovery.

Now I'll spend less time at her bedside and more simply at her side in her home on Rosemary Way, when, on Tuesday, she makes that happy trip to Lynden. It'll be different than a hospital room as I continue to tend to ongoing needs. She will immediately face the six weeks of daily radiation, which could exhaust more of her strength. And there will be continuing rehabilitation at the home. So "at her bedside" broadens out into being at her side in the kitchen, or the car, or the doctor's office as I continue to be privileged to escort her and her care team into this new phase of her journey into a future known only to our Father, who never leaves her side. It is all privilege. And I know that being at her side, I represent your hands and your hearts, your voices, and your smiles.

Kay Koeman

Let Youth Praise Him

Such is the title of a songbook that I and thousands of other youngsters sang out of in our elementary years while attending a CSI Christian School. The book was published by what was then called the National Union of Christian Schools, a first edition in 1949. It includes 155 songs intended to be attractive and meaningful to children.

My recollection is that we started most school days with 10 or 15 minutes of singing. Most of the classrooms had pianos, and often the teachers could play piano. Sometimes we would team up with another class.

The book had another unique feature in that there were 23 pictures sprinkled throughout the book, usually across the page to enhance the song with a poignant picture. When I talk to folks of my age group, many of them remember the images and the song that attended.

My sister Marge wanted her own copy of the book, but my practical mother was less than willing to buy one for her. Instead, she made a deal that if Marge would cut off her ponytail, she then would buy her one. Mom thought that ponytails were too much hassle—a pixie would be easier. To this day, Marge believes she got the raw end of that deal.

Like so many things in life, the book eventually fell out of favor and by the hundreds likely ended up in a dumpster, although many families also had copies and they passed them on to the next generation. So it was in Nana's family, so we had a copy throughout our married life, though rarely did we use it.

That changed in 2011 when the dreadful cancer was found in Nana's brain. Much of the last nine months of her life were spent in bed, resting and sleeping. When people came over, we often visited in the bedroom. A wonderful habit developed that we engaged in nearly every day—we sang! Before going to sleep at night or whomever was visiting during the day, we most often would sing, and usually it was from that previously seldom-used, reddish *Let Youth Praise Him* songbook, published in 1949 by the National Union of Christian Schools in Grand Rapids. It was a providential gift the Lord comforted us with.

In the course of all that singing, it became so clear to me that the book shaped me far more than I had realized. Virtually all the songs had an underlying biblical truth or theology that influenced both a worldview, but also a way of life. They expressed a faith that applied to day-to-day living. At this point in my life, I marvel with thanksgiving for all the Christian principles that were embedded in our minds and hearts.

A few examples:

#1 "The Lord is My Shepherd" with a close versification from Psalm 23, in metered poetry from the 1650 Scottish Psalter. So we essentially learned that most precious Psalm from singing it. And the picture across the page was a shepherd boy driving the sheep toward home.

#2 "You Cannot Hide from God" was a short but memorable song based on Psalm 139 (by A.H. Auckley) that got our attention and reminded us that "his eyes were fixed" on us. I suspect that song kept us out of some mischief.

#5 "He Loves Me Too" is accompanied by a picture of a little girl watering the pansies and a song that talked of little things like birds and flowers; and if God loves them, "I know he loves me too." Maria Straub was the lyricist.

#11 "For God So Loved the World" was another song that used the actual words of John 3:16, so we not only memorized it, but we learned the deepest truth of the gospel that God loves us and offers us everlasting life.

#16 From "This is My Father's World", one of the great hymns of the church written by Maltbie D. Babcock, we learned early on that our world belongs to God. Meaningful phrases like "though the wrong is oft' so strong, God is the ruler yet," and "He shines in all that's fair" reflect the providence of God.

#21 "The Seed Song" was one of my "farm kid" favorites, because of the picture of a farmer with his team of horses pulling a sulky plow. The words, by Frederick A Jackson: "Farmer, farmer, sow your seed, up the field and down, but God will make the golden corn grow where all is brown." We learned from whence the harvest came.

#29 "Wonderful Words of Life" impressed on us that the Bible was filled with "beautiful words, wonderful words" that teach us "faith and duty" and "offer pardon and peace to all." Indeed, words of life from Philip P. Bliss!

#37 We all loved the rousing "Hallelujah, Praise Jehovah." It was one of those songs where the girls would start the phrase, and the boys would come in a few notes later to reinforce it. "Let them praises (let them praises) give Jehovah, for his name alone is high," and "his glory be exalted far above the earth and sky." Psalm 148 is the direct source of the poetry.

#43 "For the fruit upon the trees, for the birds that sing of thee, for the earth in beauty dressed, father, mother and the rest..." This and several other songs taught us that essentially all of life, and the gifts that come with it are cause to repeat three times over, "Father, we thank Thee." (Mary Mapes Dodge)

#61 Several familiar Christmas songs were included, but one that we don't so much sing anymore is from Fanny J. Crosby, "Tell me the Story of Jesus, ...write on my heart every word..." Only the first verse refers to the birth of Christ, but the rest of the song tells the fuller story. It was this song that my young sister Marge and I sang at the "Grandma's Christmas program." It was our debut in singing publicly.

#70 "Master the tempest is raging. The billows are tossing high." And then the chorus would start low and softer, "The winds and waves shall obey My will, Peace be still, Peace be still" And the chorus would crescendo to the end when "the Master of ocean and earth and skies, would sweetly obey,"...and end quietly "peace, peace be still." We all loved the song (a dramatic work by Mary A Baker)—and the message!

#80 "The Ninety and Nine," taught us that the priority for Jesus was that one lost sheep. And across the page was that sweet picture of Christ freeing the lamb from the thicket. Lots of theology in those five verses of Elizabeth C. Clephane.

#93 Representative of several Easter songs was a favorite by Robert Lowry, "Up from the Grave." We loved to sing that chorus, reaching down to a C note and then belting it out as the chorus progressed.

#117 A sobering song from H. R. Palmer: but "Yield Not to Temptation" was a healthy reminder "Ask the Savior to help you...He will carry you through." The songbook was not afraid to remind us of the reality of sin.

#127 A similar song by Mary Ann Kidder that would get our attention was "Is My Name Written There?" We learned early on that there was life after death, but "the blood of my Savior is sufficient..." to see our names in the book of "the Kingdom."

#135 "Dare to be a Daniel," a challenging reminder that we were to be witnesses, and "dare to stand alone, dare to have a purpose firm, dare to make it known." I doubt that anyone who sang out of that book could forget this song by Bliss, including that line "SHOUT for Daniel's band."

#137 This song, another by Fanny Crosby, became a favorite of our family, "Give, Said the Little Stream." I suspect it was later that we caught on to the fuller meaning—as the streams and rain give to make the grass green and flowers grow, so we are called in verse three to "give as Jesus gives," to give our life away.

#145 "Bring Them In" is a missionary song penned by Alexcenah Thomas with this important image on the adjoining page, that of a Navajo mother and her little boy and two little sheep. Who would have thought that we would be called to live among the Navajo people for 23 years, during which time we tried to live out the theme of the song that we grew up with.

#139 This one slightly out of order, but for good reason. "Near to the Heart of God" became the song that we sang nearly every night during the months of Colleen's sickness. "There is a place of quiet rest, near to the heart of God"—such was the comfort we claimed. We would sing all three verses from C. B. McAfee, ending with that last line of the chorus, "Hold us who wait before Thee, near to the Heart of God."

Have I made the case—that these songs taught us some the basics of our Christian faith? And I could have easily chosen another 20 titles that would have demonstrated the same or other vital themes for our faith.

Is there a lesson here? I think so—our children should be singing, a lot, and songs that are melodic and are based on good theology. And it will never leave them.

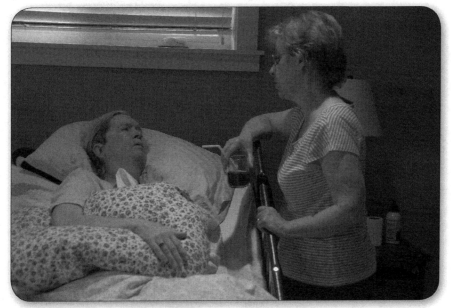

Captain Kay Koeman at bedside

Colleen Polinder
COLLEEN G. POLINDER

Colleen's perfect penmanship

Laid to Rest

CHAPTER 16

JUDY: A SECOND BLESSING

It is the sweetest of stories—the night before Colleen was to go in for surgery shortly after the brain tumor was discovered, we were alone together in her room. Out of the blue, she announced, "If I don't make it, you need to remarry."

That was the last thing I wanted to talk about, so I quickly said, "We are not going to go there—you will come out just fine." To which she responded, "And I have two women in mind for you—Judy Trull and '............'." (The second, never to be disclosed.) That ended the conversation, but not the memory.

Colleen and Judy had a long-standing friendship that leads to another story. After their 8th grade year, Judy came to Lynden from Granger, WA to live with her grandparents. She was signed up to pick raspberries in Sumas, as was Colleen at the same patch. Each morning the crew would travel on a flatbed truck to the field.

When picking raspberries, the pattern is to have two people on a row, one of each side. Neither Colleen nor Judy knew other pickers, so they were teamed together. Both being quite shy, it took them three days to begin to have conversation, thanks to some jokes coming from another row. Thus began a 40-year friendship.

Judy came back to Lynden two more summers and more raspberry picking. They took their job seriously, one year each picking a ton and thus earning a chicken dinner at Johnson's in Ferndale, which in those days was a big deal. More importantly, Colleen's family was very hospitable to Judy, calling her their third daughter.

Through the decades, there was not a lot of contact, but always a Christmas greeting, and the occasional stop as we traveled between Washington and New Mexico. That meant a grand time in their swimming pool, and thereby coming to know Judy's four kids. For Colleen and Judy, it was one of those friendships that picks up where the last visited ended—a deep, authentic friendship.

We were shocked and dismayed when one of the Christmas cards reported that Judy and husband Jim were divorcing. We had been friends, the four of us, but it did not disrupt our friendship with

Judy. During Colleen's sickness, Judy came on at least three occasions to be the caregiver for the week.

A year+ after Colleen's passing, Judy and I discovered each other one night on FB Messenger, and started chatting. Those chats became increasingly frequent, which led to a September dinner "out" for my birthday, and the start of a genuine romance. The trips between Lynden and Sunnyside increased. At some point midway we decided to have rings made by some of our Native silversmith friends Darrel and Becky Begay.

We set the date for July 19, 2014 in our backyard on Rosemary Way. Our good friend Pastor Ken Koeman performed the ceremony with his usual skill and substance. I had the privilege of singing "Shine on Us" with my two girls. It was a late morning event to which close family was invited, followed by a dinner under tent given threatening rain.

Thankfully, the weather completely cleared for our evening reception that drew a nice response from friends, relatives, and fellow-church members. We had four different styles of live music, singing off a WRS flat trailer. And Rusty's ice cream truck was a popular attraction. It was an altogether joyful event.

This was followed by an equally splendid time in Sunnyside orchestrated by Judy's friends and family. From there we honeymooned in Walla Walla and on to the Oregon Coast. It was a grand commencement to the coming years of married life. We thank God for his good providence that brought together the detail and the desire for our marriage.

Now these seven years later, we have had much joy together, though not all. As noted elsewhere, my prostate cancer has left me quite disabled with back trouble, all of which adds to Judy's load. This was especially true during the chemotherapy regimen. It also meant that I could not help as Judy moved her furniture and other household items.

Yet we have had grand times together. Judy and I somewhat at the same time developed an affection (note I did not say addiction) for Navajo rugs. Though described in detail elsewhere, we have simply had so much fun collecting—and then to watch Judy decorate with them.

Judy's eye for beauty is a gift from God. She has enhanced the Southwest theme of our upstairs and likewise enriched the Northwest/antique quality of the basement. It is so abundant, I really can't even take it all in. Many folks do not realize that she was a partner in operating a gift shop for eight years in Sunnyside, meaning she had a lot of collectables.

Most importantly is the seriousness of Judy's faith. Having faced some major trials in life, including divorce, she has not wavered from her Christian upbringing and her determination to grasp the grace of God, and to respond with a life of gratitude.

This comes to expression in numerous ways, but her ongoing role as a mother is wonderfully obvious—and I should add grandmother, and now great grandmother. She has reserved her biggest smiles for grandmothering. Likewise, she has been gracious to my kids and grandkids. Nor has she forgotten her sister and brother—she has been a good sister.

Judy also respects and reverences the church. Given several decades, she has at times been disappointed in church life, but as Sunnyside built their new building, she volunteered early and often. Too, she sees needs, people who she wants to minister to, even as they ministered to her when she was in need. And she loves good music and good preaching.

All of which is to say, we share so much, and adds to our capacity to love each other. Having experienced deep pain in the loss of Colleen, God has seen fit to give me a second blessing, and she would say the same, as we live out the years yet before us.

Courting Judy   Tieing the knot, July 2014

The whole gang

Navajo Rugs: A Beautiful (Nizhoni) Affection

The word for beautiful in the Navajo language is *nizhoni*. Judy and I have had a *nizhoni* experience in recent years with Navajo rugs, of all things—how obscure is that? Here is the story:

Navajo weavers, the vast majority being women, are incomparable to any other group or ethnicities, in terms of weaving skills. They learned the skills from the Spanish, which evolved into their own unique style, dating way back to the 1850's.

Colleen and I early on would buy the occasional rug, often smallish, but still reasonable. We did buy a couple of high-end rugs through the years from people with Rehoboth connections. Interestingly, different communities developed different styles and colors of rugs. Most of our rugs were of the "Two Grey Hills" variety, meaning they came from the area called by that name, which neighbored a community called Toadlena. Two Grey Hills rugs are a combination of black, brown, grey and white wool, often from sheep from the weaver's flock, sheered and washed, carded and spun, and woven into masterpieces, even tapestries. This is where Judy and my stories merge.

Judy's uncle Rev. Jacob Kobes and his wife Trina along with six children were missionaries in Toadlena for 37 years. Judy had never been to Toadlena, prompting me to insist that I take her there, a remote community about 80 miles north of Rehoboth. Prior to our visit, we made arrangements with the lay pastor James Belone. We were not prepared for what we saw—the church had an area five feet in diameter without shingles. Peeking through the windows, the interior damage was likewise obvious.

In meeting with James and his wife Louise, we got a fuller story—a poor community that did not have the resources to maintain a church building. After a two hour visit, we asked, "Would you like the church restored?" prompting an immediate, "Yes, we have been praying for help." Our response, "Often white folks make too many promises, so we will only see what we can do."

(From here the story gets only better, but too long for this book. It is included in our collation of appendices, available by contacting the author)

Toadlena is also famous for a collection of Navajo rugs on display at the Toadlena Trading Post. The owner, Mark Winter, has devoted his life to collecting these amazing rugs, and further, tracing the families from which they came. He has published a 600-page book *The Master Weavers*, cataloging with photos and genealogies the history and stories of the region.

Navajo Rugs on the dining table

Navajo rugs, called Ganado Reds

Navajo women preparing Frybread for youth meeting in Toadlena, c.1970

Judy, with her eye for aesthetics, became increasingly intrigued, only to learn that a 2nd cousin's estate sale in Lynden included some Navajo rugs. We got there on the second day, with just two left, both purchased with minutes of arrival. These were from the Chinle and Crystal areas of the Rez, more gold, tan, brown and white. A trip to New Mexico the next week enticed us toward three more Two Grey Hills rugs. We then discovered sales on eBay and purchased a few more. Well you get the picture!

We have had the providential privilege of becoming friends with Dave and Pat Newhouse, Sunnyside residents, though Pat grew up in Lynden, in the very same house/farm on Abbott Road where we spent 18 years. Pat is a student of cultures around the world but has come to particularly admire Navajo people and their weaving of rugs, like we do. Dave and Pat have a marvelous collection; thus we have this affection in common.

Then we met a Matt Wood in Bothel, WA, a second-generation trader with a warehouse loaded with Southwest artifacts, rugs, pots, jewelry and more. And there Judy became fond of the "Ganado Red" style, from another community on the Rez. The location was all too convenient, and it has been noted, "Matt and the Polinders became friends."

All of which is to say, we now live in what some have called the Lynden Trading Post, decorated by an unknown artist named Jude, funded by ???, enjoyed by all who enter in, marveling at the skill and artistry of mostly unnamed Navajo grandmas, master weavers indeed!

Help for Red Mesa—COVID-19 response

July 15, 2020 — Pulling a 16-foot trailer filled with donated cleaning supplies and other items, a diesel pickup truck arrived and parked in late June outside the Tohatchi Christian Reformed Church in Tohatchi, N.M.

Two couples — Marlin and Linda Hendricks and Henry and Evonne Bierlink — climbed out to be greeted by members of the church. Together, the couples from hundreds of miles away and church members joined in unloading the trailer. Working under a hot sun, they took out containers of bleach, hand sanitizers, disinfecting wipes, toilet paper, paper towels, bottles of Gatorade and even a few cans of Spam.

Also as part of this effort, undertaken by a group of mainly CRC members in Lynden, Wash., was a check for $16,000 to be used by Classis Red Mesa, the regional church body, to help people on the Navajo reservation replenish the supplies when they run out.

"We were so thankful for these gifts. We are scattered geographically and it has been very hard for us to get cleaning supplies in bulk," said Camilla Lynch, who works at Rehoboth Christian School in Gallup, N.M., and helped to coordinate the effort by offering her church in Tohatchi as a center to store the and then distribute the donated items.

"With the supplies at hand in Tohatchi," she said, "we were able to reach out to 16 churches and offer them a wide range of cleaning supplies" — not to mention the Spam, a sturdy staple from years past that a few people asked for.

Given the terrible toll COVID-19 has taken on the Navajo nation, these supplies can play a role in helping people who have not contracted the virus to stay healthy.

"People on the reservation have been especially hard hit," said Lynch. "Many families live under one roof and do not have easy access to water for cleaning."

The number of those infected by the virus has skyrocketed, now reaching 8,300 infections with more than 400 deaths, according to the Navajo Department of Health. And these numbers, per capita, place the rate of infections and deaths on a par with people in New York and New Jersey and now Florida, Texas and Arizona.

"It has been very sad," said Lynch, adding there have been days when two or more COVID-19 victims have been buried at the cemetery in Rehoboth.

Despite this harsh reality, commented Lynch, "It is a blessing beyond blessing what the people in Washington were able to do. They came wholeheartedly and with a willingness to serve."

Book Club desires to reach out, CRC News

A group of men, mostly members of the CRC, have been meeting for a book study, prayer and spiritual growth every Saturday for a decade or so in Lynden, Wash., said Allen Likkel, who worked for many years for Christian Reformed Home Missions (now Resonate Global Mission) before he retired.

Recently, the group was reading a book on the topic of social justice and they began to wonder — in this time of racial turmoil and the pandemic — what they could do, right now, to respond to the call to help those in need.

"We looked for an immediate 'hands on' project that we could do," said Likkel.

It turns out that Ron Polinder was leading the book study on that Saturday when people discussed what they could do. Given that he worked for many years at the Rehoboth Christian School, a portion of that time as superintendent of the school, he had contacts in that region — people such as Camilla Lynch — suggested they consider doing something to help the people on the Navajo reservation.

"I had had an email from a former student who told me about the situation down there and how bad it has become and about a need for cleaning supplies," said Polinder. "We talked this over and then let the Holy Spirit guide us from there."

Messages he placed on his Facebook page got a quick response, assuring him that the Spirit was indeed in the move of members of the book group to come to the aid of fellow CRC members down in New Mexico.

Using Facebook as his main tool to spread the message of the mission they were on, Polinder wrote: "We need your help—there is a desperate shortage of cleaning supplies, Clorox, wet-wipes, hand sanitizers and spray bottles.

"With a few of my Christian brothers, we are hoping to collect a big trailer full of supplies for transport to some of our churches, who in turn share them with their parishioners and neighbors, most of whom are poor and live in very remote places on the reservation."

Donations came pouring in, said Polinder, and he started to store them in his garage. As the items arrived and began to mount up, he started to wonder how they would transport the goods to the reservation.

That is when someone offered to lend his pick-up truck for that job and soon the two couples — Marlin and Linda Hendricks and Henry and Evonne Bierlink — volunteered to drive the vehicle south on a 26-hour journey to Tohatchi, NM.

In another Facebook message, Polinder wrote: "Would you believe that 40 percent of folks on the Rez do not have running water, and 30 percent do not have electricity — and this is in America, folks!

"They live in close quarters, pile into one vehicle/pick-up, travel on dirt roads from these remote areas to get to the highway" to reach grocery stores and to obtain other necessities, he said.

McKinley and San Juan counties, where many of the CRC congregations are based, are amongst the very poorest in the US, said Polinder.

In a few short days, said Polinder, he had a garage full of donated items; financial gifts were also increasing. And then came the word that the pick-up was available.

Once he connected with Camilla Lynch and they made arrangements for the church in Tohatchi to be the distribution point, the two couples headed off on the journey to New Mexico.

"I give so much credit to Camilla for doing the organizing on her end," said Polinder. "Given her efficiency, I recommended she run for President not of the Navajo Nation but of the U.S.A."

After the goods were distributed, Polinder heard from Evie Benally, who along with husband, Willie, pastor the Sanostee church.

"Evie wrote the nicest note of gratitude. Years ago, we hired her to teach at Rehoboth, prior to getting married and having kids."

In part, Evie's note reads: "Oh Praise the Lord! Ron was the elementary school principal when I used to teach at Rehoboth years ago! Send our greetings to all the Christian families! We're very thankful. God takes care of his church through caring people."

As he looks on what they were able to do, and what they will be doing because of the money being managed by Classis Red Mesa, Polinder is convinced that from the idea posed in the book group to trucking and unloading the goods in New Mexico, this was a divine venture.

"This was a mighty act of God. The Lord was in and through it—we watched and marveled," said Polinder.

Chris Meehan, CRC Publications

CHAPTER 17

RETIREMENT WORK & WRITING

20 Remarkable Trees

For a couple of years now, I have had this article in head waiting to be written. Our town is wonderful in many ways, but one that is seldom talked about relates to the remarkable trees that we have in Lynden. We should pay more attention to these incredible creations.

A long walk with Councilman Ron DeValois has motivated me to finally get to it. Ron is a student of nature—more than most he knows the names of birds and plants and trees. So he has become my partner on this project.

What's more, last Friday was Arbor Day, a good time to reconnect with our trees.

Our thought is that sometime this spring, after your Sunday afternoon nap, that you take a drive to admire these notable trees of Lynden. If you have a family, take your children with you so they learn in their early years to see these amazing structures—the scale, color, line, diversity, height, width. Consider the work that God put into growing those trees!

My former pastor, Ken Koeman, is fond of the little poem of Elizabeth Barret Browning—in fact some years ago, he had our whole Sonlight congregation memorize it:

> Earth's crammed with heaven,
> And every common bush afire with God;
> But only those who see, takes off their shoes--
> The rest sit around and pluck blackberries.

So it is with our trees—we can drive past them, sit under them, hide behind them, and maybe even cut them down without a thought of how they got there or who put them there.

So, this spring, in addition to considering the lilies, consider the trees, "how they grow: they neither toil nor spin, yet I tell you, even Solomon in all his glory was not arrayed like one of these" (Matthew 6:28-29).

Part of the fun of this would be for you to decide that ours was a lousy list, and you would come up with your own nominations. Surely, we have missed some beauties, and would welcome the challenge. Here we go:

- A good place to start is right downtown Lynden, the Judson tree across from the Post Office on 6th St. There is a little sign planted there to tell you part of the story of this massive Black Walnut.
- Drive west a few blocks on Front and 10th St., next to the 1st CRC, to look at that straight arrow, pointing to the sky, a Concolor Fir that was planted by the pastor's wife Mrs. Westra in early 1930's.
- Close by on Front and 9th St. are two lovely Redwoods, full and round and tall. Though when you get to the other side of town, at 826 Garden Drive you will see an even taller Redwood.
- This may be cheating a bit, but while on Front Street, take the time to celebrate those spectacular Pin Oak trees that line our streets. Consider the beauty of the summer canopy and their fall colors. (It's springtime—let's not think about the work they require.)
- Those Pin Oaks replaced, in 1958, Broadleaf Maples that lined the streets of Lynden. On 10th street, south of Front remain four of those magnificent maples.
- Swing over to 811 Grover Street to see a stately Grand Fir. Wow, that is a tall tree!
- There are many attractive Red Maples, and we choose the one on the corner of 7th and Liberty.
- By the war memorial on Grover and 4th street is a Black Locust, barely leafing out at this date, but it is a beauty.
- Now it is time to get out of the car for a short hike to see the huge Cottonwood Tree on the dike by Ken Stremler's property. The best way to get there is to drive down to the Water treatment plant and find the trail to the dike. That Cottonwood is approaching 8 feet in diameter. Phoebe Judson described a bear climbing a Cottonwood along the river—one wonders if it was that very tree?
- Moving east, drive past City Hall and enjoy the beautiful Western Red Cedar just north. There are also several beautiful cedars on the Lynden Christian playground.
- On Birch street in the corner of a lot is a wonderfully tall Sequoia, which can be seen quite well from Bender Road.
- Head down Brookfield Drive and notice at 8660 the comical Monkey Puzzle Tree, native to Chile. While on that street, at 8650, check out the Weeping Sequoia. These trees remind us that God is creative and playful.
- Over on Benson Road on the Isom School campus is a wonderful American Chestnut. They tell me the school was designed to make sure that marvelous tree was saved.

- The city of Lynden recently acquired the property from the Heusinkvelds on 8727 Benson Road. There are some appealing trees there, in particular two Oak trees as you enter the driveway, planted by Mr. Benson possibly before 1900. There are also two Birch trees to the North and impressive Spruce tree behind the house. This property will soon be one of Lynden's parks.
- How do you choose a favorite Douglas Fir in town? There are hundreds, but we think the stunning, stately stand in front of the Century House on 401 S BC Ave is worthy of your attention. Those 10 trees were planted by Ron DeValois's father in the 1920's. But you may know something even more striking.
- The Copper Beech tree in the Fairway Shopping Center won out over several others equally as worthy—this one is easy to get to, and shows off well in that location.
- A final visit to the eastside, on the corner of 1st and Grover is Red Sunset Maple, which will not turn red until the Fall. Remember to check it out—it will be aflame!
- And let's close with another Judson landmark, the house on the corner of Nooksack and Front St—there stands an elegant Elm (we think), likely old, and symbolic of those old-timers who had the foresight to plant trees.

Yes, we cheated—there are more than 20 trees listed here. But they all are instructive in some way—we couldn't stop ourselves. We hope you catch the spirit—go plant a tree, maybe to honor a loved one.

It was Isaiah who taught us the "trees of the field shall clap their hands" as we go out in joy (55:12b). Take a joyful ride through our town!

Board (or is it Bored) to Death

Such was the cynical comment from my friend Bob Keller when asked what he was doing in retirement. For sure, Bob meant "board," for he was the consummate board member. My life has also been chockful for board meetings.

I suspect I got this habit from my father whose life was littered with board meetings, most of which were related to the dairy business and Darigold in particular. From him, I picked up the notion that if you wanted to make a difference, if you wanted to bring about change you likely better learn to sit in the board room.

My goodness, I cannot tell all that I learned in the process, most often from smarter people than me likewise around the board room table. I thought it could be interesting to make a list:

1. It started in HS: student council, youth group, and even 4-H club where we learned at least the basics of parliamentary procedure.

2. A couple of years of Calvin University student council, in the late '60's when students were restless and insisting on things like Faculty Evaluation.

3. The Fort Wingate church steering committee, at age 21, where we, a group of four, advised our pastor and gave direction to the church—an early cross-cultural experience.

4. The Rehoboth Christian Hospital Board of Governors was a totally different experience, not an easy one, and figuring out hospital finance. We also fired an administrator during my tenure.

5. The Rehoboth Christian School Board, newly formed, and now I am an employee of the Board, a young employee. But learned much from some good leaders, though one called us "young punks."

6. The New Mexico Association of Non-Public Schools (NMANS) placing me in the company of folks of different faith traditions, particularly Roman Catholics, a grand experience.

7. The move to Washington and employment with Concerned Christian Citizens placed me under the authority of a Board, a young group with vision and passion for faith and politics.

8. My other part-time job was at Lynden Christian where I answered to a Promotions Committee. Again, great experience working with the likes of Gerrit Byeman and Donna VanderGriend.

9. A high privilege was being invited to serve on the Board for the Center for Public Justice. This enabled me to serve with the smartest people I ever met, led by Director James Skillen.

10. Co-Chair of the Task Force for Positive Teen-age Sexuality, along with Dr. Ken Gass, head of Planned Parenthood—and exercise in compromise and getting along with folks of different worldviews.

11. Answering to the Education Committee and Lynden Christian School Board—what a privilege to work 14 years with such fine men and women, in fact the first women to have served.

12. After APJ, Pastor Koeman nominated me to Classis PNW for the Calvin College Board of Trustees. I was elected and served a terrific eight years, including the selection of Pres. Gaylen Byker.

13. During the 90's, I also took on the chairmanship of the Lynden Future's Task Force, whose task it was to imagine how the unique character could be sustained.

14. At the same time I was chosen by District 7 of the CSI International Board to serve representing our region, a challenging assignment given the contention of certain Canadians.

15. Our decision to return to New Mexico meant giving up CSI. But it put me back working for the Rehoboth School Board, a grand experience, in spite of their inexperience.

16. After receiving the Gates Grant, we were given the challenge of sharing three million dollars with our neighboring schools to form the Coalition of Red Mesa Schools, of which I was chairman.

17. Upon returning to Lynden and after Colleen's passing, I was asked to chair a long-range planning effort at Sonlight. We had an excellent committee, and produced a document: The Identity and Values of Sonlight CRC, 12 statements leading us into our future (we hoped).

18. Kara Turner and I were asked to co-chair a Search Team for a new pastor, which proved to be a positive Sonlight assignment.

19. The Northwest Washington Fair board has annual election for which I submitted my name. I served six years but did not seek a third term—it's time to turn it over to the next generation.

20. Most recently, a group of us out of concern for some racial attitudes in our community formed Racial Unity Now (RUN) to address the prejudice and bigotry toward people of color.

21. Too, chosen as an Elder at Sonlight, an assignment I had previously declined given my role as a school administrator—where the meetings and game supervision are legion.

Final thought: This kind of work is not for everyone—it depends on your learning style and giftedness. But it is a way to serve your community, church, and school—which means the Kingdom of God.

Growing Up At the Fair

Often, when bragging about the Lynden Fair, I will say, "I grew up at the Fair!" Some hyperbole to be sure—I really grew up just across the river. But allow me to make my case, for that one glorious week in August. Where else but at the Fair did I learn so much about life?

It was at the Fair that I first experienced a blue ribbon. Even before I was old enough for 4-H, I remember my dad tucking a blue ribbon in his shirt pocket in the show ring between those two old cow barns, now long ago replaced. Blue was the most beautiful color. It took us a few years to discover the beauty of purple, but that came too.

Of course, this symbolizes competition, which is built into the very fabric of the Fair—one wonders how many ribbons are given out in just one year? Those ribbons reach out with lessons that we can learn. There is wholesome satisfaction in that purple if we have won well, having worked hard and competed fairly. There is also danger in purple—self-importance and pride.

There are always two ends to a class at the Fair—it's healthy if we learn how to stand on *both* ends, first and last. But the Fair helps us with those lessons, even if we are slow-learners—for some of us, it can take decades.

For me, it took way too long to give thanks to God, for he was the one that chiseled out that Grand Champion cow, or as Job describes in chapter 29:19, God gave the horse its strength and clothed its neck with a flowing mane. Those gorgeous flower baskets, those perfect vegetable boxes are first the fruit from his hand.

There are other lessons we learned—remember when mom gave us a few dollars to spend? How long did it take for those dollars to disappear? Were we broke by noon, or did we have some left at the end of the day? And now as parents and grandparents, do we teach our young ones how to measure, or do we over-indulge them, giving them a false notion that there is always more?

There were those teenage lessons, when the hormones were overactive. Lots of us learned how to flirt at the Fair. I suspect some of us overstepped our bounds—I did—with "smart remarks" that really were not very smart, maybe even hurtful. One wonders how many romances were started—can't you feel it in the air on a Friday night at the Fair? Cute girls and cute guys wondering if now is the moment to hold hands for the first time? And hoping that seat on the Ferris Wheel squeezed us closely together.

There was work at the Fair—and for months before. In part, blue and purple comes from sheer work. I suspect all of us can remember literal blood, sweat, and tears in preparation for the Fair week. Then there was getting up early for barn duty, and not only doing your own work, but helping the neighbor kid, the novice, who had so much yet to learn. No one does well at the Fair, or should do well, unless they have done the work!

Often that work happened alongside strangers, at least they started out as strangers. It was at the Fair that we got to know kids from the other schools, other clubs, other counties, and we learned to like them. That family across the aisle showing cows was a Lutheran family, and the one down further was a Catholic family, and those right next to us—I'm not sure they go to church. Strangers all—who became friends. The Fair taught us the gift of the stranger.

But finally, the Fair is not about just the youth, or even the middle-aged. It also about us old-timers. We go to the Fair in large part just to visit—just to see people that we have not seen for a year, or maybe a decade. We run into old classmates who live out East somewhere but are in town to visit their relatives. It is so good to see them! Whatever dislikes we may have had toward certain folks are long forgotten. We learn about their family, their faith, their work, their joys, and sometimes their sorrows, deep sorrows. There are mostly smiles and hugs at the Fair, but there can even be tears. So it was for me this past year. Yet, there were lots of former students ready to hug their crabby, old principal.

But aren't we thankful for this amazing week—when all of this can happen? When a community comes together, celebrating our agricultural roots, but also, celebrating each other? When city folks and country folks so easily rub shoulders, when our Canadian neighbors come to our Lynden Fair because "they just love it."

There is a grace in all of this that should be named, respected, and sustained. It is like God is blessing us to "Fair thee well."

Ron Polinder
November 2012

Who Owns the Fair?

Many will think that an odd question, until you try to answer it. When I first became a Board member, now three years ago, I confess my own answer was fuzzy at best. I suppose my first response and best answer would have been the Northwest Washington Fair Association, which consists of about 80 members who meet annually and elect the Board.

But some of the Association members don't quite picture themselves as owners and thus believe the Fair Board must own the Fair. Association members play a more modest role. But the Board of Directors has no more or less ownership than anyone else, (and by the way are all strictly volunteers).

As a new board member, I thought of dozens of folks who seemed more likely owners than me. Some exhibitors have been at it for 50 years, and there are department superintendents who have held their volunteer position for 30. They must be the real owners.

Then there are those, like my grandkids, who just love the Fair; showing their calf, preparing their Lego exhibit, working with their 4-H club—I think lots of those kids think this is "their" Fair.

There are also the elderly folks who have been coming to the Fair for decades—they wouldn't miss it. They love the six-horse hitches, a good fair hamburger, the smells that only a fair can produce. They check out those ever-larger tractors and wonder what one of the monstrosities actually costs? If the relatives visit from out of town, they will quickly say, "You need to come a day with us to see 'our' Fair." And they will have a grand time seeing old friends and relatives that maybe they haven't seen for years. If they get tired of walking around, they can rest in the shade of those giant fir trees.

Before I come closer to answering my own question, I should quickly note who does not own the Fair. It is not the State of Washington—we get a modest grant from them for our premiums, but there is no ownership. Well how about the County—isn't this a "County Fair?" Actually, it is not a county fair, and thus we receive no annual support from the Whatcom County government. We are a regional fair, officially the Northwest Washington Fair and Event Center. We even pay taxes?

When I got elected to the Board, I was surprised to discover—*we are a non-profit*. I surely thought that we had some larger connection to the State or County and would get a big, fat check each year from one or both. Nope—we are a non-profit like dozens of other non-profits in our community. You know what that means—we have to watch our finances very closely to make ends meet. Thus, that roof with the rusty surface—it may be a few years before that is replaced. And those bleachers that need some new 2' by 12's for better seating, we got some of them replaced by don't have the cash to complete the job.

Thus, a major task of the Board and Staff is to make careful financial decisions—which means we have to raise the price of admission periodically and set aside a "rainy day" fund in case of emergency.

Yet our Fair, given sound management, it in pretty good shape. We are making improvements each year. But if you were to examine those big barn-like exhibit buildings by the North entry, you would quickly note how tired that facility is. We must replace it, and soon! Some of you likely have heard rumors about an Agriculture Education Center being planned for the fairgrounds. The rumors are true—even now we are in the quiet fund-raising phase to produce a 1st class Ag. Ed. Facility, which would replace those aging exhibit barns. Actually, we have received nice grants from both the State and the County toward this educational effort. Stay tuned for more refreshing news on this project.

But now back to the original question—who owns the Fair? I get my answer when I sit in my brother's open tack room in the dairy barn, the southeast corner. It is a busy corner with all manner of people walking through. Lots of moms and dads with two, three, or four kids wanting to touch the cows, wanting to know their names, hoping a new calf will be born.

There are the teenagers, a chummy boy and girl, likely more interested in the holding hands than studying the cattle. The Fair is multi-purposed. J

There are our Canadian neighbors who love the Fair. They celebrate its cleanliness, family-friendliness, and it has actual grass—unlike the PNE in Vancouver. Retired Canadian farmers who just want to come and see some good cows again.

Are you beginning to sense a reasonable answer to the question? WE ALL OWN THE FAIR!!! If you read this full article, you are interested and thus you are an OWNER. It is YOUR Fair. As Whatcom Country community, we have the joy of being PARTNERS and OWNERS of the Northwest Washington Fair.

Claim it, enjoy it, sustain it—the gift is rich!

Ron Polinder, Chair, 360-325-3449
Community Linkage Committee
Northwest Washington Fair

Board member privilege—riding up on the wagon

Cows resting at the Fair

Debbie—the best cow ever at Ronelee Farm

CHAPTER 18

PERSONAL

My Prostate Cancer

I can't imagine a title like this will invite very many readers. Yet, this is one of the realities of life, and cancer has certainly influenced my life and that of our extended family. Most memorable was my Dad's prostate cancer that eventually was the cause of death after a horrible final month of suffering.

Thus, in November of 2009, when I was likewise diagnosed, it immediately raises memory and fears. As of this writing, that was nearly 12 years ago. Some of you, especially men, will be interested in my journey—we tend to compare notes.

Our first decision was a treatment plan. We decided to do robotic surgery in Seattle and have the prostate gland removed. The robot is less invasive, but it still meant a night in the hospital and a couple weeks with a catheter. When the lab work arrived, unfortunately, cancer had already in one small area escaped the capsule. That led to radiation treatments, 28 in number, in Bellingham, that I endured with almost no side effects.

A couple years later, my PSA number showed some resumed activity. The number was low, and treatment normally begins as it rises. In the meantime, I had heard from a couple of friends elsewhere in the country about a Dr. Vogelzang in Las Vegas who was a noted researcher in prostate cancer. Also, my very good friend, Shirley Vogelzang Hoogstra with whom I served on the Calvin Board of Trustees is a first cousin to Dr. Nicholas. Shirley was more than willing to write a note to her cousin encouraging him to take me on as a patient, which he willingly did.

I first met Vogelzang in 2014 in Las Vegas. After a thorough study of my case, he asked if I would be willing to participate in a trial at the National Institute of Health in Bethsaida, MD, at no expense to me. We quickly signed on for that, was accepted, and started on a special pill. After about two months, I had two incidents of temporary memory loss, both of which I reported. After the second, they took me off the pill and out of the trial. Though at first disappointed, I have since wondered if that medication has contributed to some of my short-term memory loss.

My next visit to Las Vegas, the good doctor urged me to get a special kind of exam called C-11, which reveals more accurately the location of cancer. It was costly and required a special trip to Phoenix. However, it did show exactly which lymph nodes were affected. Dr. Vogelzang thereafter devised a plan of both chemotherapy and medication. The chemo would be a 30-week regimen, which began in the summer of '16, at the Cancer Center in Bellingham. The infusions were every three weeks.

By the second round, the side effects became all too obvious: change in appetite and extreme weariness. My favorite food became Campbell's Chicken Noodle Soup, and the heretofore chocolate addiction disappeared. Worse by far was the fatigue. I recall two Sundays when I dressed for church, but when it came time to brush my teeth, I simply did not have the energy to do it. After the typical six treatments of the proposed ten, I ask via text the doctor (he always answered within 24 hours) why we were doing ten. He responded, "Well, you want to live a little longer, don't you?" Ten it was to be.

I survived but knew I would have to face some additional radiation, which in turn presents dangers of burning certain organs. In the meantime, Seattle had opened a Proton treatment center. Proton treatment enables the radiation beam to be pinpointed, and given the C-11 scan, they could design a treatment accordingly. This however would require a daily trip to Seattle, five days a week for five weeks. Thankfully, friends volunteered in the summer of '17 to drive me, leaving Judy on duty once a week.

All went very well, on what was a five-minute treatment, until the final week when it became painful in my back coming off the stainless-steel table, a table I claimed was "harder than Pharaoh's heart." The pain was so intense, it took usually two or more people to get me to my feet. As I recall after a week, the pain subsided in my everyday life. However, in February, I was on playground duty, catching the basketballs for Henry and tossing them back for his next shot. I felt a tweak in my back, and it has never gone away, only intensified.

Thus a whole new chapter in this journey. I finally visited a neurosurgeon in Bellingham who after an MRI reported that I had at least two compression fractures, and a third that appeared to be healing. Also called Osteoporosis, the prognosis for these compression factures is not promising. A referral to Seattle to the best in the state indicated a 12-hour surgery, a long recovery and likely a 15% chance of a failure. This was not encouraging—even the doctors were obviously reluctant.

The result is that I walk with a cane, though at short distances, use a walker for longer distance, and graduate to a scooter if needed. That is the bad news—my mobility is seriously compromised, and my lower torso is deconditioned.

Now for the good news:

- I feel good, very normal
- I sit without pain, mostly in my recliner
- I sleep pretty good, mostly in the recliner
- My PSA has been undetectable for nearly five years, the best news

So I give thanks for my extended years, and trust the Great Physician to decide when He will call me home.

Our leisure pursuit, Navajo Rugs

Polinder 6 horse hitch of Black and White
Clydesdales, driven by Courtney Polinder

Weeklings—terrific brothers

More of the gang

The Weeklings

What for a title is that? It goes back to England where there was a group called the Inklings. They were writers, some of them very famous, like C.S. Lewis and J.R. Tolkien, who in the 30's and 40's would get together most every week. They would read their latest work to each other and ask their friends for critique.

We kind of imitated that name, though we are not sure we are Weeklings or Weaklings. We are not writers, but we read books, good books, almost all about our Christian faith—and sometimes a book of the Bible. We always have good discussions.

Our group started 40 years ago when some men from Sonlight church gathered around the principles of 3D—devotion, discipleship, and diet. Given a dynamic visit to Lynden by speaker and author Richard Foster, our group evolved into the principles of *Renovare*, with a spiritual formation emphasis. Each week, we read together a litany. One paragraph is as follows:

In utter dependence upon Jesus Christ as my ever-living Savior, Teacher, Lord, and Friend, I will seek continual renewal through spiritual exercises, spiritual gifts, and acts of service.

We also focus on the following themes, one each week: **Contemplative, Holiness, Charismatic, Social Justice, Evangelical, and Incarnational.** We are called on to see how God may have worked in our lives for the theme of that week. Occasionally, but rarely, we pass if nothing comes to mind. The Lord's Prayer is offered each week, and we close with the Doxology.

Over those many years, there has been turnover and even death. We were profoundly saddened when Pastor Ken Koeman, our "elder statesman," died after a short bout with cancer. He had been one of the original members and was so often who were depended on for the "right word" when we were in a quandary.

I will not include the names of members, past and present, because we pledge to each other to hold in confidence what was shared and discussed. Often our prayer times are full of personal or family struggles that "are to stay within these wall—this is how we help each other."

So what are the takeaways in what for me has been 30 years. Considerable intellectual and spiritual stimulation is gained by reading important literature from diverse traditions and points in history. Further, my fellow Weeklings are thoughtful guys whose insights are always helpful.

Additionally, a bond of friendship is formed that is unusual in our culture. We care deeply for each other, praying for each other and our families. We can also cry, Papa being the weepiest of the group. And we can laugh, really laugh.

In closing, how I hope and pray that my grandchildren and great grandchildren will likewise confess the opening words of Psalm 90:1, "Lord, you have been our dwelling place throughout all generations." My friends are weaklings, **I am a weakling**, and you will be too—it's our nature. May in God's good providence, you find some weeklings.

Closing Doxology

Lord, through all the generations, we your children, see your grace
In our fears and tribulations, you have been our dwelling place
On us let grace and beauty, of the Lord our God remain
Strengthen us for noble duty that our work is not in vain

From the Blue Psalter, Paraphrased from Psalm 90,
Henry Richards, born 1819

A STATEMENT ON APPENDICES

Not attached, but under separate copy at home are a few coil-bound booklets which are collations of writing on various topics. Our first experiment with this was the making of copies of the Caring Bridge pages when Colleen was living with brain cancer. The response to her sickness was overwhelming, in part because our kids were scattered around, and Colleen and I had lived in different places. We received 135,000 hits on Caring Bridge, many beautifully written pieces to Colleen. And my kids and sisters and certain friends wrote meaningful pages updating her condition.

We made six copies to share with family and friends and would be pleased to loan them to those who may be interested.

Of different substance is a collection of a dozen stories, articles, speeches, essays that are just too long to fit in the book. Yet, they are not unimportant to the total what I have tried to communicate—the big ideas, big events, big stories. Again coiled, but available for modest cost at my house by calling (360) 325-3449, or stopping by 205 Rosemary Way, Lynden, WA 98264. Here is that list:

Stories:

- Alejandro and Celina—the story of a Hispanic, homeless mom and three kids who walked into the lobby of Sonlight church on a cold December day in 2013 and wound up in our basement. Later joined by the dad of the two little boys, it is a story of pain and blessing, hopelessness and hope, trust and friendship. Now eight years later, we continue to walk together in facing ongoing uncertainty, yet marveling at the providence of God.

- Toadlena: "Make Straight in the Desert a Highway for our God"--the story of an obscure community on the Navajo Reservation where the church building was recently abandoned to the elements. Family and friends of long-time missionary and his wife Rev. Jacob and Trina Kobes who pastored there for 37 years, Uncle and Aunt to Judy, rallied to restore the church and thus make room for the gospel.

Chapter:

- "Loving the Land in Lynden" is referred to in this memoir as to how it came into being, referencing Bob Keller who presented the invitation. The full chapter is in "Whatcom

Places" and would be too long for this venue. It remains the most significant invitation I have received as a "writer." It is a fabulous book describing our county. A second edition was published and now out of print. The photography in the book is outstanding—worth looking for as a used book.

Speeches:

- Speech to the Education majors at Calvin College, now University, in 2003. Niece Sarah Bos VanderPlas was one of the graduates, having done her student teaching at Rehoboth under Elsie Belone, a veteran Native teacher. The theme of the speech was to challenge the graduates to live out what they have been taught at Calvin, to listen for God's calling, even to obscure places in His Kingdom.

- Speech to L.C. graduates in 2001, following our decision to move to Rehoboth beyond the one-year leave of absence. Using the question of Madonna's song, "So What Happens Now?", students were challenged to "Go Lyncs, Go, Fight, Win," spiritualizing the cheers used for years at our basketball games.

- Speech to the leadership and regional directors of Christian Reformed Home Missions, highlighting the successes and challenges of Rehoboth Christian School. Further, noting the withdrawal of the CRC in the financial support not only of Rehoboth School, but of the 15 low-income Reservation churches, in essence breaking covenant with the Native community, all the while failing to recognize the cross-cultural contribution that Native people have made to our denomination.

- Speech to the Calvin College Faculty and Board of Trustees at the annual Faculty/Board Conference. A faculty member and board member were called on to respond to marvelous speech given by retired Wheaton philosopher/professor, Arthur Holmes. What was a very intimidating assignment, but well-received by the distinguished audience.

- Speech at a CACE (Center for the Advancement of Christian Education) conference in Washington DC in the Fall of '21. It was an honor to be asked to speak to 90 leaders from the Christian school movement from around the continent. I titled it "70 years of Christian Schooling."

Assignment:

- "Christian Athletics: By What Standard?' The preface of this piece is included in the Memoir above, but the substance uses the Creation, Fall, Redemption triad that Reformed theology is noted for. applying it to athletics: God created us to play, the Fall has disrupted God's intention, but Chrisitans are called to return play to the way it is supposed to be—a guide to Christian school athletic activities.

Public Statement:

- Statement of "Confession and Reconciliation" published in the "Gallup Independent" and "Navajo Times" in 2003, the 100th anniversary of the founding of Rehoboth Mission School. Following a "Day of Reflection" during the summer celebration, Edward T Begay recommended that we publish a summary of the proceedings, to which the School Board agreed. I was given the assignment to create the full-page ads for the papers.

Educational/Curricular Outcomes:

- In a phone call from my friend Dan Beerens, an outstanding educational consultant, when learning I was writing a memoir, he urged me to include the following "40 Outcomes," noting that he routinely shares this with nearly every workshop he conducts. I had not read them for at least a decade, so I quickly re-read the document. Fortunately, I discovered I still agreed with myself. J Too long for the book, they are added here, I was pleased to learn that ACSI used them to craft a similar statement.

Whereas I was able to include in the book several of the op-ed pieces written for the Bellingham Herald and the Gallup Independent, I have copied 20 additional articles to include in this collation. Each of these are a standard 750 words on a wide range of topics, again on subjects that I was willing to address publicly for the purpose of rendering opinion.

Ron Polinder,
March, 2022

AFTERWORD

Two overwhelming feelings:

1. How many wonderful stories and people were neglected, people who blessed us with love and prayer and friendship, whose stories are equally precious to those who made it into the memoir. For example, I think of my numerous colleagues at Lynden Christian, but with a larger staff, how does one decide who to include? Or terrific students, or not so terrific students, who have blossomed beautifully?

2. How amateurish it seems, compared to friends and acquaintances whose writing is much more creative and professional. And who have I unknowingly offended, even my own family? So this goes to the publisher with a prayer, that the Holy Spirit will make something good of it, that it will be a blessing, that this work of "my" hands will be established.

Ron Polinder, 2022